THE FAMILIES of
ELEANOR of
AQUITAINE

THE FAMILIES of ELEANOR of AQUITAINE

A Female Network of Power
in the Middle Ages

J.F. ANDREWS

For my daughters

A female network of power

First published 2023

The History Press
97 St George's Place, Cheltenham,
Gloucestershire, GL50 3QB GL50 3
www.thehistorypress.co.uk

British Library Cataloguing in Publication Data.
A catalogue record for this book is available from the British Library.

ISBN 978 1 80399 121 4

Typesetting and origination by The History Press
Printed and bound in Great Britain by TJ Books Limited, Padstow, Cornwall

Trees for LYfe

CONTENTS

LIST OF ILLUSTRATIONS

14. Double tomb of Leonor and Alfonso at Las Huelgas (Wikimedia Commons, John Robinette / Javi Guerra Hernando. Reproduced under a Creative Commons Licence)
15. Blanche of Castile is crowned queen of France (British Library MS Royal 16 G VI, fol. 386v)
16. Joanna and her brother Richard greet King Philip Augustus of France (British Library Yates Thompson MS 12, fol. 188v)
17. Philip Augustus gives his sister Margaret in marriage to Béla III of Hungary (British Library MS Royal 16 G VI, fol. 341r)
18a and 18b. Esztergom castle (Pixabay)
19. Effigy of Berengaria of Navarre at L'Épau abbey (Wikimedia Commons, Mossot. Reproduced under a Creative Commons Licence)
20. Arthur of Brittany pays homage to Philip Augustus (British Library, MS Royal 16 G VI, fol. 361v)
21. Magna Carta (British Library Cotton MS Augustus II 106)
22. Effigy of Isabella of Angoulême at Fontevraud (Wikimedia Commons, UAltmann. Reproduced under a Creative Commons Licence)

FAMILY TREE

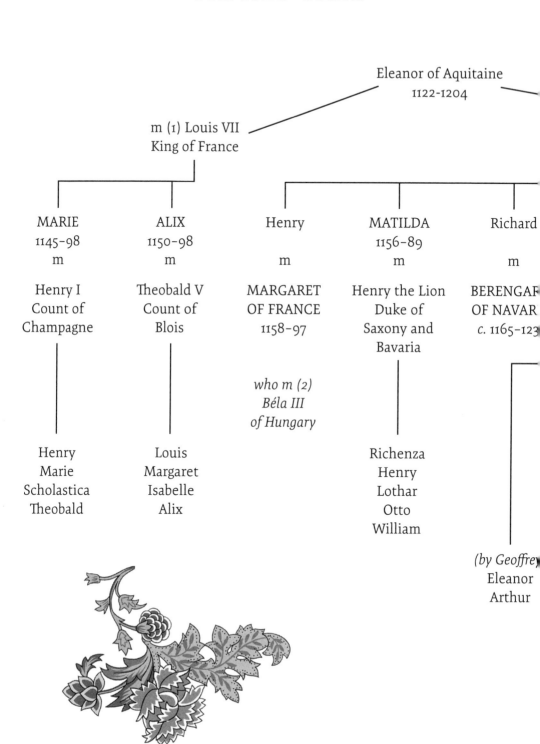

Eleanor of Aquitaine
1122–1204

m (1) Louis VII
King of France

MARIE	ALIX	Henry	MATILDA	Richard
1145–98	1150–98		1156–89	
m	m	m	m	m
Henry I Count of Champagne	Theobald V Count of Blois	MARGARET OF FRANCE 1158–97	Henry the Lion Duke of Saxony and Bavaria	BERENGARIA OF NAVARRE c. 1165–1230

who m (2)
Béla III
of Hungary

Henry Marie Scholastica Theobald	Louis Margaret Isabelle Alix		Richenza Henry Lothar Otto William	

(by Geoffrey)
Eleanor
Arthur

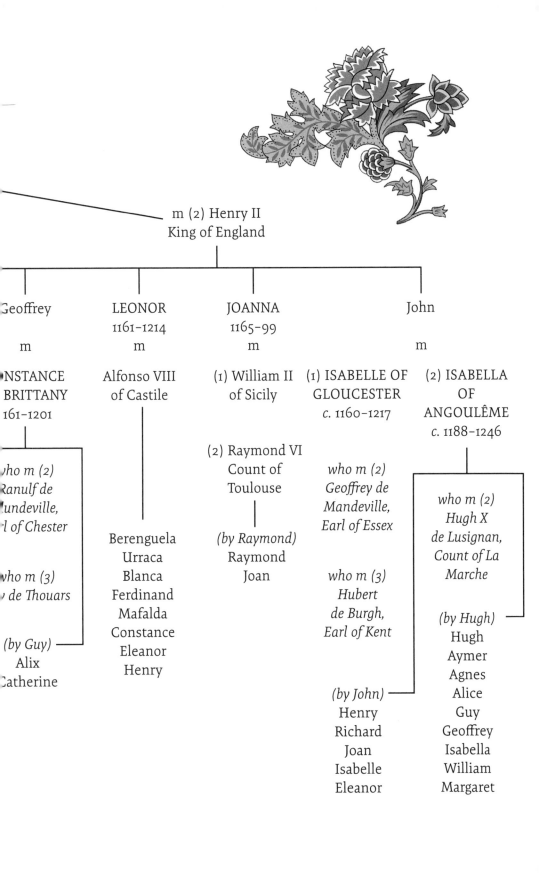

m (2) Henry II
King of England

Geoffrey	LEONOR 1161–1214	JOANNA 1165–99	John
m	m	m	m
NSTANCE BRITTANY 161–1201	Alfonso VIII of Castile	(1) William II of Sicily	(1) ISABELLE OF GLOUCESTER c. 1160–1217

(2) ISABELLA
OF
ANGOULÊME
c. 1188–1246

(2) Raymond VI
Count of
Toulouse

who m (2)
Ranulf de
undeville,
l of Chester

who m (2)
Geoffrey de
Mandeville,
Earl of Essex

who m (2)
Hugh X
de Lusignan,
Count of La
Marche

who m (3)
, de Thouars

Berenguela
Urraca
Blanca
Ferdinand
Mafalda
Constance
Eleanor
Henry

(by Raymond)
Raymond
Joan

who m (3)
Hubert
de Burgh,
Earl of Kent

(by Guy)
Alix
Catherine

(by Hugh)
Hugh
Aymer
Agnes
Alice
Guy
Geoffrey
Isabella
William
Margaret

(by John)
Henry
Richard
Joan
Isabelle
Eleanor

MAPS

England

0 25 50 75 100 Miles

N

North Sea

Irish Sea

SCOTLAND

Edinburgh
Berwick-upon-Tweed
FORTH
CLYDE
TWEED

Carlisle
TYNE
Durham
TEES

Belfast

Dublin

ENGLAND

York
RIBBLE
OUSE
HUMBER

Lincoln
TRENT
Nottingham   Newark-on-Trent

WALES
SEVERN

King's Lynn   Norwich

Worcester   Warwick   Ely   Bury
USK   GREAT OUSE   St Edmunds

Gloucester   Oxford   STOUR
TAFF   THAMES   St Albans

Cardiff   Bristol   Reading   LONDON
Sandwich

Devizes   Marlborough   Rochester
Windsor   Canterbury   Dover

EXE   Salisbury   Winchester

Exeter   Southampton   Arundel   Hastings
Corfe

English Channel

N

Le Havre   SEINE

FRANCE

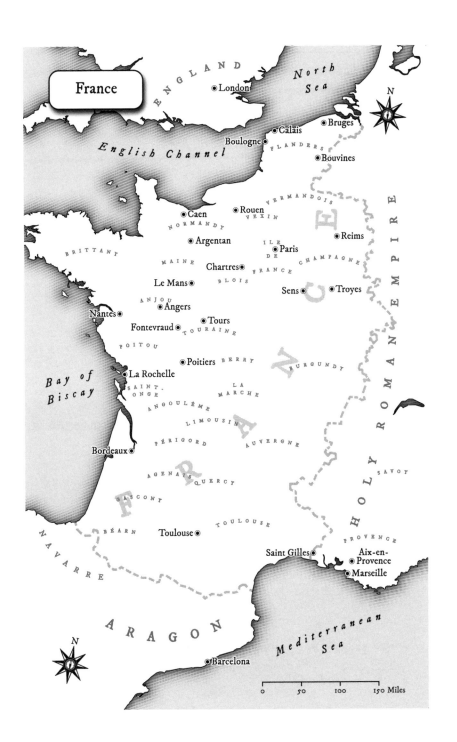

The Empire *and the* Kingdom of Sicily

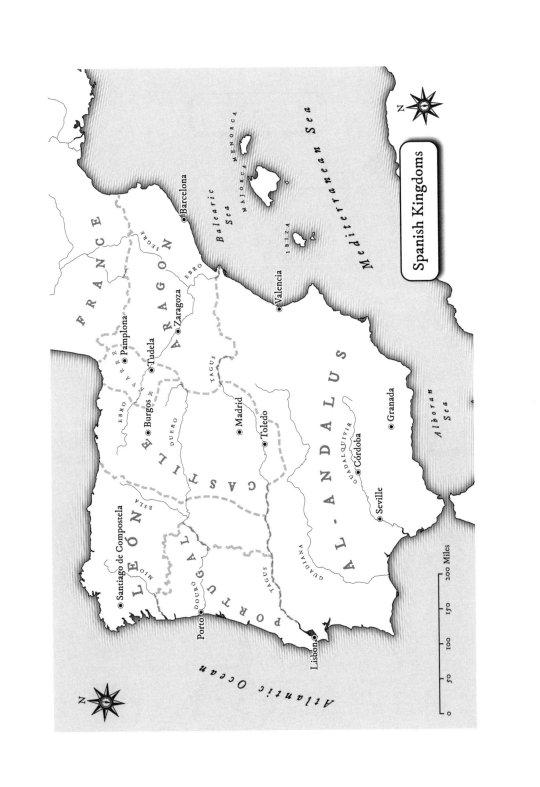

Spanish Kingdoms

N

FRANCE

NAVARRE
Pamplona
Tudela
ARAGON
Zaragoza
Barcelona

SEGRE

EBRO

EBRO

Balearic
Sea

MAJORCA
MENORCA

IBIZA

Valencia

Mediterranean Sea

LEÓN
Burgos
CASTILE

ESLA

DUERO

TAGUS

Madrid
Toledo

AL-ANDALUS

GUADALQUIVIR

Córdoba

Granada

Alboran
Sea

Santiago de Compostela

MIÑO

PORTUGAL

DOURO

TAGUS

GUADIANA

Seville

Porto

Lisbon

Atlantic Ocean

N

0   50   100   150   200 Miles

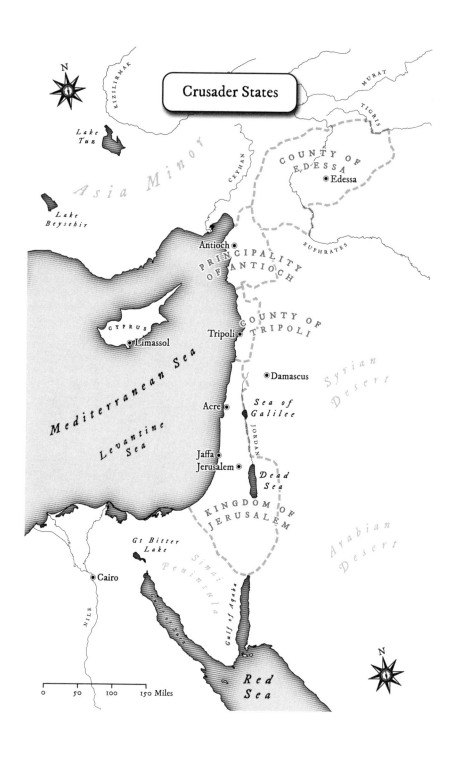

ACKNOWLEDGEMENTS

I'd like to express my gratitude to the group of academics known collectively as #TeamQueens, who are producing some wonderful scholarship that brings to light the lives and experiences of royal women in the Middle Ages, and the crucial political roles they played throughout Europe and beyond. The advice of these scholars and the references they provided were invaluable. I would also like to thank those colleagues who kindly shared details of forthcoming publications so that I was able to consult the most up-to-date research.

ELEANOR OF AQUITAINE

In early 1137 William X, the widowed duke of Aquitaine, was planning to go on a pilgrimage to Santiago de Compostela in the Spanish kingdom of León. Like any long-distance travel, this undertaking was a risky one, so he needed to ensure that he made arrangements both for the duration of his absence and for the possibility that he might not return. He had no son, but two daughters: Eleanor, then aged around 14 or 15, and Petronilla, who was probably 11 or 12. Until such time as William might return, remarry and father a legitimate son, Eleanor was the heir to Aquitaine, and she needed to be placed under the protection of a powerful guardian lest anyone should seek to gain the duchy by marrying her against her father's will.[1] William confided both his daughters to the care of the man who was nominally his overlord, King Louis VI of France, and they were sent to the castle of Bordeaux for safe-keeping.

Duke William died on his pilgrimage, meaning that no future male heir could supplant Eleanor, and overnight she became the richest marriage prize in western Europe. King Louis took the obvious course of action and immediately dispatched his son and heir, the 17-year-old Louis the Young, south to marry her. The wedding took place on 25 July 1137, bride and groom having almost certainly never met before. This was, of course, not unusual for royal couples, whose marriages were not matters of personal preference but rather arrangements centred on lands and dynastic concerns.

Louis VI, who had been ill for some time, died just a week after the wedding, meaning that his son ascended the French throne as Louis VII and Eleanor, after a whirlwind six months, was not only duchess of Aquitaine in her own right but also queen of France by virtue of her marriage. The royal relationship would go on to experience much upheaval, with the pious Louis complaining of Eleanor's vivacious behaviour while she in turn felt that she had 'married a monk, not a king'.[2] The situation was compounded by the lack of an all-important male heir for the French crown: after thirteen years of marriage Eleanor had borne just two daughters, Marie (b. 1145) and Alix (b. 1150), and no son.

A difficult decision lay ahead for Louis, who was by that time 30 and had the question of the succession hanging heavily on his mind. Divorce and remarriage might give him the chance to father a son to continue his royal dynasty, but he would lose the rich duchy of Aquitaine, which would stay with Eleanor as duchess in her own right. Eventually the concerns of the French crown won out and the marriage was dissolved on 21 March 1152, officially on the grounds of consanguinity.[3] Divorce, in the sense that we now understand it, was not permitted; the only option was annulment, which theoretically meant that the parties had never been married in the first place because their union was invalid. This had implications for any children, but Marie and Alix were declared legitimate by the Church on the slightly fudged reasoning that the parties had originally entered into the marriage in good faith. Custody of them was granted without question to Louis; children were legally the property of their father.

With Aquitaine as a prize, Eleanor had no shortage of suitors for a second match, but she evaded all offers (and several kidnap attempts) so that she could marry the man of her own choice. He was Henry of Anjou, duke of Normandy and claimant to the English throne, later to be Henry II. They were married in Poitiers on 18 May 1152, just eight weeks after the annulment of Eleanor's marriage to Louis.*⁴

Louis was, understandably, furious. If Eleanor were to bear Henry a son, the French king's elder daughter Marie would lose her status as the heiress to Aquitaine, which he would have hoped to control in her name in due course. The union also linked Aquitaine with Normandy, and potentially England as well – an intimidating prospect for a French king who exercised direct control over only a small part of his kingdom, and who needed to be wary of over-mighty vassals. Louis's fear was soon to be realised as, making a mockery of French criticism of her fertility, Eleanor and her second husband started a family very quickly. Their short-lived firstborn, William (1153–56), was followed by Henry (b. 1155), Matilda (b. 1156), Richard (b. 1157), Geoffrey (b. 1158), Leonor** (b. 1161), Joanna (b. 1165) and John (b. 1166).

None of Eleanor's children were born in Aquitaine, despite the fact that she was duchess there for more than sixty years. Instead their birthplaces of England, Normandy and Anjou showcased the huge agglomeration of lands over which she and Henry ruled. This makes it a little more difficult to refer to the children of this marriage as being 'English' or 'Angevin', in the same way that Marie and Alix can safely be called French,

---

* Eleanor's marriage to Louis had been dissolved on the grounds of consanguinity, but in fact she and Henry were almost as closely related: all three of them were direct descendants of Robert II the Pious, king of France 996–1031.

** This daughter was christened Eleanor, the same as her mother; in order to avoid confusion I have chosen to call her Leonor, the name by which she was known in Castile after she married its king, and by which she is referred to in many modern works of scholarship.

so for the purposes of this book I will call them 'Plantagenet', even though they did not use the surname themselves.[*]

Eleanor's children were her family, but they were not a 'family' in the sense that we might understand the word now. Never – not once in her long life – was Eleanor in the same place at the same time as all of her children, nor indeed even with all the children of her second marriage. A twelfth-century royal family was not a close-knit group of people with emotional ties who lived together; rather, it was a political and strategic unit in which each member was expected to act in order to bring advantage to the whole, regardless of their own personal feelings.[5]

Marriages for members of the family were of crucial importance: peace treaties might depend on them and valuable international alliances might be sealed by them. This worked both ways, so the wives of Eleanor's sons coming into the family were just as important in dynastic terms as her own daughters marrying out of it – indeed arguably more so as they would (it was hoped) ensure continuation of the male line. This is why Eleanor's daughters-in-law are included in this book along with her daughters. They were Margaret of France (b. 1158), married to Henry; Berengaria of Navarre (b. *c.* 1165), married to Richard; Constance of Brittany (b. 1161), married to Geoffrey; and Isabelle of Gloucester (b. *c.* 1160) and Isabella of Angoulême (b. *c.* 1188), both married to John.[**]

---

[*] 'Plantagenet' was the soubriquet used by Henry II's father, Geoffrey of Anjou. It was not a hereditary surname and Henry did not use it himself, but it has become accepted shorthand for his family from this point on, and has been widely used for this purpose in other publications.

[**] Both of John's wives are referred to in different sources interchangeably as Isabelle and Isabella; in the interests of clarity I will consistently use the spelling 'Isabelle' for Isabelle of Gloucester, and 'Isabella' for Isabella of Angoulême.

Eleanor's own daughters were all sent away at very young ages to be brought up in the homelands of their intended husbands. It is probable that Eleanor did not have much say in their destinations – however, it is equally probable that she approved of the high status of the husbands in question and that she would not have wanted her daughters to make inferior marriages simply in order for them to stay near to her.[6]

In the normal course of events, these unions between different kingdoms, and the distances involved, meant that Eleanor would not really have expected ever to see her daughters again, though they would certainly have anticipated corresponding. No letters between Eleanor and her daughters survive, but that does not mean there were none; royal women engaged in frequent correspondence. Henry II would certainly have kept in touch with the husbands he had arranged for his daughters, for an alliance would be of little use if the parties never communicated. As it transpired, however, fate would bring Eleanor into close contact with all three of her daughters by Henry II as the years passed, and she would have widely varying personal relationships with her daughters-in-law. She had much less interaction with her daughters by Louis, though they also formed part of the strategic web that would influence the course of events in France and England – and further afield – throughout the late twelfth and early thirteenth centuries.

The lives of the ten women featured in this book spanned almost exactly a century, from the birth of Marie in 1145 to the death of Isabella in 1246. Between them, they would form a great international network of political alliances that linked their siblings, their husbands and their children. Their stories stretch from England to the Holy Land, from Spain to Sicily, from France to Hungary, thus giving them a combined sphere of influence that extended across many kingdoms and thousands of miles, while the actions of each influenced the lives of the others even across great distances. None of them had a say in the choice of their (first) husbands, but they all took on the challenge of carving out a life and a position for themselves, some in unpredictable ways and all with differing degrees of success. Some of them found happiness; others endured lives of turmoil and conflict. Some of them had close relationships; others never met. But two things linked them all: their connection to Eleanor and the kingdoms over which she reigned, and their determination to exert authority on their own terms in a male-dominated world.

PART I

DAUGHTERS
OF FRANCE

1

MARIE AND ALIX

In the spring of 1145 King Louis and Queen Eleanor of France had been married for seven and a half years. No child had been born to them in all that time, and hopes were fading for a royal heir. But Eleanor had at last conceived and, despite all the potential dangers, she had carried the pregnancy to term; she was now confined (literally shut into a room with her female attendants, as was the custom at the time) and news was expected any day.[1] Finally, a message from the birthing chamber reached the king, but it was not the one he had hoped for. In one respect, of course, the labour had been a success, in that both mother and baby had survived – but in another it was a catastrophic failure, because the new arrival was not the all-important and much-anticipated son, but a daughter.

Marie, known as Marie of France and sometimes later as Marie of Champagne, was Eleanor's firstborn.[*2] A child had been long desired, but this little girl was not exactly treasured by either of her parents and was not destined to have the sort of close and loving relationship with them that a modern 'miracle baby', born after years of childlessness, might expect. She was separated from them very early in her life, being barely 2 years old when both her parents left France to embark on

---

* Marie should not be confused with her near-contemporary, the writer and poet Marie de France, who was unrelated to the French royal family.

what would later be known as the Second Crusade; they would be away for more than two years.

By the time they returned to France, Louis and Eleanor's relationship had deteriorated to the point where the dissolution of the marriage was openly talked of. The pope, Eugenius III, was aware of the national and international implications of such a split and he made a last-ditch attempt to reconcile the couple: he 'forbade any future mention of their consanguinity' and 'strove by friendly converse to restore love between them'. He also, perhaps more pertinently, 'made them sleep in the same bed, which he had had decked with priceless hangings of his own'.[3] This intervention saved the marriage in the short term and even resulted in another pregnancy. It was hoped, certainly by Louis and undoubtedly by many others in France, that this time Eleanor would bear a son, but when she was confined in the summer of 1150 her baby was another girl. They named her Alix and began to make plans to separate.

The annulment of Louis and Eleanor's marriage on the grounds of consanguinity, when it occurred on 21 March 1152, did not affect Marie and Alix's position to any great extent; they remained princesses of France, their legitimacy confirmed by the same ecclesiastical council that had been convened to examine the circumstances of the marriage. Nor did the split particularly alter their relationship with their parents. They would see very little of them from now on, but actually that had always been the case, with royal infants being fed and cared for by wet-nurses and other women employed for the purpose.

When a marriage ended, custody of any children was always the prerogative of the father, and there is some doubt as to whether Eleanor ever saw either of her daughters by Louis again, with the possible exception of a brief meeting with Marie more than forty years later. Eleanor has sometimes been accused of 'abandoning' Marie and Alix when she left the French royal court, but given the situation it is difficult to see what else she could have done; they were their father's property in law, and he would have been perfectly entitled to deny Eleanor access to them even if she had remained in Paris. Meanwhile Louis was, like most medieval kings, a distant father; if the girls did remain at his court for a while once Eleanor had left it, he is unlikely to have spent a great deal of time with them personally. Their only consolation – and even this only as long as they remained in Paris – was that they were probably housed together.

Eleanor's second marriage, to Henry, duke of Normandy, just weeks after her separation from Louis and all too obviously the result of a prior arrangement, enraged the French king. He was 'highly incensed [...] because she had delivered over to the Duke of Normandy the fertile province of Aquitaine, the lawful inheritance, in his opinion, of the daughters he had by the queen', and he 'flew to arms and began very violent attacks on the duke'.[4] Louis sought to make alliances against Henry, and these same dispossessed daughters would be the means by which he achieved his aims. In early 1153, Marie and Alix were betrothed, at the ages of 7 and 2, to the brothers Henry I, count of Champagne, and Theobald V, count of Blois, who were 25 and 22 respectively.

These two men were among France's most powerful nobles: Henry had accompanied King Louis on the Second Crusade as one of his most loyal commanders, and Theobald was shortly to be named seneschal of France.* Their whole family was exceedingly well placed; in addition to Henry and Theobald being two of France's most powerful counts, their other brothers were Stephen, count of Sancerre, and the cleric William

---

* 'Seneschal' can have different meanings in different contexts; in France in the twelfth century the royal seneschal was the most senior of the officers of the crown, heading up the royal household and responsible for raising and organising troops when necessary. The position was not hereditary, and could be awarded or rescinded at the king's pleasure.

Whitehands, who would go on to become archbishop of Reims, France's most senior ecclesiastical position. They also had six sisters, one a nun at Fontevraud and others involved in various high-ranking political marriages. Henry and Theobald were also, as it happened, the nephews of King Stephen of England and therefore not well disposed towards his rival Henry, duke of Normandy. In connecting the counts to the French royal family through his daughters, Louis hoped with their help to profit at the expense of his ex-wife and her new husband, who between them now controlled more of France than he did.

It was customary, at this time, for a child bride to be sent to the lands of her future husband so that she could be brought up and educated in what he considered the most appropriate manner. This is what happened to Marie and Alix, separated now not only from both parents but also from each other. Marie was dispatched to Champagne, probably to the abbey of Avenay, and Alix to an unidentified but no doubt similar foundation in Blois. We should note, at this point, that being educated in a convent by no means indicated that a child was intended for holy orders. The care of infants of both sexes, and of girls as they grew older, was considered a female concern, and convents were centres of female literacy. It thus made sense for royal and noble girls – and boys if they were under the age of about 6 or 7 – to be educated there, though it was certainly a different and more rigorously academic sort of upbringing from the one that might be supervised by a mother or prospective mother-in-law. We do not have the exact details of Marie and Alix's education but it would have been substantial, as befitted the daughters of a king: literacy, Latin, religion, training in how to organise and administer a large estate and a good grounding in politics would all have been included, as well as pursuits that we might consider more traditionally 'feminine'.[5] Noblewomen were expected to be their husbands' able colleagues and deputies, not just the mothers of their children.

As they studied and grew up, Marie and Alix's positions in the dynastic and political order shifted. In 1153 the birth of a son to Eleanor and Henry meant that Marie was no longer the heiress to Aquitaine, a blow both to her father and to her intended husband, who might have hoped to rule it in her name one day. In 1154 Eleanor became queen of England, so the girls found themselves in the unique position of having a crowned parent on both sides of the Channel. In that same year Louis married again; his bride was Constance of Castile, who was at the time somewhere between 14 and 18 years old, and to whom he was actually related even more closely than he was to Eleanor, which demonstrates that the 'consanguinity' excuse for the annulment was nothing more than a convenient fiction.* However, he was again to be disappointed in his quest for a son and heir, as Constance bore him two more daughters: Margaret in 1158 and another Alix (normally referred to as Alice, to avoid confusion – a convention we will follow in this book) in 1160, during which labour Constance died.[6]

Louis, now in his forties and more desperate than ever for a son, married again just five weeks after Constance's death, and his choice of wife was to throw the family relationships and the genealogical record into total confusion. His new queen was Adela, sister to Counts Henry of Champagne and Theobald of Blois, the future husbands of Louis's daughters. This meant that the young men would in due course be Louis's brothers-in-law as well as his sons-in-law, and Queen Adela would be Marie and Alix's stepmother as well as their sister-in-law.** We do not know Adela's exact date of birth, but she was almost certainly still in her teens at the time of the marriage, and thus nearer in age to her stepdaughters than to her husband.

---

* Constance of Castile was a direct descendant, via her paternal grandmother, of King Robert II of France.

** Seriously, try drawing that on a family tree.

The new and complex family situation was cemented in 1164 when the marriages of both sisters took place. Alix was 14, criminally young now but at the time not an unusual age for a noble girl to be married. Marie was a more mature 19; she had already given her personal and binding 'consent' to her marriage some years previously, when she was 14 or 15, but it seems that it was politically expedient to have both weddings take place at the same time, hence her wait until her sister was considered old enough (by twelfth-century standards at least) to consummate her union. Marie and Alix now moved from their places of education to take up residence at their husbands' courts, Marie in Troyes and Alix some 130 miles west of her in Chartres.*

As the king still had no son and Marie was his eldest daughter, Count Henry of Champagne would have been one of the prime candidates to succeed Louis on the French throne had the situation continued thus, though his claim might be contested by the king's younger brother Robert, count of Dreux. But the prospect of conflict over the crown was avoided when Queen Adela – after what must have been a highly stressful and pressured childless five years of marriage – gave birth to a son, Philip (later known as Philip Augustus), in August 1165. There were huge celebrations in the streets of Paris, perhaps motivated by relief as much as joy. A second son for insurance purposes was now Louis's goal but his sixth and final child, born in 1170 when he was 50, was another girl, Agnes.

Following Philip's birth and her own consequent demotion in the line of succession, the now 20-year-old Marie's future was more clearly mapped out as the countess of Champagne, and she soon began a family of her own in order to continue her

---

* Because of the traditional and fixed locations of these comital seats, the count of Champagne was sometimes referred to in contemporary documents as 'the count of Troyes', and the count of Blois as 'the count of Chartres'.

husband's line. She gave birth to a son and heir, Henry (later Henry II of Champagne), in July 1166, and would go on to have three other surviving children: Marie, Scholastica and Theobald. Given the large age gaps between the four – Theobald was not born until 1179 – Marie may have endured stillbirths or infant losses in between, but there are no records either way. Alix also had a family: tragically, three of her four sons died young, but the other, Louis, survived, as did three daughters, Margaret, Isabelle and Alix. It is perhaps worth noting that neither Marie nor Alix called any of their daughters Eleanor, although how much choice they were actually able to exercise in the naming of their children must remain a matter for conjecture.

The exigencies of dynastic politics meant that matches were arranged for Marie's children while they were still very young. No marriage alliances between Champagne and Blois could be considered, of course, as the children were closely related to each other twice over, but other proposed unions offered the potential to spread the family network wider. Marie's two eldest children, Henry and Marie, were betrothed to Isabelle and Baldwin, the two children of Count Baldwin V of Hainaut, when Henry was 5, his fiancée Isabelle about 18 months, and Marie and Baldwin still babies in their cradles. These were matches of great political significance in France, for Baldwin V was not only count of Hainaut in his own right but also the heir to prosperous Flanders via his wife, Margaret, who was sister to the childless Count Philip of Flanders.

It would appear that Marie and Alix had very little opportunity to see each other during the years of their education and early in their marriages. Alix and Theobald visited Marie and Henry in Troyes at Christmas in 1166, and it is possible that this was the first time the sisters had seen each other since they had been separated thirteen years previously.[7] If this was the case, then Alix, who had only been a toddler at that time, can hardly have remembered Marie at all. As with many members of Eleanor of Aquitaine's extended family, Marie and Alix's ties to each other were strong because of their shared blood and their dynastic and political concerns, not because they enjoyed a close personal relationship.

By this time Marie and Alix had a full complement of half-siblings from their mother's second marriage as well as from their father's. Marie, perhaps surprisingly given the complex family circumstances, would become close to the three eldest of the Plantagenet brothers, Henry, Richard and Geoffrey; possibly there was in this an element of compensation for the lack of personal contact with Alix or with any of their French half-siblings during their formative years. Having said that, Marie would later become deeply attached to one of Louis's other daughters through a very strange event: in a confusing arrangement that we will explore more fully in Chapter 5, her paternal half-sister Margaret would marry her maternal half-brother Henry.

Henry, known as the Young King because he had been crowned during his father's lifetime in order to secure the succession (a practice common in France but unknown in England either before or since), was in the early 1170s actually on better terms with his father-in-law than he was with his own father. He thus spent much of his time in France, either on the tournament circuit as a protégé of Count Philip of Flanders, or at Louis VII's court in Paris. In 1173 his disaffection with Henry II resulted in open rebellion, and he, Richard and Geoffrey (supported by Queen Eleanor) conspired against the English king with the French alliance of King Louis and Counts Henry of Champagne and Theobald of Blois. This put Marie and Alix in the position of having their mother and their father siding together against a common enemy, but it did not result in a personal meeting: Eleanor's three sons travelled to Paris but she remained in Aquitaine. All of them, however, had underestimated Henry II, and he soon put down the revolt, forcing his sons to come to terms and imprisoning his wife. None of Eleanor's older children would see her again for quite some while.

While she was Count Henry's consort during the early years of her marriage, Marie was not heavily involved in Champagne's politics or governance, although this would change later. She thus had the time, in between her childbearing duties, to pursue her own interests and to carve out a life of her own, and she became a noted literary patron.

At this time all secular writers – that is, those who were not cloistered monks – needed a patron to support them financially. While monks tended to concentrate on religious texts or chronicle histories, those who lived in the great royal and comital courts produced many other types of literature, including poems and tales of courtly love (a concept we will explore more fully in Chapter 2). During the 1170s Marie supported many poets and writers, including one of the greatest of them all, Chrétien de Troyes. Under her patronage Chrétien wrote five Arthurian romances, clever and intriguing texts that interweave the legendary and fantastic elements of the story with recognisable geography and contemporary political events.* The realm depicted in his first work, *Erec et Enide*, for example, is the England of Henry II, not that of King Arthur; and one of the characters in *Cligès* seems to have been based on Count Henry of Champagne as a young man.

Chrétien's *Lancelot, or the Knight of the Cart* is explicitly dedicated to Marie in a lengthy (and, it must be said, somewhat sycophantic) opening passage in which he credits her

---

* At this time a 'romance' meant a work composed in the vernacular, rather than in Latin; it does not necessarily imply anything 'romantic' in the modern sense.

not just with patronage but also with giving him the idea for the story:

> Since my lady of Champagne wishes me to begin a romance, I shall do so most willingly, like one who is entirely at her service in anything he can undertake in this world. I say this without flattery, though another might begin his story with the desire to flatter her; he might say (and I would agree) that she is the lady who surpasses all women who are alive [...] I will say nothing of the sort, though it is true in spite of me. I will say, however, that her command has more importance in this work than any thought or effort I might put into it. Chrétien begins his book about the Knight of the Cart; the subject matter and meaning are furnished and given him by the countess, and he strives carefully to add nothing but his effort and careful attention.[8]

Another high-profile writer who was based in Troyes was Andreas Capellanus (the soubriquet translates as 'the chaplain'), who was a witness to a number of Marie's charters and acts in the 1180s and may have been a member of the comital household. His most famous work is a Latin treatise called *De amore* (*On Love*), part of which depicts noblewomen pronouncing judgements on a number of different theoretical love-related scenarios. Although both Marie and her mother are listed among those ladies who sit in in this so-called 'court of love', it has long been recognised that the episodes are fictional and that they were not really in each other's company while Andreas was writing. As one of the other ladies depicted at the imaginary court was Eleanor's niece Elizabeth of Vermandois (the daughter of her younger sister, Petronilla), who was already dead by the time the work was completed, it seems that Andreas was simply using the names most likely to be recognisable to his intended audience.[9]

However, Marie's literary patronage might still have been a means of connecting her with Eleanor across the miles that separated them. Literature was not confined by national borders; Andreas's and Chrétien's works were known in England and other realms as well as France, so it is not impossible that Eleanor heard her daughter's name mentioned when the texts were read to or performed for her.*

In May 1179 Marie's life took a dramatic turn when her husband Count Henry departed on crusade, leaving her to rule Champagne in his stead. Despite modern preconceived images of a male lord ruling his lands while his wife sat sewing, this was in fact a very commonplace scenario; a husband might be absent for long periods for any number of reasons, and there was generally no better person to leave in charge than his wife – they were, after all, effectively one legal entity. This is why the education of royal and noble girls included politics and administration as well as religion, reading and music.

A woman left in such a situation did, however, often have to prove herself to her husband's vassals by asserting herself as and when the need arose. In Marie's case, she was greatly assisted by being the daughter of a king as well as the wife of a count, and she employed this status to good effect; the seal that she used to signify her authority had the style 'daughter of the king of the Franks' appearing ahead of her title of countess. We can see from surviving documents and letters that Marie was authoritative: one representative example starts with the unapologetic formula, 'I Marie, countess of Troyes,

---

* Works of secular literature were designed for oral performance, not solitary quiet reading, so Eleanor and Marie (and others) would have heard them spoken aloud.

make known to the present and future that [...]' and ends with a firm, 'Which I have confirmed with my seal so that it may be held valid'.[10] It is also noticeable that no regency council was employed to support or govern her actions; she was in sole charge and had the full authority of her husband. As an additional insurance policy, however, Marie enlisted the support of the pope, Alexander III, who wrote a letter to her that was meant to be made public in order to confirm that he had acceded to her request:

> To his beloved daughter in Christ, noble woman countess of Troyes. Though we are debtors to all by the ministry of the office we have accepted, we are more inclined to protect the rights of those who show purer devotion to us and the church and do not refuse to travel to lands across the sea to defend the Christian name. Induced by that reason and *inclined by your requests*, we take the land of our beloved son, the noble man H[enry] count of Troyes, your husband, and you with everything pertaining to you under the protection of St. Peter and us until his return and we affirm under the patronage of this document that no man is permitted to weaken the letter of our protection or to oppose it by reckless boldness. If anyone should presume to attempt this, he should know that he will incur the anger of almighty God and of the saints Peter and Paul the apostles.[11]

Marie was therefore safe under the protection of both a royal and a spiritual father, but she and Alix were not to remain daughters of a reigning king for much longer. In November 1179 their younger half-brother Philip Augustus was crowned as 'junior king' of France, but by that time Louis was already gravely ill, incapacitated after suffering a stroke during a pilgrimage to Canterbury in August to pray at the shrine of St Thomas Becket; he had travelled there to implore the saint's intercession as his only son was gravely ill and thought likely to die, a situation that would have been catastrophic for the French succession. Louis's prayers were answered and Philip recovered, but Louis never regained his own health.

At the time of his accession Philip was on good terms with the Plantagenet brothers, and Henry the Young King, Richard and Geoffrey were all present at his coronation. This was not an opportunity for Marie and Alix to meet with their English family, however, for they were not in attendance, and neither was Philip's mother, Adela of Blois. This was an early indication of the rift that would soon occur in the family. The French crown had long been on the closest terms with the houses of Champagne and Blois, but now this relationship was elbowed aside in favour of the new king's partiality for the combined Flanders–Hainaut faction. Philip Augustus was simultaneously very much under the influence of Count Philip of Flanders while also wanting to stamp his own authority on the kingdom, and he was not afraid to offend his closest relatives in order to achieve his aims.

Although only the 'junior king', the 14-year-old took up the reins of power straight away due to Louis's incapacity, and immediately made a series of provocative moves. He confiscated his mother's lands, forcing her to flee to the court of her brother Theobald, Alix's husband. He dismissed Theobald from his position as royal seneschal. Then, in April 1180, Philip decided to marry, and he took as his bride none other than Isabelle of Hainaut, who had long been betrothed to Marie's son Henry. Politically this had its advantages for the junior king: he gained Isabelle's dowry of the county of Artois and formalised his alliance with Counts Philip and Baldwin while simultaneously preventing the planned Champagne–Hainaut–Flanders coalition, which would be a threat to his own interests. However, it was a huge insult to his eldest sister, and it caused a rift between them that would sour relations for some years. King Louis's infirmity meant that there was no possibility of

Marie appealing to him; he died in September 1180, having never recovered sufficiently to resume governance of the realm, and leaving France to the increasingly authoritative Philip.

In the early spring of 1181, Marie's husband, Count Henry, returned from the Holy Land after a two-year absence. He had endured some difficult experiences abroad: he had been the sole survivor of a massacre in Anatolia, and was subsequently captured and imprisoned before being ransomed. Following his release, he set off home, but the rigours of crusade and captivity had taken their toll. Marie welcomed him home to Troyes, but he died just weeks later in March 1181.

Marie now found herself, at the age of 36, a widow with four young children. There was no question that her elder son, Henry (now Henry II of Champagne), would succeed to the county; however, as he was still not quite 15 and the age of majority for French noblemen was 21, Marie would need to act as his regent for the next six years.* She appears to have managed the transition with very little fuss, her previous experience of acting for her husband no doubt being of great use. Once again, no voice was raised against her, for it was just as normal to see a mother ruling on behalf of a son as it was to see a wife acting for her husband. Having women in positions of authority was not a problem to contemporary patriarchal society, so long as that female authority was acting within

---

* As we have already noted, Philip Augustus took over the reins of power from his ailing father when he was 14 and became sole king at 15, without a regent; the normal comital rules do not appear to have applied to the French crown. Philip was the youngest king of France to assume full independent power, and must have been very much on the borderline – when his grandson Louis IX later acceded at the age of 12, he was subject to a regency.

male constraints. That is to say, it was perfectly acceptable for a woman to exercise power on behalf of a male relative; trouble would only arise if she sought to rule in her own name.* Marie was extremely careful in this respect, noting in her acts that she had the consent of 'my dearest son Henry' or opening her letters with 'I, Marie, countess of Troyes, and my son Henry' to emphasise their joint authority.[12]

In June 1183 Henry the Young King, the eldest of Alix and Marie's English half-brothers and the husband of their French half-sister Margaret, died. It does not appear that either of them attended his funeral, held in Rouen, but a year later Marie was one of the participants at a memorial service, after which the widowed Margaret came to stay with her in Troyes. Margaret had spent some time there previously, while Young Henry had been on the tournament circuit in the late 1170s, and these two sojourns enabled the sisters to develop a close relationship that would be lifelong. Also at the memorial service was another half-brother, Geoffrey, along with his wife, Constance of Brittany; Geoffrey had by this time 'so won over the minds of King Philip and all the great men of France that, by their unanimous wish, he was created seneschal of France', and he spent a great deal of his time at the French court.[13] Unfortunately, he would not long survive his eldest brother; he was killed in a tournament in Paris in August 1186. Geoffrey's death seems to have struck Marie particularly hard. She was by this time reconciled to Philip Augustus, and attended the funeral with him in Paris, at which point she endowed a

---

* The obvious example here is Empress Matilda (Eleanor of Aquitaine's mother-in-law), who was lauded as the consort and occasional regent of her first husband in Germany, vilified when she sought to rule in her own name in England, as the only surviving legitimate child of Henry I, and then appreciated once more when she later ruled Normandy on behalf of her son. Her death in 1167 was well within living memory, and Marie would have wished to avoid attracting any of the same sort of criticism.

chaplain to celebrate Mass on the anniversary of Geoffrey's death in perpetuity, something she is not recorded as doing for any of her many other half-siblings.[14]

In the summer of 1187, Marie's son Henry celebrated his twenty-first birthday and thus reached his majority. He assumed full control of his estates, and Marie decided to retire to a convent – possibly taking her younger son, Theobald, who was still only 8 years old, with her. She did not take any vows, and nor was there a need for her to do so: it was just as normal for noblewomen, particularly widowed ones, to live in convents as guests as it was for noble children to be educated in them. In such an institution a widow could live retired from the secular world, free from the presence of men and from the pressure of marrying again, but without needing to become a nun. Convents would have guest houses or apartments for this purpose and would expect a significant financial contribution in return, which Marie could easily afford. For her, of course, life in a nunnery would have been a familiar and perhaps comforting return to the routine of her youth.

We cannot be sure whether Marie intended her stay to be a temporary one as she planned her next move (she was still only in her early forties), or whether she intended to lead a quiet, retired life until she died, but the question was soon taken out of her hands. She can barely have settled into the convent when she was called upon to leave it again; only six months after his assumption of full authority, Henry II of Champagne decided to follow in his father's footsteps and head east on a crusade. He was single, having turned down an offer from Count Baldwin V of Hainaut to marry his second daughter as a consolation prize for the eldest having married King Philip, and with no wife to leave in charge, the obvious person to name as regent was his well-regarded and experienced mother.

Marie returned to Troyes and Henry set off on what would later become known as the Third Crusade, together with his paternal uncles Theobald of Blois and Stephen of Sancerre and with the rival kings Richard of England and Philip of France – both also his uncles, thanks to his mother's family connections. As it happened, the two kings also left their mothers in charge during their absence, Eleanor of Aquitaine acting as regent in England and Adela of Blois in France.

The departure of Count Theobald on the crusade in the spring of 1190 meant that Alix, too, was now acting as regent in her county. Like her sister's, her regency moved from husband to son when Theobald died in January 1191 at the siege of Acre; their one surviving son, Louis, was at that time still a minor.

Marie ruled in Champagne without incident for some while, a familiar figure to the nobles and to the people, but then some strange and surprising news reached her in the summer of 1192: her son Henry was now the king of Jerusalem. The background to this is complex, but in short, Queen Isabelle of Jerusalem held the title in her own right, and her husband and consort Conrad of Montferrat had been assassinated, thus leaving her in need of a new partner who could lead the crusaders' military efforts.[15] There was much jostling for position but Henry II of Champagne, as a close relative of the kings of both France and England, was seen as a good compromise candidate. He was pressured to marry Isabelle and the ceremony took place just eight days after Conrad's death, even though she was heavily pregnant with Conrad's child at the time. Henry, in fact, does not seem to have been particularly gallant about the situation, being pushed into it by King Richard:

The king spoke to the count and told him that he wanted to give him this lady, but he explained that she was pregnant by the marquis and if she bore a male heir he would inherit the kingdom. To this the count replied 'And I shall be stuck with the woman. You will know why I cannot then go to Champagne.' The king said, 'I shall give you more than you would ever get by going back to Champagne.'[16]

This was hardly a reflection of the courtly behaviour espoused by the literature that was patronised by Henry's mother. But, however willingly or unwillingly the marriage was undertaken by either party (we do not know what Isabelle of Jerusalem thought of it herself), it had significant consequences for Marie. As king of Jerusalem, or as regent for a newborn boy who would experience a very long minority, Henry was unlikely ever to return from the east. He would become the leader of the crusading forces in the Holy Land once King Richard left for England (King Philip was already back in France by this time). As it happens, the child Isabelle bore posthumously to Conrad in 1192 was a girl, Maria, so Henry remained king of Jerusalem in right of his wife. Marie's regency in Champagne thus took on an air of permanency, although Henry did correspond with her to some extent, sealing documents *in absentia*. He and Isabelle would have three children together, all girls, and Marie would never meet these granddaughters of Jerusalem.[*]

King Richard departed the Holy Land in October 1192, but he was captured on the way home and imprisoned in Germany (we will explore this in greater depth in Chapters 4 and 6).

---

* Due to a lack of male heirs, the crown of Jerusalem passed to four queens regnant in a row between 1186 and 1228. This was remarked upon at the time as a weakness, but actually it had the advantage that a king (taking the throne by marriage) could be chosen for his ability and prowess, rather than the position passing to a man who might be weak or unsuitable even though he was born as the hereditary heir.

His incarceration was to last for some time while an enormous ransom was collected, and one of the ways in which Richard kept himself occupied was in writing a poem that he sent to Marie. In it he addresses her as 'Countess sister' and writes of her 'sovereign worth', but it is not in any way a poem in praise of her in the traditional courtly style – it is more like an extended complaint at how long it is taking to raise the ransom money. One interesting point that it does seem to confirm is that Richard was on much better personal terms with Marie than he was with Alix: far from describing her as another 'countess sister', he writes of Alix that 'I do not speak about the one in Chartres, Louis's mother'.[17]

The person most instrumental in ensuring that the ransom was raised was Eleanor of Aquitaine, and once she had amassed sufficient cash and treasure, she chose to travel in person to Germany in order to hand it over. As her route would logically have taken her through Champagne in December 1193, it is just possible that she might have met Marie again in person for the first time in over forty years – but, frustratingly, there is no specific evidence either way.[18] The ransom effort involved hostages as well as money, and several members of Richard's extended family would be called upon to this end; this reminds us once again that a king was supported by a large kinship network that included female members, even when they had married into far-flung lands.

By the late 1190s, Marie was in her fifties and Alix in her late forties. They were by no means old – and certainly not in comparison to their indefatigable mother – but they were nevertheless at an age where they might start to think about slowing down, and Marie had already made one attempt to retire to a convent before her duty called her out of it again. Alix's regency in Blois came to an end when her son Louis reached his majority, but Marie's was to continue under tragic circumstances when her son Henry died at Acre in September 1197, never having returned to France.* Although he had three daughters from his marriage to Queen Isabelle, they would remain in the east and he was succeeded in Champagne by his younger brother, Theobald. Theobald was still in his teens at the time, so this meant that Marie's rule continued, with only the name of her 'dear son' changed in her acts. This time, however, she was not able to put as much energy and vigour into her actions, crushed as she was by the heartbreak of Henry's death and by the second loss that had occurred in the Holy Land at almost exactly the same time: that of her half-sister Margaret of France.

This double tragedy sent Marie into a depression, one that was considered so grave that in February 1198 Pope Innocent III wrote to three French bishops to warn them that she was so seriously affected that she might cause herself harm.[19] The toll on Marie's mental and physical health was severe and she seems to have retired again, possibly even taking the veil this time. Whether or not this was the case, she died (apparently of natural causes) very shortly afterwards, in March 1198. She left three surviving children: Marie, who was by now countess of both Flanders and Hainaut by right of her marriage to Baldwin VI, which had proceeded as her mother had originally planned all those years ago; Scholastica, who had married a minor local count; and Count Theobald III of Champagne, now 19 and able to take over his affairs himself, although he was technically still underage. He arranged for Marie to be buried in Meaux cathedral and, among other bequests in her honour, paid for a candle to be kept burning perpetually in memory of her.[20]

---

* Henry died in an unfortunate accident: he was killed when a balcony or trellis gave way beneath him and he fell from a first-floor window of the palace in Acre.

Marie had continued to be a literary patron through all the intervening years, and a writer who was undertaking a commission at her request was in the middle of it when she died. He broke off to insert some heartfelt words about her:

> All women now living should take her as an example, for from her all good things are derived. All other women are honoured by her [...] She has taken away the wicked blame the world bestows on other women, so that great honour abounds in them. She kept the land well and maintained it, nor was anything she had in her hands lost; she was so gracious, and wise and worthy and courageous.[21]

As readers will no doubt have noticed, there has been rather more about Marie in this chapter than about Alix. The reason for this is that we simply do not have anything like the same amount or quality of evidence for Alix's life; we can only glean information from passing mentions. She faded from the historical record completely following her son Louis's majority in 1193 and the consequent cessation of her regency; it is probable that she died in 1198, the same year as her sister. Alix left four surviving children: Louis I, count of Blois, who would die in Constantinople in 1205 during the Fourth Crusade; Margaret, who later became countess of Blois in her own right after the childless death of Louis's only son; Isabelle, married to a minor lord in Touraine and also later countess of Blois following the deaths of Margaret and her children; and her namesake Alix, a nun who was later abbess of Fontevraud abbey.

Marie and Alix led lives that were almost completely separate from the other members of their extended family, and indeed from each other. Despite this, Marie felt strong ties of kinship to her half-siblings, as they were part of the same dynastic unit. The sisters' network of relationships meant that, although they never left France, their influence stretched across international borders as far as Constantinople and the Holy Land. At home they were held in great respect, not only because of their birth and their noble marriages, but also because of their independent actions. Alix was a capable regent for her husband and son in Blois, and Marie ruled the great county of Champagne almost uninterrupted for two decades, not only keeping it in good order but enhancing its prestige both politically and culturally.

Marie and Alix are fine exemplars of medieval noblewomen. They had no say in the choice of their life partners, but they made their mark on the world by working within the constraints they were given. Nobody expressed surprise that these women should be asked to rule lands and estates on behalf of their husbands or sons; nobody expressed surprise when they did it effectively and with authority. These daughters of France knew their duty – to both their birth family and the families they acquired by marriage – and they acted in the manner best designed to execute it, just as their sisters and sisters-in-law were called upon to do in their different ways in other realms.

PART II

DAUGHTERS OF ENGLAND

MATILDA

Matilda was the first daughter born to Eleanor of Aquitaine from her second marriage, to Henry II. She was also the first of Eleanor's girls whose arrival was not a profound disappointment to the father: Henry had already seen his wife bear him two sons in the first three years of their marriage, so he was not ill-disposed to a daughter who would be useful to him in forming a marriage alliance later on. Matilda was born in England in June 1156 and was baptised at Holy Trinity Church in Aldgate, London, by Theobald of Bec, the archbishop of Canterbury; she was named for her paternal grandmother, Empress Matilda, from whom Henry derived his right to the English throne.[1] The elder Matilda was at this time ruling Normandy as Henry's regent while he concentrated on stamping his authority on England, where he had acceded to the throne some eighteen months previously following a civil war that had lasted the best part of two decades.

In marked contrast to her elder half-sisters Marie and Alix, little Matilda spent much of her infancy and early life in her mother's company, travelling with Eleanor as she crossed and re-crossed the Channel to visit the different parts of the vast domain formed by the union of her lands and Henry's. Matilda can barely have been 2 months old when she made her first journey overseas, taken with Eleanor's household as she crossed to Normandy in the later summer of 1156. With them was the boy who was by now the heir to the English throne,

Eleanor's second son Henry; her eldest, William, had died at the age of 3 during that same summer, though we do not know if this was before or after Matilda's birth. They all returned to England in the spring of 1157, Eleanor in the early stages of another pregnancy, and Matilda would remain in her mother's household and her care (if not necessarily by her side) in England, Normandy and Anjou between that time and 1167, when she turned 11.[2] During this time she would have received the sort of comprehensive education that royal girls expected; she was certainly both literate and pious, and as an adult she demonstrated a firm grasp of international politics. She may also have learned to speak the language now known as Middle High German, in order to prepare her for what was to come.

Matilda's experience of an itinerant lifestyle at a young age would be good training for the future, for by the time she reached what would now be the end of primary-school age, plans for her wedding were already in train. As the eldest daughter of the king of England, she would naturally be expected to make a marriage of international significance, and so it proved: in early 1165 a match was arranged between the then 8-year-old Matilda and Henry the Lion, duke of Saxony and Bavaria, a cousin and powerful ally of the Holy Roman Emperor Frederick Barbarossa. Some thought had perhaps been given to an alliance with the emperor's more immediate family, but his son Frederick was only a year old, significantly younger than Matilda, and age gaps were less acceptable that way round. Henry II succeeded in negotiating a betrothal for his second daughter, Leonor, with young Frederick, but this match never came to fruition.

On a personal level, the prospect of a union with Henry the Lion cannot have been entirely enticing to a young girl – he was a divorcee in his mid-thirties with two daughters older than his new fiancée – but Matilda's opinions on the matter, of course, carried no weight with King Henry and are unlikely to have been canvassed at all.[3] It was a prestigious match for her, and that was all that mattered. Henry the Lion might be a duke, not a king, but the size of the Empire meant that his lands were just as extensive as those of some monarchs, and this, coupled with his proximity to the imperial throne, meant that he was one of the most powerful uncrowned men in western Europe. The marriage would give Matilda the scope to be politically ambitious, regardless of what her personal feelings might have been.

Duke Henry sent envoys to England to collect his bride in September 1167, and Matilda said goodbye to her mother, who accompanied her as far as Dover, for what she probably expected would be the last time. She reached Germany in safety and was married to Duke Henry on 1 February 1168, still aged only 11.[4] This was the start of her new life and she must see what she could make of it, both in personal terms and on behalf of her birth family.

One point in favour of the marriage, one consolation for an apprehensive young girl in a strange country, is that Matilda could expect to be treated with courtesy and honour. Although it came with a lack of agency in the choice of marriage partner, her position as the representative of a dynasty had its advantages: she was no friendless girl but the embodiment of the Plantagenet family, and thus to treat her with anything less than respect would be to disparage Henry II. Insulting King Henry was not, and never would be, a particularly astute political move, so his status offered his daughter a great deal of protection. The marriage also bolstered Duke Henry's prestige, a royal title being the only thing he was lacking, and he emphasised his new wife's status whenever possible. For example, Matilda is mentioned in three surviving charters of her husband's, and in two of them she is given the style *filia regis* ('daughter of a king').[5] Moreover, Matilda's family background had additional significance in Germany: Empress Matilda, the grandmother for whom she was named, was – as her title implied – a former empress. She had been very popular during her tenure, known as 'the good Matilda' when she reigned as the wife and consort of Emperor Henry V (Barbarossa's great-uncle) in the early twelfth century.[6]

The splendour of young Matilda's lineage was also accentuated by the rich items she brought with her to her marriage, either as personal possessions in a trousseau or as part of the dowry she was bringing to her husband. A contemporary narrative notes merely that she was sent 'with an immense sum of money, and in very great state', but the English Pipe Rolls (financial records) for the year of her departure give more detail, listing the expense of travel for Matilda and her retinue, as well as sumptuous clothes and furs, horses, and household goods including tapestries and furniture.[7]

So Matilda, in February 1168, found herself a married woman – or, to be more precise, a married pre-pubescent. Duke Henry, with no surviving son from his first marriage, would naturally have been keen for a male heir, but none appeared for some while. It is not clear whether this was because Henry held off from consummating his new union, in view of Matilda's tender age, or whether he did sleep with his young wife but she either did not become pregnant for several years or endured early miscarriages that were not recorded. Such events were so common that contemporary commentators rarely mention them, so there is no way of knowing.[8] For her sake we may hope it was the former.

Matilda evidently made the best of the situation she had been compelled to accept, growing into her role as duchess. In 1172 Duke Henry set off on a pilgrimage, travelling to Jerusalem 'with a large retinue of soldiers, full of mighty designs' and with treasure that he 'distributed with a liberal hand among the poor and the churches of the Holy Land'.[9] While he was away, he left Matilda as regent for his domains, even though she was still only 15 or 16, and we have no reason to believe that she was not up to the task; as far as we can see from the evidence, matters under her control continued to function smoothly. As would later be the case for her half-sister Marie in far-off Champagne, Matilda was not subject to a regency council, instead ruling alone in her husband's name.

As Matilda began her stint as her husband's regent, she was pregnant, and while he was away in the Holy Land she bore him a daughter, who was named Richenza.* It is difficult to know exactly how much input Matilda had in the naming of her children but this choice was suitable for both families, being that of Duke Henry's grandmother, Empress Richenza, and also the female form of Richard, the name of one of Matilda's brothers. Henry may have been disappointed at the arrival of a third girl, following the two from his first marriage, but after his return to Germany in 1173 his familial ambitions were amply fulfilled as his still-teenaged wife bore him three sons in the next four years. These were an heir, Henry (a name again diplomatically commemorating members of both families), and then two others given the more traditionally German names of Lothar and Otto.

Henry the Lion was a first cousin of the Holy Roman Emperor, Frederick Barbarossa (Henry's father and Frederick's mother having been siblings), and in Germany he was second only to the imperial family in dignity and ambition. 'No one holds

---

* This is the name she is given in German records. In English chronicles this daughter is often called Matilda, though whether this is because the writers thought it was an alternative version of the same name, or whether they were confusing her with her mother, or whether they were simply not particularly bothered about the exact name of a daughter, is not clear.

such extensive possessions as he has [...] for he has forty cities and sixty-seven castles, besides very many towns', wrote one impressed contemporary.[10] His two duchies, Saxony in the north and Bavaria in the south, did not border each other and it might have been expected that – like many other lords with extensive holdings – he would travel frequently between the two. However, he chose to reside almost entirely in Brunswick in Saxony, intending to develop it into not only a magnificent ducal residence but also a rich cultural hub. His royal wife, thanks to her connections and the money she had brought with her to the match, would be crucial to these ambitions.

In 1173 Henry and Matilda founded and began the construction of a church dedicated to St Blaise and St John the Baptist, better known today as Brunswick cathedral. Like all such building projects, this was an enormous undertaking that would take decades to complete and it was intended as a statement of the glory and prestige of the founders as well as the glory of God. While construction was underway, the ducal couple commissioned magnificent liturgical objects to be placed in the cathedral when it was complete, including an illuminated psalter, a pyx for the main altar and a sumptuous gospel book intended for the altar of the Virgin Mary.

This gospel book was produced sometime in the 1170s or 1180s, and it still survives today.[11] The fact that this was a joint enterprise of Henry's and Matilda's is evidenced by their appearances together at several points within the volume: they are both mentioned in the dedication poem, both pictured in the miniature that accompanies the dedication, and both appear in a separate illumination known as the 'coronation miniature', in which they are depicted being crowned by God (with a crown of eternal life as a reward for their piety, not as secular king and queen) while a collection of saints look on. Matilda's royal and imperial lineage is emphasised in this image by the inclusion behind her of Henry II and Empress Matilda;

the inscription calls her 'Duchess Matilda daughter of the king of the English'.[12] She was not merely the wife of Henry the Lion but the representative of her royal dynasty and the means by which her husband could be connected to it.

Ostentatious piety was expected of those who were in positions of privilege, and gifts from the couple to other religious foundations included a donation of intricately embroidered vestments to Hildesheim cathedral. Matilda herself seems to have been the driving force here, as the cathedral's chapter book specifically notes that the gift was from 'Duchess Matilda [...] together with her husband Duke Henry', a form of wording that would be unusual if he had been the primary donor.[13] The extent of Matilda's enthusiasm for, and her generosity to, religious foundations would seem to indicate that she possessed a deep and genuine piety rather than merely donating out of conventional expectation, although she could certainly use her gifts to her own and her family's advantage where necessary.

One way in which Matilda achieved this was through the propagation of the cult of St Thomas Becket in Germany. Becket, of course, was a very recent saint; he had been the archbishop of Canterbury until he met his death in the cathedral there in December 1170, and in an unusually speedy process had been canonised in February 1173. It may seem odd that a man murdered when in dispute with Henry II (whether at his direct order or not) should be venerated by the family, and indeed to begin with King Henry tried to suppress Becket's cult. However, when it became clear that the momentum of the cult was unstoppable, and when stories of miracles began to circulate and to be widely believed, he changed tack. After a very public penance and display of reconciliation, the king appropriated the cult as his own, which had two advantages: in embracing it publicly he fought against the widespread perception of his culpability for the archbishop's death, and it also meant that he could claim Becket as a special saint particularly linked to his family.[14]

Henry II invoked the name of St Thomas Becket at every available opportunity when it would be advantageous for him to do so. For example, the saint's favour was apparently confirmed when Henry's men captured King William I of Scots at Alnwick on the very day that Henry was praying at Becket's tomb during the war of 1173-74. This coincidence was remarked upon by contemporaries: 'The king of England [...] had made his peace with St Thomas on that very morning when the king of Scots was made prisoner and led away', notes one, adding later that when Henry heard the news he exclaimed, 'Thanks be to God, and to St Thomas the Martyr, and to all the saints of God!'[15]

It was therefore in the interests of Henry II's dynasty to promote the cult of Becket and their special relationship with him, and Matilda took up the idea with enthusiasm. There is evidence of this in the gospel book mentioned earlier in this chapter: Becket is one of the saints depicted in the coronation miniature, placed directly above Matilda's grandmother Empress Matilda. Given that there were so many saints to choose from and that Becket had only recently been canonised, this seems a deliberate choice. Becket's martyrdom is also depicted in a wall painting in Brunswick cathedral; the fresco dates from after Matilda's death, but he would be an unlikely subject for a cathedral in Saxony unless there was a particular reason for his inclusion, and Matilda's propagation of his cult seems by far the most plausible explanation. Matilda's eldest son, Henry, would later establish Thomas Becket as the patron saint of the duchy of Saxony.[16]

During the 1170s, Duke Henry was involved in various disputes with other magnates and bishops in Germany, relying on his close relationship to the emperor to aid him. However, towards the end of that decade he lost Barbarossa's support and even quarrelled with the emperor, a hazardous course of action. He was summoned several times to answer charges in front of an assembly, but refused to appear, which eventually resulted in January 1180 in a sentence of outlawry being passed against him and in the confiscation of his estates.[17]

None of this, of course, was Matilda's fault, but like all wives she would bear the consequences along with her husband. Duke Henry refused to accept the sentence, and a year and a half of campaigning followed. The results were not favourable to him:

> The emperor, with a great army, entered the territories of the duke of Saxony and laid them to waste with fire, and sword, and famine, and reduced the duke to such extremities that he placed himself at the mercy of the emperor, abjured his territory, and placed the same for seven years at the mercy of the emperor.[18]

By 1182, therefore, Duke Henry found himself no better off for all his attempted resistance. He was forced to go into exile and to agree not to return without the emperor's consent. Matilda was to accompany him, but it appears that her royal status and her connections could have spared her, as a chronicler explains: 'The emperor granted to Matilda, duchess of Saxony, in consideration of the love he bore to the king of England, her father, permission to remain at perfect liberty and under his protection, and to enjoy all her dowry freely and quietly.'[19] Barbarossa evidently did not wish to pick a fight with the only other man in western Europe whose power approached his own.

Whether Matilda declined this offer from the emperor on her own behalf, or whether Duke Henry would not countenance her staying in Brunswick while he had to leave, is not clear, but in either case the couple left the Empire together in

July 1182 along with their daughter and two of their sons, Henry and Otto. Their other son, Lothar, remained in Germany, probably as a hostage for his father's good behaviour. Unlike many refugees, they knew exactly where they were going: the family's destination, unsurprisingly, was the domain of Matilda's father, where they would be guaranteed safety.

Matilda was at this time heavily pregnant, which must have made the 630-mile journey from Brunswick to Argentan, in Normandy, particularly trying. Travelling was arduous at the best of times. Nobody of Matilda's status would walk, of course, but the only other options were horseback, a swaying horse litter or a slow, springless, jolting wagon – none of which were comfortable for a woman in the late stages of pregnancy. The hardship duly took its toll. The party arrived at Argentan before the end of the summer, at which point Matilda gave birth to a fourth son. He is not named in any source and never mentioned again, so we can only assume that, tragically for Matilda, he died shortly after birth.[20]

Matilda, Henry and family remained in Normandy for the next year and a half, relying on her father for support. The king was generous: he 'expended large sums of money in his [Duke Henry's] behalf', wrote one chronicler, while another adds that the duke 'was there supplied three [*sic*] years by the king's munificence with all things necessary in great abundance'.[21] This eased their situation somewhat, but there was still no possibility of a return to Germany, so in spring 1184 the couple travelled with Henry II to England. It was yet another uncomfortable journey, this time over the sea, and Matilda was pregnant once more.

Matilda arrived in the land of her birth for the first time since she had left it as a young girl, but she encountered a less than ideal family situation. Queen Eleanor was at that time a prisoner of her husband, having been kept in captivity since the failed uprising of her sons back in 1173–74 (which we mentioned briefly in Chapter 1, and which will be explored in greater depth in Chapter 5). This was not harsh imprisonment in a dungeon – it was more akin to what we might now call 'house arrest' – but it still made the family reunion extremely awkward. However, Matilda's presence helped: it is perhaps overstating the case to say that the intervening decade had mellowed the king, but his daughter's arrival either coincided with, or was the catalyst for, some relaxing of the restrictions on Eleanor. Mother and daughter were thus able to spend as much time as they liked in each other's company – a luxury few queens experienced with their married daughters – and Matilda benefited from Eleanor's presence when she gave birth to a fifth and final son, William, at Winchester in July or August 1184. The choice of name is interesting: there was no precedent for a William in Henry the Lion's family, but there were several illustrious examples in Matilda's, including William the Conqueror on her father's side, the many Williams who were dukes of Aquitaine on her mother's, and of course Matilda's own eldest brother who had died as a child. The choice of name was almost certainly a deliberate attempt on the ducal couple's part to associate their newest son with England, the place of his birth, and with the side of the family that was at present best suited to advance him.

Matilda and Eleanor spent much of the rest of that year together, and in December 1184 Matilda found herself at the royal Christmas court at Windsor not only with her father and her mother, but also with all three of her surviving brothers, Richard, Geoffrey and John (Henry the Young King having died the previous year), an unexpected circumstance that could hardly have been predicted a few years previously. By this time Matilda's elder sons were growing up – Henry aged around 10 or 11, Otto 8 or 9 – and the family gathering gave them a chance to get to know their uncles, forming an important personal connection to the men who would be their political allies in the years to come. Otto in particular would grow up to be a favourite with both Richard and John.

During all his time in exile, Duke Henry had never ceased lobbying for the recovery of his lands and possessions in Germany, something that would have been all but impossible had it not been for the weight of his wife's family connections. In 1185 he was reconciled with the emperor, a contemporary noting that this came about 'by God's assistance, and by the energy, power and riches of the king of England'.[22] Matilda's place, of course, was at her husband's side, so in May of that year she said goodbye to her mother once more and set off on the journey back to Germany. It might have been a wrench, personally speaking, but the two women had spent more precious months together at that stage of their lives than either of them would ever have expected.

Matilda and Duke Henry took the opportunity of renewed ties to the English court to ensure future benefit for their children: they left Richenza (now entering her teens and thus approaching marriageable age) and baby William (who was less than a year old but had a specific connection to England as he had been born there) behind them to be brought up under the auspices of Henry II. There is no indication that young Henry remained also; as he was the eldest son and therefore the heir to all his father's German lands, it is probable that he returned with his parents to Brunswick. There is no evidence either way as to whether Otto went or remained at this stage, although if he returned to Germany he did not stay there long, as he was back in England by 1189.

To modern sensibilities it might seem surprising that Matilda would either suggest or agree to the separation from her children, particularly in baby William's case, but as the product of her dynastic upbringing she would recognise that her children would be best served by her utilising her royal connections on their behalf rather than by her personal presence. This was the primary means by which she could expand her own and her family's network – and her ambitions for her sons would have been particularly high at this point, as Henry II had no other surviving grandsons.*

When Matilda made it back to Germany, she may or may not have been able to see her second son, Lothar, for the first time in several years; he was still a hostage, but it is unclear precisely what the restrictions on him were. Being a young noble hostage did not generally mean imprisonment, but rather being brought up and educated at the court of the holding lord, while hopefully also developing some personal loyalty to him. Even if she were not able to see Lothar in person, therefore, Matilda could rest assured that he was being treated according to his rank.[23]

There is unfortunately little evidence to inform us of Duke Henry's and Matilda's precise activities during the years that immediately followed their return from exile. They probably remained in Brunswick for the most part, Henry of course having a great deal of catching up to do with the administration of his vast estates after his lengthy absence. We might also conjecture that he would have been keen to keep his head down in order not to further strain his newly patched-up relationship with the emperor. As for Matilda, her childbearing years were over, although as she was still not quite 30 at the time of their return, she might not have realised that for some time. Whatever her thoughts or hopes, the cessation

---

* Matilda's younger sister Leonor had by this time, the spring of 1185, borne three sons, but heartbreakingly all of them had died in infancy. She had one surviving child, the 4- or 5-year-old Berenguela, but as the daughter of a daughter Berenguela was unlikely to figure in Henry II's plans. His only other grandchild was Eleanor, a baby daughter born to his son Geoffrey in 1184. Unless and until a grandson was born to him in the male line, Henry might have been well disposed to favour Matilda's sons if they were continually under his eye and he could supervise their upbringing.

of frequent pregnancies and their attendant recovery periods did give her more time to focus her attentions on other, more intellectual, pursuits.

Like Marie of Champagne, the half-sister she never met, Matilda was both a patron and the dedicatee of a number of literary works, including poems by troubadours, who were composers and performers of works that generally dealt with the theme of courtly love. This is a complex subject, but in short: a 'courtly' love was one that, while evincing sexual attraction, was platonic rather than physical in nature, as it was a love felt by a knight for an unattainable lady, generally one far above him in rank. He would perform knightly deeds of chivalry in her name, being spurred on to great feats by thoughts of impressing her.[24] There was a specific link between Matilda's family and this genre of literature, as Queen Eleanor's grandfather, Duke William IX of Aquitaine, had been one of the earliest and greatest of the troubadours.

While Matilda was at Argentan between summer 1182 and early 1184, during her period of exile from Germany, she came into contact with one of the most well-known troubadours of them all, Bertran de Born. He was a baron from the Limousin region of Aquitaine, and thus a vassal of Henry II. Bertran had previously fought alongside Henry the Young King and had composed a lament in Young Henry's honour when he died. Now, giving Matilda the pseudonym 'Elena' (a variant of Helen, presumably in reference to Helen of Troy), Bertran made her the subject of two poems of courtly love. In one, he wrote, 'The boredom and vulgarity of Argentan nearly killed me, but the noble, lovable body and sweet, mild face and good companionship of the Saxon lady protected me.' This might sound a little risqué, but courtly love, as we should remember, was all about longing for an unattainable object rather than a real relationship, so after some frank speculation about what Matilda would look like without her clothes, Bertran clarifies in another stanza:

> So it is right for love to kill me, for the loveliest one in the world, and all in vain, for when I watch her fine ways I know she'll never be mine. If she wants to she can choose among the noblest castellans and the most powerful barons. She holds the mastery of virtue and courtesy, noble gifts, and most exquisite behaviour.[25]

Matilda also played a fundamental role in having some works of Old French and Anglo-Norman literature translated into German, thereby increasing their reach and making them available to a new international audience. One of the oldest and most famous works of French literature was the epic *Chanson de Roland* (*Song of Roland*), an eleventh-century poem telling of the Battle of Roncevaux Pass during the reign of Charlemagne; a version of this text was produced in German as the *Rolandslied* by Conrad of Regensburg in the 1170s. In his epilogue, Conrad wrote that he composed the work at the request of the noble spouse of Duke Henry, who was herself the daughter of a king; this can only mean Matilda.[26]

In 1189 Emperor Frederick Barbarossa was planning to set off on the high-profile Third Crusade, along with King Philip Augustus of France and Matilda's brother Richard, who was by now the heir to the English throne (and actually its king by the time he departed). Perhaps not wanting to leave such a powerful yet troublesome vassal behind him during an absence of uncertain duration, Barbarossa demanded that

Duke Henry either go with him to the Holy Land or resume his exile until he returned.[27]

Henry chose to take refuge in England once again, taking with him (either by choice or by order) his eldest son and heir, Henry, by now in his mid-teens. His other available sons, Otto and William, were already at their grandfather's court, so it would be something of a family reunion. However, Duke Henry reached England only to discover that King Henry was in France, where he was embroiled in conflict with his son Richard and with Richard's ally Philip Augustus. He thus re-crossed the Channel, but met his father-in-law in Normandy only for the ailing king to die a few weeks later on 6 July 1189. The English throne passed uncontested to Richard, which might have caused some difficulties for a duke known to be such a close ally of Henry II, but Henry the Lion's family connections saved him once again and he attended his brother-in-law Richard back to England for his coronation.

Matilda did not accompany her husband on his second period of exile, instead remaining in Germany alone to defend his interests. How well she would have done this, and what difficulties she would have faced, are not known, because it was not long after his departure that she died, on 28 June 1189, at the age of just 33. We have no idea of the reason, but we may assume some kind of regular cause such as illness or accident, as the manner of her death did not raise an eyebrow among the contemporary chroniclers. If she had been killed in an unusual or remarkable way (in defending her husband's castles, for example) somebody would have been sure to mention it. Duke Henry rushed back to Germany when the news eventually reached him – an indication, perhaps, of a personal bond between them as well as of his political concerns – but the message had taken some while to arrive and his return journey was a long one. By the time he got home, Matilda had already been buried, in the still-unfinished Brunswick cathedral.

Matilda left five children ranging in age from 5 to 17. Given their birth, their rank and their ancestry on both sides, it was perhaps to be expected that they would go on to great things, and Matilda may have comforted herself with this thought on her deathbed; however, as it transpired, most of them did not and none left a great dynasty behind them.

Otto was the only one who raised himself to great eminence, though some of his methods were questionable, to say the least. Having spent much of his youth in England, he was a favourite of his uncles Richard and John, and this brought him his initial advancement. Richard named him earl of York and count of Poitiers (a subsidiary title of the duchy of Aquitaine, and the one by which Richard himself had been known while Henry II was alive), and tried to arrange a marriage for him with the elder daughter – and, at the time, heir presumptive – of William I of Scots. When Richard was captured on his way back from the Third Crusade, and subsequently released, Otto was one of those who was detained as a hostage until the ransom was paid in full, which earned him Richard's gratitude.[28]

There was even some speculation, in the late 1190s, that Richard might name Otto as his heir, but the death of Emperor Henry VI (Frederick Barbarossa's son and successor) in 1197 created a power vacuum in the Empire and Otto left his English and French lands behind in order to make a bid for the greater prize of the imperial crown. He succeeded, but only following a long struggle and after his principal opponent, Philip of Swabia (Henry VI's younger brother), was conveniently murdered. Otto was widely suspected of having a hand in this, and he certainly benefited from it; the path ahead of him was clear and he was crowned, sealing his claim by marrying Philip's 14-year-old daughter and heir, Beatrice. She, perhaps equally conveniently for Otto, mysteriously died three weeks after the wedding.

As Holy Roman Emperor, Otto allied himself with John, by then king of England, in a campaign against Philip Augustus of France, but this eventually led to his downfall and his death in disgrace. He left no children.

Richenza, Matilda's only daughter, was married in her teens to Geoffrey, the count of Perche in France. The couple's only surviving son, Thomas of Perche, would later die childless, fighting against Richenza's cousin Henry III during a war over the English crown.[29] Matilda's eldest son Henry would succeed to some of his father's lands, including the duchy of Saxony, but he would die while embroiled in conflict with Emperor Henry VI, leaving two daughters but no son of his own. Lothar would die at the age of 15 or 16, not long after his mother and still apparently a hostage. The only one of Matilda's sons to leave a son of his own was her youngest, William of Winchester. He married Helena of Denmark, sister to Cnut VI and to Ingeborg of Denmark, queen of France, and their son – another Otto, who was known as Otto the Child as he inherited young and to distinguish him from his uncle – would eventually become heir to all the family lands.

Matilda's children did not forget her. In a charter of 1223 her eldest son, Henry, described her as his 'dearest mother of most happy memory', and he would commission the tomb effigy of her that lies next to that of her husband (who, despite the large age difference between them, outlived her by six years) in Brunswick cathedral.[30]

Matilda's was a short life, but a well-travelled and well-lived one. She wielded a great deal of influence, both politically and culturally, spreading the Plantagenet network to encompass Henry the Lion's Brunswick court, which became known as an enlightened hub of culture.[31] She carried her family's dynastic connections across Europe into the eastern half of Germany, leaving children who would play significant roles on the international stage – though, like some other family members, she did it in almost total isolation from the others. It is perhaps not surprising that she never met her French half-sisters Marie and Alix, but she had almost as distant a relationship with her two full sisters, Leonor and Joanna, who were destined to travel even further than she did.

LEONOR

In the autumn of 1167, when Matilda left England to travel to Germany for her wedding, her younger sister Leonor was just turning 6 years old. For all of her life so far, Leonor had been by Matilda's side in their mother's household, and it must have been a wrench to part with her older sister. Unhappily for them both, the separation was to be permanent: they would never see each other again.[1]

It might have been different. As we mentioned briefly in the previous chapter, Leonor had been betrothed to Frederick, the eldest (and, at the time, only) son of Emperor Frederick Barbarossa, when she was a toddler and he a baby. If this arrangement had proceeded according to plan, she and Matilda might both have spent their adult lives in the Empire, not exactly together but able to meet with relative frequency. However, little Frederick died in 1170 at the age of 6, and it would seem that the betrothal had already fallen through by that stage. This was probably due to concerns about his health, as implied by the fact that he had been overlooked in the emperor's succession plans; in 1169 it was Barbarossa's second son, Henry, who was crowned king of the Romans, the recognised title for heirs to the Empire, even though Frederick was still alive at the time.[2]

There was no attempt to transfer the arrangement and affiance Leonor to Henry, and in 1168 a very different match was arranged for her. Her new intended husband was Alfonso VIII, king of Castile, meaning that she would be sent to a completely different geographical and political milieu from the one that had originally been envisaged, and that she would be separated from her elder sister by a distance so great that it would make personal meetings all but impossible.

In one respect Leonor was luckier than Matilda, in that her intended husband was much nearer her own age. At the time of the betrothal she was 7 and Alfonso just shy of 13, although he had been on the Castilian throne for ten years already. Their marriage would not take place straight away, but the delay was not a lengthy one. In the summer of 1170, Castilian ambassadors travelled to Bordeaux (where Leonor and her mother were at that time staying) to collect the little bride. She said what she probably thought was a permanent goodbye to Eleanor and headed off to her new life among strangers.

As ever, no contemporary writer thought to comment on how all this might affect Leonor personally, so we can have no insight into her feelings, but it was certainly a momentous event in her life and one that she would have remembered, for good or ill. She and Alfonso were married at Burgos, the Castilian capital, in the first half of September, around the time of her ninth birthday; he was 14. The first of many charters in which the young king of Castile would note that he was acting 'together with my wife Queen Leonor' is dated to 17 September 1170.[3]

The reasons for the union were, of course, political rather than personal, with benefits accruing to both kings. Henry II gained an ally whose lands were to the south of Aquitaine, and the new relationship went some way to counterbalancing the earlier Castilian alliance of Louis VII, who had married as his second wife Constance of Castile, Alfonso VIII's aunt. Constance was by this time dead but her two daughters, Margaret and Alice, were Alfonso's cousins and King Henry might have wanted to head off any potential close friendship between France and Castile. Henry also gained by marrying Leonor into royalty – rather than merely aristocracy, as had been the case for his eldest daughter – and thus further enhancing his own prestige, particularly in the eyes of anyone who might point out that although his mother had been an empress, his father had been only a count.

Alfonso, meanwhile, was young and involved in a territorial dispute with his more experienced neighbour Sancho VI the Wise of Navarre, so the king of England would be a powerful ally. Alfonso would make much of the relationship right from the start: in the document that confirms Leonor's dower allocation, he refers to 'the illustrious king of England my father' and calls Eleanor of Aquitaine 'my mother Eleanor, illustrious queen of England'.⁴ The terms 'dower' and 'dowry', incidentally, are sometimes confused; it is worth explaining the difference here, as we will encounter both words frequently as we go along. A *dower* comprised lands that were allocated by a husband to his wife for her financial support if he predeceased her; a *dowry* was the lands or goods a woman brought to a marriage, which were then controlled by her husband.

In marrying Leonor, Alfonso would avoid the common royal problem of consanguinity, which was particularly prevalent in the Spanish kingdoms. Finally, the occasion of his marriage was a convenient opportunity for him to declare his minority ended, so he could rule Castile in his own right.⁵

The young Leonor must have found the whole experience both bewildering and something of a culture shock. As she made the long, slow journey further and further south, away from her family and the temperate lands of her birth and upbringing, over the high, snow-capped mountains of the Pyrenees and down into the heat of her husband's Spanish kingdom, she was entering a complex environment – not to mention one where people spoke a foreign language – with which she would need to get to grips very quickly.

The Iberian peninsula was at this time divided into six regions. Five were Christian kingdoms: Portugal (which covered approximately two-thirds of its modern area), León, Castile, Navarre and Aragon. The sixth was the southern region of Al-Andalus, then under Muslim control and thus the frontier of Christianity and the scene of crusading warfare. The monarchs of the various Spanish kingdoms were both rivals and relatives in varying degrees, and Leonor's husband was situated in the middle of an intricate web of relationships. Sancho VI of Navarre – with whom Alfonso was in dispute – was his maternal uncle, while Alfonso II of Aragon, a firm ally, was his uncle by marriage. There were even closer ties with León: Alfonso VIII's grandfather, Alfonso VII, had been king of two realms, but he had left Castile to his eldest son (Sancho III, who had died in his twenties, leaving the crown to the 2-year-old Alfonso VIII) and León to his second, meaning that Ferdinand II of León was both Alfonso's paternal uncle and his heir presumptive until he had children of his own.

We have few details of Leonor's life for the next few years, but it undoubtedly involved the same sort of education experienced by royal and noble girls throughout western Europe. We know from later evidence that she was politically aware, literate and pious. As was the case for her elder sister in faraway Germany, Leonor's rank and the benefits of the alliance she brought to her husband's kingdom would mean that she was treated with the greatest respect, and as there were no other royal women at court (Alfonso's mother had died when he was a baby, he had no sisters and his only living aunt was the queen of Navarre), she could not be considered anyone's rival. Leonor could learn and grow up in peace.

Meanwhile, Alfonso made use of his relationship to the king of England. In August 1176 he and Sancho VI of Navarre submitted their quarrel to Henry II for arbitration, and in the spring of 1177 their representatives met with the English king at Windsor.[6]

The result was perhaps not the complete victory Alfonso might have been hoping for; Henry II had a growing reputation as an international mediator to protect and his decision was even-handed. He criticised Sancho for the actions he had taken against Castile while Alfonso was a minor and an orphan, but as part of the agreed settlement, Alfonso, although styled as 'our dearly beloved son', was obliged to return some cities he had taken and to pay an indemnity to the Navarrese king.[7]

There had, of course, been no question of Leonor being expected to consummate her marriage immediately after her wedding at the age of 9. Indeed, indications are that the couple did not engage in sexual relations until she was in her later teens, and Leonor's first child was born in early 1180, when she was 18. Given that she was almost perpetually pregnant throughout the rest of her childbearing years, it would seem logical that abstinence was the reason for the years that passed between her marriage and the birth of her first child, although, as ever, there is the possibility that she suffered earlier miscarriages or stillbirths that were not mentioned by contemporaries.

Of all her sisters, Leonor would be the most fecund, but she would experience a great deal of loss and much concern about the question of the Castilian succession, which was all the more urgent as Alfonso had no siblings, nephews or nieces. The child born to them in 1180 was a daughter, Berenguela; this may have come as a slight disappointment to all concerned, but with her fertility now proven, Leonor could look forward to the birth of a male heir in due course. However, she and Alfonso then experienced several years of tragedy and heartbreak, during which she bore three sons and a daughter who all died as infants. The loss of four babies in a row must have been all but unbearable. Infant mortality was much more common in the twelfth and thirteenth centuries than it is now, but that does not mean that parents felt the loss of their beloved and beautiful children any less.

These deaths occurring in quick succession led Alfonso and Leonor to consider the possibility that Berenguela would be their only surviving child, and she was named in several documents as heir presumptive to the throne. The tragic cycle of infant losses was broken in 1186, but with the birth of another daughter, Urraca; she was followed by a third girl, Blanca, in 1188. Then, amid great celebration, Leonor bore Alfonso a surviving son, Ferdinand, in November 1189 – more than nineteen years after their wedding and at a time when despair of a male heir might have been setting in.

Given their previous heart-rending experience of infant mortality, Leonor and Alfonso would have wanted another son to secure the succession, but their next three children were all girls: Mafalda, Constance and Eleanor. Finally, a second boy was born to them in April 1204, by which time Leonor was 42, a grandmother, and had been almost continuously pregnant or recovering from childbirth for twenty-five years.[8] This second son was given the unusual name Henry (Enrique), unprecedented in Castilian royal history and presumably in tribute to Leonor's father.

During these many years of pregnancy and childbirth, Leonor was also busy with the usual occupations of a twelfth-century queen. Among the most important of these was the education of her many children: the boys only until the age of around 7, but the girls for as long as they remained with the family. The royal daughters would, of course, be expected to make the same sort of political alliance that Leonor had herself, and she trained them with this in mind.

The first to marry was, unsurprisingly, Berenguela, who was much older than her surviving siblings. As a child, and at a time when she was the heir presumptive to her father's throne due to the lack of a male heir, Berenguela had been betrothed to Conrad, a younger son of Emperor Frederick Barbarossa. This arrangement had fallen through, however, partly as a result of the birth of her brother and the consequent diminution of her prospects, and an alliance nearer to home was found. In 1188 Ferdinand II of León had died, to be succeeded by his son Alfonso IX; this Alfonso married as his first wife Theresa of Portugal, but after she had borne him three children, their marriage was dissolved by Pope Celestine III on the grounds of consanguinity, as she was his first cousin. Rather than learning his lesson and looking further afield for a new bride, Alfonso IX of León turned to the family of another first cousin, Alfonso VIII of Castile, and he and Berenguela were married in 1197.

So Leonor bade farewell to her eldest daughter. Given that the kingdoms were neighbours, the separation was never likely to be as permanent as hers from her own family, but she might have been surprised by just how quickly she saw Berenguela again. Berenguela bore her new husband four surviving children in quick succession, only to see their union annulled by order of Pope Innocent III (whose immediate predecessor, Celestine III, had never given a dispensation for it in the first place) due to consanguinity. By 1204 Berenguela was back in Castile and, unusually, she brought her children with her.* Leonor thus welcomed into her household four grandchildren who were all older than her own newborn son, Henry.

As was customary, Leonor's elder son, Ferdinand, had been removed from female guardianship at a young age in order to

---

* As we saw with regard to Eleanor of Aquitaine's separation from Louis VII of France in Chapter 1, children normally remained in the custody of their father in such situations. Alfonso IX of León might have been more amenable to letting Berenguela take the children because the two of them remained on very good terms (having fought off the possibility of separation as long as they could) and because their kingdoms were close neighbours.

enter the world of men, but with six daughters, Leonor was able to have children about her for many years as she educated and prepared them for their future roles. Three of the others would also be queens: in 1200 Blanca married the future Louis VIII of France; in 1206 Urraca married the future Afonso II of Portugal; and in 1221 Eleanor married James I of Aragon.

To be a queen consort at this time was not merely to be 'the wife of the king'; it was a position in its own right. Queens underwent the ritual of coronation alongside their husbands (or upon their marriages, if their husband had already been crowned) and there were specific expectations laid upon them. They had to be good and virtuous wives and mothers, of course, setting an example not just to their own children but to all the subjects of the realm. They also had to exhibit great beauty: looks were not the primary motivation for royal marriages, but no king would stand for an ugly bride and he would expect to be assured of a potential wife's attractiveness before he agreed to a match.[9] They had to demonstrate piety and religious devotion in exactly the right quantity – too little and a queen might be seen as flighty, too much and she could be accused of neglecting her secular duties – while engaging in acts of patronage. They were responsible for their own household and anyone who had been placed within it, and needed to oversee the administration of their dower estates. As it was recognised that queens had a great deal of personal influence over their husbands, they were also expected to put this to good use in acting as peacemakers or intercessors, particularly in any interactions between their birth families and the families into which they had married.

In all of these duties Leonor succeeded admirably, and she was held up as an exemplar of queenship both at the time and after her death. Indeed, she appears to have attained personal happiness as well, becoming one of the lucky few whose arranged marriage resulted in real bonds of affection. She and

Alfonso formed a contented domestic unit, remaining together almost constantly, much more so than was usual for a reigning king and queen.[10] Politically, Leonor was given direct control of many lands, towns and castles as part of her dower, exerting much influence there, and she was also important to the king on a national level. Alfonso consistently noted in his charters that he was acting in concert with his wife, and in his will, drawn up in 1204, he stipulated that if he died, Leonor should rule alongside their son Ferdinand.[11] As the boy was by then 14 (the same age as Alfonso had been when he declared himself of full age), this indicates respect for Leonor's abilities.

Like the rest of her birth family, Leonor was a founder and supporter of numerous religious institutions – and, like them, she promulgated the cult of St Thomas Becket. In 1179 she endowed an altar dedicated to him in Toledo cathedral, allocating lands to pay for its upkeep and a chaplain. That she, and not her husband, was the primary mover in this affair is indicated by the charter granting the endowment: it is sealed with her seal, and is in the name of Leonor, 'by the grace of God queen of Castile, together with my husband, King Alfonso', whereas we would expect Alfonso to be mentioned first if he had initiated the endowment.[12]

Leonor also founded the abbey of Santa María la Real de las Huelgas, which was for Cistercian nuns, rather than monks. Her daughter Constance would take the veil there, as would at least one of her granddaughters, and it would later become a family mausoleum. The idea of a foundation that was subject to an abbess rather than an abbot was perhaps modelled on her mother's favoured establishment, Fontevraud abbey (in France, situated on the border where Poitou, Anjou and Touraine met), to which Leonor also made gifts, including in June 1190 an annual payment for prayers for the soul of her father, Henry II, who had been buried there some months previously.

A surviving set of liturgical vestments attests not only to Leonor's donations to religious institutions, but also to the fact that she continued to associate herself with her birth family long after her marriage. The lavish stole and maniple, now among the treasures of the monastery of San Isidoro de León, are woven of coloured silk embellished with metallic thread, and woven into the stole is the inscription 'Leonor, queen of Castile, daughter of Henry, king of England, made me in [1197]'.[13] The 'made me' (*me fecit*) does not necessarily imply that Leonor made the vestments herself; it is more likely that she caused them to be created by commissioning a professional silk weaver. In doing so, she associated herself with her father as well as her husband, even though it was eight years after the former's death and twenty-seven years since she had last seen him. We do have other evidence that Leonor had kept in touch with her birth family: in July 1181 Henry II sent her a gift of silver plate and clothing to celebrate the birth of her first son, Sancho (who, sadly, was one of those who did not survive), which implies that she must have informed him of the event.[14] Leonor was well aware that her duty was twofold: not only to be a good wife to her husband, but also to be a good daughter and sister to the members of her birth family and to act as a bridge between them all.

Early in the year 1200, almost thirty years after her marriage, Leonor was unexpectedly reunited with her mother.

By this time all of Leonor's siblings except the youngest, John, were dead, and John was the king of England. We will hear more of John in later chapters, but to summarise briefly here, he had been in dispute with King Philip Augustus of France, a dispute that was ended (temporarily) by the Treaty of Le Goulet.[15] The normal way to cement such agreements was by marriage, and Philip's son and heir, Louis, was 12 years old and available. The problem was that John did not have any children of his own, so in order to find a bride for Louis, he was obliged to turn to his nieces. Some consideration was given to his only niece in the male line, Eleanor of Brittany, the daughter of John's deceased brother Geoffrey and his wife Constance of Brittany; however, for reasons we will explore further in Chapter 7, this was problematic and the idea was dropped. John's eldest sister, Matilda, had borne one daughter, the Richenza whom we have already met, but she was by now in her late twenties and long married. So that left the daughters of John's next sister, Leonor.

The proposed marriage was an important one for the future relationship between France and the Anglo-Norman realm, and the bride would in due course be the queen of France, one of the most powerful kingdoms in Europe. Close attention therefore needed to be paid to the selection, so early in the new year of 1200, Eleanor of Aquitaine travelled to Castile in order to scrutinise the candidates personally. That a woman in her late seventies should volunteer for a long overland journey (and one that involved crossing a mountain range, at that) in the winter may seem surprising, but perhaps the prospect of seeing her only remaining daughter after such a long separation was an incentive.

Eleanor arrived in Burgos in January 1200, remaining there for two months while she recovered from the rigours of the journey and made her selection from among Leonor's daughters, of whom there were five (the youngest, Eleanor, had not yet been born). Berenguela was already married, and Mafalda and Constance were very young, so the two prime candidates were 14-year-old Urraca and 12-year-old Blanca. After spending some time with them, Eleanor decided in favour of Blanca, who evidently gave some indication of the steel she would show in later life. A tale that Eleanor chose her simply because of her name (Blanca, meaning 'white', could easily be rendered into the more French Blanche, but Urraca would sound foreign however it was pronounced) appears to be apocryphal, appearing only in the sixteenth century. In any case, such an idea hardly fits with Eleanor's reputation as one of the shrewdest women in Europe at that time – and if the name of the bride were the most important factor, why bother travelling to meet them?[16]

In March 1200 Leonor bade farewell to her daughter, and Blanca set off with her grandmother for her new life. They had reached Aquitaine by April, but by that time Eleanor, 'being fatigued with old age and the labour of the length of the journey',[17] stopped and retired to the abbey of Fontevraud, charging the archbishop of Bordeaux to escort Blanca the rest of the way to Normandy, where her wedding to Louis was celebrated in May. The child newly-weds then returned to Paris to continue their upbringing at the court of Philip Augustus. In an indication of the dynastic nature of the marriage, the contemporary Roger of Howden (the chronicler we have just quoted, who noted Eleanor's fatigue) gives a full account of the journey and the marriage arrangements in which Blanca is referred to twice as John's niece, five times as Alfonso's daughter and once as Louis's wife, without her actual name being mentioned at all.[18] Despite Eleanor's efforts to choose the girl best suited to the task (from an admittedly small pool), Blanca's individuality was less important to the match than her place in the family network.

Blanca's fate resembled her mother's in several ways, from the trivial to the significant, both personally and politically. From the time of her marriage she was known as Blanche, just as Leonor was called by the form of her name used in her husband's language rather than her own (a convention we will follow in this book from here on). Blanche was married to a husband of almost her own age, with whom she developed deep bonds of affection that would be lifelong, and in his will, he would name her as regent in the event that his heir should be a minor.

Given her advanced age, Eleanor of Aquitaine probably thought that after her retirement she would remain at Fontevraud until her death; however, this was not to be the case, as we shall see in Chapter 7. When her life did reach its end, in April 1204, this was the catalyst for a war that would pit Leonor's two families against each other.

Following receipt of the news of Eleanor's death, Alfonso made a somewhat surprising claim to Gascony (the southern part of Aquitaine), on the basis that it had been promised to him as part of Leonor's dowry when they married, to be handed over to him upon the death of her mother. There were several issues with this claim. Notable among them were that there was no written record of it anywhere; that it seemed unlikely that Henry II would have agreed, even verbally, to such a large part of the lands under his control being ceded; and that all those who had been involved in arranging the union were by now dead, except Alfonso and Leonor. The official inheritor of Aquitaine, Eleanor's only surviving son, John, had been 3 years old when Leonor's wedding took place.[19]

Either Alfonso was more confident in his claim than the evidence at our disposal would suggest, or he was convinced that he could defeat the already beleaguered John – who was simultaneously in the process of losing Normandy to Philip Augustus, the marriage of Louis and Blanche notwithstanding – because in 1205 the Castilian king launched an invasion of Gascony. His troops entrenched themselves in Montaubon (about 130 miles south-east of Bordeaux and 30 miles north of Toulouse) and all seemed to be going his way, but unfortunately he was to be on the receiving end of one of John's few military victories. The king of England moved into Gascony and laid siege to Montaubon, where he scored a notable success:

> And when, after fifteen days, they had destroyed a great part of the castle by the incessant assaults of their petrariae, and the missiles from their ballistas and slings, the English soldiers, who were greatly renowned in that kind of warfare, scaled the walls and exchanged mortal blows with their enemies [...] the well-fortified castle of Montaubon was taken.[20]

John was then forced to break off and move back north, because King Philip was building upon his success in Normandy by marching as far as the border of Poitou (the northern part of Aquitaine). He did not actually invade it, but the threat was enough for John to sue for peace, and a truce was agreed on 26 October 1206 that would last for two years. Alfonso was not able to take sufficient advantage of John's distraction, and the barons of Gascony resisted the idea of submitting to a Spanish monarch. He was eventually recalled to Castile by the threat of Muslim incursion on his own southern border, and his interest in Gascony waned. One Castilian at least was pleased: 'O happy day, one always delightful to the kingdom of Castile, on which the glorious king ceased in his perseverance and quit this undertaking!'[21]

We have no specific record of Leonor's opinion on her husband's claim to Gascony, and she was not directly involved in the military incursion; her family background was in effect just a good excuse for Alfonso to push his claims. However, as the wife of one party and the sister of the other, she was naturally considered an ideal person to engage in the traditional peacemaking role of queens. In 1206 John granted her a safe-conduct, which implies that she was ready to travel to his lands to meet with him and discuss the situation, but unfortunately there is no evidence either way as to whether she made the journey or not.

In 1211 Leonor suffered a double tragedy. At some point that year – we do not know exactly when – her daughter Mafalda died, in her early teens and apparently on the point of being betrothed. This explains the absence of details about her death, as girls were of interest to chroniclers primarily in terms of their marriages; the demise of an unmarried girl barely rated a mention, even if she happened to be the king's daughter.

We have more details about the second family tragedy of that year, as it involved the loss of Leonor's elder son and the heir to the throne, Ferdinand. He was 21 and had begun to take his place in the adult world, acting on his father's behalf, so the devastating loss was all the more keenly felt. In the summer of 1211 he had been on campaign against the Muslims in southern Spain; military campaigns tended to be seasonal affairs, and as summer turned to autumn he began the journey home. He had only reached Madrid when he fell ill with a fever, and he died there on 14 October.

The anguish of his parents was extreme. On hearing the news, Alfonso wept with 'inconsolable grief' and was 'sick at heart'.[22] Leonor's pain was expressed publicly:

> The most noble Queen Leonor, hearing of the death of her son, wished to die with him and lay down on the bier on which her son lay, and placing her mouth on his mouth and folding her hands over his hands, she strove either to bring him to life or to die with him. Thus, those who saw it claimed that such a grief as this never had been seen.[23]

As we have already noted, it was all too common in the Middle Ages for parents to lose children, not only in infancy and childhood but also once they had grown or almost grown to adulthood. It happened so often that the temptation for modern readers is to wonder whether medieval parents could possibly love their children to the extent common today; the answer is that they did, and they felt their losses just as keenly regardless of how frequently they occurred, as Alfonso and Leonor's evidently wrenching grief shows. Every time we write 'the eldest surviving son of', or words to that effect, we should remember those who did not survive and the grief of those who felt their loss.[24]

In this case, Ferdinand's death had repercussions not just for the family but for the whole realm of Castile. He had been the heir to the throne since birth, and – perhaps surprisingly, given his age and position – he was unmarried and therefore left no children of his own. This meant that the succession now rested on the slender shoulders of Leonor and Alfonso's youngest child and only remaining son, the 7-year-old Henry, and after him his five surviving sisters and their children.

King Alfonso's dedication to the crusade against the Muslims in southern Spain was not dampened by Ferdinand's death, and the following summer he led a campaign there himself, together with his neighbouring kings and cousins Sancho VII the Strong of Navarre (who had succeeded Sancho the Wise in 1194) and Peter II of Aragon (who had succeeded Alfonso II in 1196). They were normally his political rivals, but they all put aside their differences in the name of Christianity as they made their way south.

Leonor remained in Burgos, where she anxiously waited for updates. Alfonso was by now in his late fifties, not a prime age for the sort of physical effort that was needed for armed combat in extreme heat, and this must have added to her worries. When the news came, however, it was spectacular:

Alfonso VIII and his allies had won a great victory at the Battle of Las Navas de Tolosa on 16 July 1212. The occasion prompted correspondence between other members of the family, and we are extremely fortunate that a letter written by Leonor's daughter Berenguela (now back in Castile following the annulment of her marriage) to Blanche in France has survived. It contains a great deal of military terminology and specific detail, showing that royal women – or these ones, at least – were by no means ignorant of military matters:

> I have joyful news for you. Thanks to God, from whom all power comes, the king our lord and father conquered in pitched battle Ammiramomelinus [emir Muhammad-el-Nasir], in which we believe the honour won was outstanding, since up to now it was unheard of for the king of Morocco to be overcome in pitched battle. [...]

> The manner of the war was the following. Our father, as I reported to you another time, obtained the castles which are between Toledo and the port, awaiting battle. Seeing Ammiramomelinus coming, he began to cross the port. But the exit from the port on the other side was a narrow place. Then Ammiramomelinus ordered his men to make sure that ours could not cross. [...]

> Our father divided his men into three battle lines [...] The first line rushed against the Saracens and removed them from the place, but they, once they had absorbed the force, pushed us back for the most part, the first line into the second. Seeing this, our father anticipated attack from the side of the two lines, joining his line to the previous one and repulsed the Saracens with force and pressed them back, so he restored the first line to its place and then returned to his own place with his whole line. Again the Saracens, as they had done before, attacked

our men and again our father, seeing it, joined his wing to the first wing and again pressed the Saracens back to the line of Ammiramomelinus.[25]

The Battle of Las Navas de Tolosa was Alfonso's greatest moment of triumph during his fifty-six-year reign, and Leonor surely rejoiced along with her daughters, in relief at his survival as well as in celebration of his success. Although we have no surviving correspondence of Leonor's, Berenguela's letter to Blanche (and particularly the line 'as I reported to you another time') indicates that these royal women were in frequent contact with each other, keeping their network alive despite the physical distance between them.

In September 1214 Alfonso and Leonor were on their way to visit the Portuguese royal court, along with Berenguela, her sons, and their own surviving son, Henry, when the king fell ill with a virulent fever. He died on 6 October, leaving Leonor distraught with grief for the man who had been her husband for forty-four years and since she was 9 years old. She did not suffer for long, however, as she succumbed to the same illness. She was not well enough either to oversee Alfonso's funeral arrangements or to take up her duties as regent, and she died just three weeks after him, on 31 October 1214. She was buried at the abbey of Las Huelgas that she had founded, in a joint tomb with Alfonso and alongside her beloved son Ferdinand.

The new king of Castile was Leonor's only surviving son, Henry, who was just 10 years old and suffering from the trauma of having lost both his parents so suddenly. Leonor's will had stipulated that the regency should pass to her eldest daughter, Berenguela – who was old enough to be Henry's mother anyway – and Berenguela devoted herself to him even as she buried both her parents and looked after her own children. Tragically, Henry was killed in an accident just three years later (he was playing with some other children outdoors in Burgos when a tile fell from the palace roof and hit him on the head), at which point Berenguela inherited the throne of Castile in her own right.[26] Perhaps mindful of her maternal family history – most notably the struggles of her great-grandmother Empress Matilda in seeking to rule in her own name in England – Berenguela chose not to rule as sole queen regnant but to have her eldest son crowned as Ferdinand III.

This arrangement was initially not popular. On a spiritual level, the pope (now Honorius III) considered Ferdinand illegitimate, as Berenguela's marriage had been dissolved on the grounds of consanguinity. Moreover, the nobles of Castile were not keen on being ruled by the man who was also the heir to the throne of León, fearing that their realm would be subsumed when he inherited there. They therefore came up with what was probably an entirely fictitious stipulation said to have been left by Alfonso VIII, that if his son Henry should die without heirs, the Castilian throne should pass to his daughter Blanche and her heirs. Blanche had by now been married to Louis of France for seventeen years, but fortunately for all concerned they declined this offer firmly, for both themselves and their sons, and no conflict ensued.[27] Ferdinand, Leonor's eldest grandson, went on to rule peacefully for more than thirty years.

Leonor was considered by many contemporaries to have been an ideal queen consort, and we can see that she amply fulfilled the criteria. She was beautiful and of royal birth, and in marrying her husband she brought him an alliance with one of Europe's most powerful kings. Once married she demonstrated fertility, piety, generosity, dignity and unstinting support of her husband, while at the same time remaining modest and quiet, not influencing him to an undue extent or seeking to act in a more powerful, 'masculine' way. She and Alfonso enjoyed a mutual respect, spending most of their time together, unlike many royal couples.

Robert de Torigni, the Norman abbot and chronicler who was also Leonor's godfather, said of her marriage to Alfonso that her 'advice and assistance have been productive to him of many happy results'.[28] Even Gerald of Wales, a contemporary who wrote disparagingly of the marriages of Henry II's other children, was forced to acknowledge that 'one will be able to hope for some good to come from the Spanish one from the happy bond of marriage'.[29] The Castilian chronicles were equally complimentary: to them Leonor was 'of noble lineage, chaste and pure, and very wise'; and 'exquisitely educated, quiet and calm, very beautiful, greatly charitable, very kind to her husband, and honourable in all her dealings with the people of her realm'.[30]

Despite spending less than ten years of her life with her birth family, Leonor never forgot them. She continued to associate herself with them and was shaped and influenced by her dynastic position. She followed in her mother's footsteps in exercising female authority, and she passed it on to her own daughters. Urraca and Eleanor were both queens consort in Iberian realms; Berenguela was an effective regent and a queen in both León and Castile; Blanche was the sole regent of France for many years and thus actually ruled the kingdom until her son came of age. Constance, who took holy orders, became known as the 'Lady of Las Huelgas', a unique role that she established and that was later reserved for royal women who were nuns there and who used their position and influence to good effect. Leonor's line continued: her great-granddaughter and namesake, Eleanor of Castile, would re-forge the alliance between Castile and England when she married King John's grandson, the future Edward I, and would become one of the great queens consort of England.

. Louis's disappointment
t Eleanor bearing only
wo daughters during their
marriage was one of the
easons why the relationship
nded. Here Louis consults
with his council on the
ubject of a divorce.

la meelines la oewnnairete. quar tan
toft li rendi ces . ij . chaftiaus que il li a
uoit tolluz . Ci feuift le . xxij . chapitre
et commence . le . xxiij .

Dies ce aunnt que ne lai
quner gens du lignage
le roi umdrent à lui et
li furnt entendant si com
me uous eftoit : que il

2. Louis became desperate
for a male heir. Here he prays
and is rewarded when his
third wife, Adela of Blois,
gives birth to the future
Philip II Augustus.

in uie et pais.
Lj . xvij . comment rollo ligmus
qui puis fu baptizie: pnst nonnendie

Ci commence le premier chapitre des mr
du bon roi pleippe. qui parole comment
il fu nez et de lannfion son pere.

3. A genealogical roll shows the eight children Eleanor bore to her second husband, Henry II: from left to right, William (who died in infancy), Henry, Richard, Matilda, Geoffrey, Leonor, Joanna and John. Also depicted are some of Eleanor's grandchildren: Matilda's sons Henry and Otto, Geoffrey's children Arthur and Eleanor, Leonor's daughter Blanche and Joanna's son Raymond.

4a and 4b. Fontevraud abbey was Eleanor's favourite religious foundation. She retired there in later life, her daughter Joanna later sought admittance and her granddaughter Alix was for some time the abbess.

5. Eleanor's effigy at Fontevraud abbey.

6. Marie's seal, which she employed to demonstrate her authority when ruling the great county of Champagne.

lee tuillee et ce fu pour mieulx femy contre febre

Clarelot paffa le pont de lefpec et ey paffat retardoit la Royne demeure abne tour

7. Marie was the patron of Chrétien de Troyes, who dedicated his work *Lancelot, or the Knight of the Cart* to her. In an illustration from a later manuscript of the work, Lancelot is seen crossing the sword bridge to reach Guinevere.

8. Chartres cathedral. Chartres was the seat of Alix and her husband, Count Theobald V of Blois.

9. Matilda and her husband, Henry the Lion, are depicted being crowned in this miniature from the gospel book they commissioned. The two figures immediately behind Matilda are her father, Henry II, and her grandmother, Empress Matilda.

10. A fresco in Brunswick cathedral depicting the martyrdom of Thomas Becket. Matilda was instrumental in propagating the cult of the saint throughout central Europe.

11. The tombs of Matilda and her husband, Henry the Lion, in Brunswick cathedral.

12. Leonor and Alfonso formed a lifelong partnership that was both loving and politically effective.

3a and 13b. Leonor founded the abbey of Santa María la Real de las Huelgas. Her daughter Constance would be a nun there, as would at least one of her granddaughters, and it would later become a family mausoleum.

14. Leonor and Alfonso died within a fortnight of each other, and were interred in a double tomb at Las Huelgas.

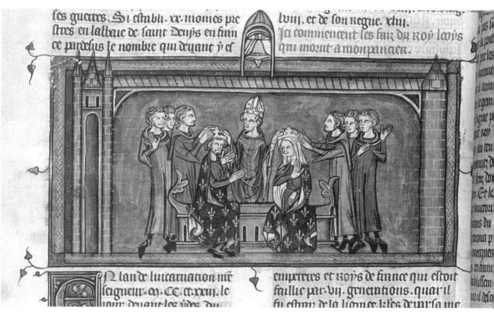

15. Leonor's daughter Blanche of Castile later became queen of France. Here she is crowned alongside her husband, Louis VIII; he cited her family connections in his claim for the English throne.

16. Joanna and her brother Richard (left) greet King Philip Augustus of France when they arrive at Acre during the Third Crusade.

au roi de hongrie et de la mort le con te giffroi de bretaigne.

17. After Young Henry's death, Margaret married Béla III of Hungary; here her half-brother, Philip Augustus, receives the Hungarian embassy and hands Margaret over to them.

18a and 18b. The Hungarian royal seat was Esztergom castle.

9. The effigy of Berengaria of Navarre at L'Épau abbey.

10. Arthur of Brittany, Constance's son, was a pawn in the conflicts between Philip Augustus and the kings of England. Here he pays homage to Philip after Richard's death, Philip favouring him over John for the succession.

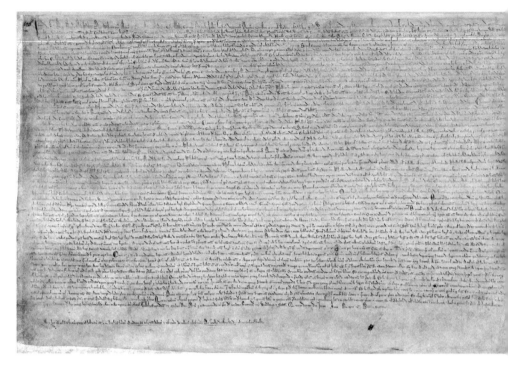

21. One of the extant copies of Magna Carta. Isabelle of Gloucester sided with the barons against her first husband, King John.

22. Isabella of Angoulême left England after John's death, married again and raised a second large family. She was buried alongside her first husband's relatives at Fontevraud abbey.

JOANNA

Joanna, Eleanor of Aquitaine's ninth child and youngest daughter, was born in October 1165 in Angers, in the heart of her father's ancestral lands.[1] She was destined to have a more peripatetic life than any of her sisters and half-sisters, and indeed one that was lived almost entirely separately from all of them. She never met Marie or Alix, and although she spent the very first years of her life in the company of Matilda and Leonor, she can hardly have remembered them at all later on: she was barely 2 years old when Matilda was sent to Germany and 4 when Leonor travelled to Spain, and she would never see either of them again. Unlike her sisters, however, Joanna would enjoy close relationships with two of her brothers: John, her only younger sibling, during their shared early childhood; and Richard, eight years her senior, in later life. She would also spend several years in close company with her sister-in-law Berengaria and would act as a pivotal point in the family network.

Queen Eleanor was based in Poitou, the northern part of Aquitaine, from early 1168 until the summer of 1174, and for much or most of this time Joanna and John lived at Fontevraud abbey, where they were educated by the nuns.[2] As we noted in Chapter 1, this was not an uncommon way for young royal children to receive an education, and it does not imply that either of them were destined for holy orders – their sojourn was only ever intended to be temporary.

Their peaceful schooling ended rather more suddenly than anyone had anticipated when their eldest brother, Henry the Young King, rebelled against their father in 1173–74. Eleanor supported her son against her husband (much to the outrage of the Church, which had a thing or two to say about disobedient wives) and she was to suffer the consequences when Henry II defeated the rebellion. She was transported to England as her husband's prisoner in July 1174, and Joanna and John, then aged 8 and 7, were removed from Fontevraud to be taken with her. Upon their arrival in England, John was sent away from the female household to be brought up in the realm of men, but Joanna stayed with her mother, firstly at Salisbury and then at Winchester.

As she was the daughter of a king, it was natural that the question of Joanna's marriage would be raised sooner rather than later. The idea of a match with King William II of Sicily had first been mooted in the early 1170s but had been delayed by various issues, including Henry II's dispute with Thomas Becket and the rebellion of Henry the Young King. With these both now brought to a conclusion in their different ways, the proposal could be considered again, and in May 1176 a Sicilian embassy arrived in England.

The attraction of the match for King William was obvious: he would be the son-in-law of Henry II, one of the most powerful monarchs in Europe. There were also a number of potential advantages for Henry II. William was an unmarried crowned king and thus a member of a rather select group, meaning that Joanna would be settled according to her rank. The kingdom of Sicily (which at this time comprised southern mainland Italy as well as the island of Sicily itself) was rich and prosperous, and its geographical location made it a convenient stopping point for those travelling on crusades or pilgrimages to the Holy Land, something that was at this point an unfulfilled ambition of Henry's. The Hauteville dynasty that ruled Sicily was of Norman origin; Norman invaders had conquered it in the eleventh century and formally constituted the kingdom in 1130, so there were some historical links with the Anglo-Norman realm over which Henry reigned. Sicily had been the scene of unrest during the reign of William's father, William I (whose soubriquet was 'the Bad'), but William II – known by contrast as William 'the Good' – had brought peace, so it was a stable kingdom with which to form an alliance and a safe environment in which Henry could place his daughter.[3] Finally, William was, as it happened, the first cousin of Leonor's husband, Alfonso VIII of Castile, as their mothers had been sisters. William had previously been in amicable contact with Henry II, sending the English king a letter to congratulate him on putting down the rebellion against his rule in 1173–74.[4]

Queen Eleanor, then in captivity following that same rebellion, is unlikely to have had any say in the choice of husband for her youngest daughter, but when she heard of it, she might have approved of the choice both in terms of rank and location. She had been to Sicily herself back in 1149 (accompanying her then-husband Louis VII on the Second Crusade) and had enjoyed the splendours of the royal court there under William II's grandfather, Roger II.

King Henry, whose opinion was the one that mattered, was well disposed towards the match and entered willingly into detailed negotiations. The members of the Sicilian delegation were permitted to visit Joanna at Winchester, where they inspected the 10-year-old and came away 'satisfied as to her beauty'.[5] One of the main issues to be discussed was the question of Joanna's dower, and William made a very generous and lucrative offer, assigning her the whole county of Mount Saint Angelo and the coastal towns of Siponto and Vieste, all in Apulia on mainland Italy.[6]

As we might expect, we have no information whatsoever on what Joanna herself thought of the match. She was simply told whom she was to marry, instructed to say goodbye to her mother and packed off to the port of Southampton for the first leg of what would be a very long and arduous journey. She was conveyed in style, of course: the Pipe Rolls record the expenses for her Channel crossing as £7 10s to equip her ship, along with £10 13s for seven accompanying vessels, and she took with her a sumptuous dowry that included gold, silver and clothing.[7]

The arrangements for the marriage of his youngest daughter gave Henry II an opportunity to showcase his family's power and the extent of the lands they ruled, and Joanna barely needed to set foot outside Plantagenet-ruled territories for the whole overland stage of her journey. From her father's kingdom of England she sailed first to Normandy, where she was met by her eldest brother, Henry the Young King, who escorted her through the duchy and into Poitou. At Poitiers Henry handed Joanna over to their brother Richard, who took her south through his duchy of Aquitaine and into the county of Toulouse, over which he claimed hereditary overlordship (much to the annoyance of the counts of Toulouse).

In November 1176 Joanna was met at the port of Saint Gilles by a fleet of Sicilian ships sent by King William. There she embarked along with the retinue that was to accompany her the whole way, including such luminaries as her uncle, Henry II's half-brother Hamelin of Anjou, and Richard of Dover, the archbishop of Canterbury.[*]

---

[*] Henry II's two legitimate brothers, Geoffrey and William fitzEmpress, were by this time both dead, neither having left any children. His half-brother Hamelin of Anjou, also known as Hamelin Plantagenet or Hamelin de Warenne (*c.* 1130–1202) was the illegitimate son of Henry II's father, Geoffrey Plantagenet, by an unnamed mistress. As Henry II derived his claim to the English throne from his mother, Empress Matilda, this meant that Hamelin was not a rival and the two men appear to have got on well. Henry had arranged for Hamelin to marry one of the realm's richest heiresses, Isabel de Warenne; he took her name and was by this time earl of Surrey in his wife's right.

Unfortunately for Joanna, she fell ill during the long Mediterranean voyage, reportedly suffering from extreme sea-sickness. This necessitated a change of plan and the fleet had to dock at Naples in order to allow her to recover before the rest of the journey was made overland, except for the brief hop over from the mainland to the island of Sicily. Then it was another 140 miles westwards by wagon or by horse litter before the exhausted and overwhelmed 11-year-old finally arrived in Palermo in January 1177.[8] There was to be no rest, however, no private respite; she was thrown straight away into the public pomp that came with being royalty. The Sicilians had been ruled for over a decade by a king who had no children and whose brothers had all died one after the other, leaving him with no heirs, so they were delighted to welcome a new young queen.*

A contemporary described her reception:

> The whole city welcomed them, and lamps, so many and so large, were lighted up, that the city almost seemed to be on fire, and the rays of the stars could in no way bear comparison with the brilliancy of such a light [...] The daughter of the king of England was then escorted, mounted on one of the king's horses, and resplendent with regal garments, to a palace, that there she might in becoming state await the day of her marriage and coronation.[9]

---

* William II had originally had three brothers, but they all pre-deceased him. Two had been older than him, but Robert had died in 1160 and Roger in 1161 (the latter allegedly as a result of being kicked to death by their father), at the ages of 7 and 9 respectively, meaning that William had inherited the throne when it fell vacant in 1166. His one younger brother and heir, Henry, had died of a fever in 1172 aged somewhere between 12 and 14, leaving the Sicilian succession hanging by a thread.

The 11-year-old Joanna was married to the 23-year-old William on 13 February 1177, and she was crowned on the same day. This meant that there were now no fewer than three queens in Sicily, as the widows of William's two predecessors were still living: Margaret of Navarre, his mother, and Beatrice of Rethel, his step-grandmother. In some respects this would have been an advantage to Joanna, providing her with experienced female company from whom she could learn the ways of Sicily and its royal court. However, the presence of two dowager queens, especially her mother-in-law, was not entirely positive. Margaret of Navarre lived for another seven years after Joanna's arrival, during which time she retained the style 'queen' and some of her previous authority, however informally it must now be exercised. William II had acceded to the throne at the age of 12, so his mother had acted as his regent for many years, and even after his majority and his marriage, it is possible that it was she, rather than the young Joanna, who was seen as the pre-eminent woman at the royal court. Joanna certainly does not seem to have enjoyed the same sort of influence as her sisters Matilda and Leonor: there is little evidence of any literary or religious patronage of hers (the cult of St Thomas Becket did reach Sicily, but this seems to have occurred before Joanna arrived so she cannot be credited with instigating it) and her name does not appear on any surviving charter of William II except the one assigning her dower.

Despite any possible tension over status, Joanna was able to benefit from the advantages of her new position and her sunny, warm new home. Settling in would have been made easier by the fact that – unlike her sisters – she did not have to learn a new language, for the *lingua franca* of the Sicilian royal court was Norman–French, the same as at her father's court in England. Any similarity between the two places ended there, however, for due to its geographical location, Sicily was a cosmopolitan, even multi-cultural, place. The kingdom was something of a crossroads in the Mediterranean where Latin Christians, Greek-speaking Christians, Muslims and Jews co-existed in an unusual state of relative tolerance. Immigration was encouraged and Sicily was a centre of academic learning.

Due to her extreme youth at the time of the wedding, it is likely that Joanna continued her education in some form after her arrival in Sicily, and unlikely that she cohabited with William straight away, but we do not have any firm information either about her studies or about her personal relationship with the king. William was known as a cultivated and pleasure-loving man who brought peace to his realm, and he had actively sought the marriage, so we have no particular reason to suspect that he was not kind to his young wife on a personal level; plus, of course, Joanna benefited from the same family prestige and protection as her sisters, in that any mis-treatment of her would be an insult to Henry II. The question of an heir to the throne could not be put off forever, of course, so Joanna would have been expected to consummate her mar-riage as soon as she was considered physically capable of it.

One of the strangest aspects of the lack of information we have about this period of Joanna's life is that we do not know whether she bore William a child or not. Only one chronicler, Robert de Torigni, thinks that she did, noting that she had a son in 1181 or 1182 – a plausible date, as Joanna would have been between 15 and 17 at that time. As Robert's text is generally reli-able, historians have on the whole tended to believe him and this child is often listed as Joanna's in modern works. However, Robert was nowhere near Sicily (he was the abbot of Mont St Michel in Normandy) and it seems odd that he should be in possession of information that nobody nearer to or resident in that kingdom was aware of. Moreover, he does not seem to be completely sure of his source himself, saying only that '*we have been informed by some people* that Joanna, the wife of William, king of Sicily, the daughter of Henry, the king of England, had for her eldest son a child named Bohemund'.[10] Phrases such as 'we have been informed that' are often used by medieval chroniclers when they do not have first-hand information and are unsure of their sources, so it is possible Robert was relying on hearsay, especially as the 'some people' are not named. Against the idea of Bohemund's existence is the total lack of any mention of him in any other text, whether chronicle or charter, and the fact that in her will of 1199 Joanna made bequests for the welfare of the souls of her father, mother, brothers, sisters and first husband, but made no mention of a child. If she had borne a son to William, no matter how short-lived, it is likely that she would have remembered him at such a time.

If Bohemund did ever exist, then he died after a very short life, as nothing is heard of him thereafter. Joanna and William would have no (or no other) children, but despite their barren marriage, he made no move to have it annulled, so we may infer that their union was contented and that it remained politically useful.[11]

Unfortunately for Joanna, her happiness in Sicily was to come to an abrupt end when William died in November 1189, aged just 35. After twelve years of marriage with no surviving child, William had been obliged to give some thought to the question of the succession, and he had named as his heir his only surviving relative in the Hauteville line. This was Constance of Sicily, who was his paternal aunt although she was actually several years younger than he was.* There was no official bar to female succession, but the problem for many of the Sicilian nobles, and particularly a number of crown officials, was that Constance was married to Henry, the eldest son

---

* William II's grandfather, Roger II, had been married three times, and his eldest child had been thirty-five years older than Constance, his youngest. Constance was born after Roger's death to his widowed third wife, Beatrice of Rethel, by which time her older half-siblings already had children of their own.

and heir of Emperor Frederick Barbarossa. They had no wish to be ruled by a Hohenstaufen who would one day also inherit the imperial throne of Germany and Italy (probably fairly soon given that Barbarossa was in his late sixties), and they feared that Sicily might be subsumed into the imperial domains.

At the time of William's death, Constance and Henry were in Germany, and unable to leave it as he was acting as regent in the absence of Emperor Frederick, who had set off to travel overland to the Third Crusade. This meant that there was a power vacuum in Sicily and the throne was quickly seized by William II's cousin, Tancred of Lecce. Tancred's father had been William's paternal uncle, and thus a Hauteville, but Tancred himself was illegitimate and so had been overlooked in the succession plans. In the normal course of events, it might be expected that such a usurpation would be condemned by the pope, but Clement III made no move to do so, fearing that the union of Sicily with the Holy Roman Empire that might occur under Henry and Constance would threaten his own interests. Tancred was therefore almost unopposed, and he was crowned king of Sicily in early 1190. In June of that year, Barbarossa died on his way to the crusade and Henry of Hohenstaufen became Emperor Henry VI, meaning that he had much to attend to in Germany and was not in a position to claim his wife's Sicilian rights.

All of this put Joanna in a very difficult position. She had supported Constance's claim to the throne on the basis that this had been her late husband's wish, but she could do nothing practical against Tancred by herself. He seized the dower lands that were meant to provide her with an income following William's death, and then captured and imprisoned Joanna herself. Such was the fate of many other women in the Middle Ages, those whose actions or whose very existence challenged the ambitions of powerful men, and had Joanna been a member of any other family, her story might have ended there, with a note that she remained incarcerated until her death. But Joanna was a member of a very powerful family indeed, and despite not having seen any of her close relations for over a decade and living at the other end of Europe, she could expect them to act on her behalf. Her story was not over, not by a long way.

By early 1190, when Tancred seized the Sicilian throne, Joanna's father, Henry II, and her eldest brother, Henry the Young King, were both dead. The English crown had therefore passed to the next surviving son, Richard. No sooner had it been placed on his head than he announced his intention to take part in the Third Crusade, and he set in motion plans to travel to the Holy Land via the Mediterranean alongside King Philip Augustus of France. The location of Sicily and the timing of events were thus exactly suited for him to amplify a sense of family outrage at this insult to his sister and, by implication, himself.

As the Third Crusade was an extremely well-documented affair, with several chroniclers travelling in the kings' retinues and writing eye-witness accounts, we are able to reconstruct the course of subsequent events much more easily than the previous decade of Joanna's life in Sicily. Richard arrived at Messina on 23 September 1190 with a fleet of more than 100 ships and immediately demanded Joanna's release and the restoration of her dower lands. For good measure, he also added on his own behalf a demand to Tancred for 'a golden table 12 feet long, a silken tent, a hundred first-class galleys with everything necessary for them for two years, 60,000 quarters of wheat, 60,000 of barley, 60,000 of wine, twenty-four golden cups and 24 golden plates'.[12] He attacked and took the city of Messina and allowed his troops to rape and pillage there. Tancred, hearing of this, 'realised that danger could arise if disagreement continued, as he had learnt that King Richard would not give up his efforts once he had begun until he had got what he wanted'.[13] He agreed to release Joanna on 25 September and she arrived in Messina three days later, less than a week after Richard's arrival.

Joanna's feelings on hearing of her brother's triumph and anticipating her own impending liberty can only be imagined, but we may safely assume that she was very happy to see him and to know that she was under the protection of such a powerful monarch. The siblings would certainly have noticed some differences in each other; the last time they had met, he had been a youth of 19 and she a child of 11, while he was now a king in his prime and she a queen of over a decade's standing.

Philip Augustus, the French king, was also at Messina by this time and he visited Joanna after her arrival there. There is a possibility that he was considering her as a potential bride; he had been widowed earlier that same year and had only one young son, not enough to secure the French succession given that he had five sisters but no brothers. If this match was ever formally proposed, it came to nothing, either through lack of interest or due to the complicated spiritual difficulties caused by the fact that Philip's father had once been married to Joanna's mother – although that had not prevented a different inter-family wedding, as we will see in Chapter 5.

Richard, meanwhile, was far from finished with Tancred. He had his sister back, but equally as (or perhaps more) important to him were her dower lands and the revenue they represented. He made further demands for them and would not leave Sicily – even for the crusade – until he was satisfied. He was still there in November 1190 when Tancred offered money instead of land, an offer that Richard accepted on his sister's behalf, resulting in the handover of 40,000 ounces of gold.[14] Richard would spend the entire sum on his crusade expenses and Joanna would never see a penny of it, which – if she had ever doubted it – gave her an indication of where the power lay in their sibling relationship.

As part of the deal with Tancred, there was some thought that Richard would arrange for the marriage of the young Arthur of Brittany ('our nephew, and, if we shall chance to die without issue, our heir') with one of Tancred's daughters, but in the event this came to nothing.[15] As a childless king, Richard had very few bargaining counters available to him in the marriage market, so perhaps he felt that Arthur, his only nephew in the male line, was best held in reserve for something more prestigious. Joanna was still only in her early twenties, with many years of potential childbearing still to come, so as a young widow she was now a valuable asset to Richard in that same marriage market and it was decided that she would travel with him while he continued on his crusade.

Before this could happen, Joanna had a second encounter with a member of her family whom she had probably never expected to see again: in late March 1191 Eleanor of Aquitaine arrived in Sicily. The dowager queen had made the journey in order to deliver to Richard his intended bride, Berengaria of Navarre, and she was able to take the opportunity to spend a few days in the company of her youngest daughter before she had to leave at the beginning of April to return to England – with the union still not solemnised and with Richard seemingly in no hurry for it. Eleanor may well have stressed to Joanna that it was her family duty to make sure that Richard did not forget about the wedding altogether.[16] But she had little choice but to leave them, being required urgently in England, where Richard's absence was already being felt and the authority she exercised in his name was needed. He had left his kingdom in December 1189, nearly a year and a half previously, and had not yet even reached the Holy Land, though he intended to remedy that now. With his business in Sicily concluded and with Joanna and Berengaria in tow, Richard sailed on 10 April 1191.

This was to be the start of a new chapter in Joanna's life. She had escaped the fate of many unfortunate women who were kept imprisoned for political reasons not of their own making, and must have been enjoying her liberty, but was she really free? She had no choice but to accompany her brother to one of the most dangerous places imaginable, and she was now additionally responsible for the safe-keeping and morale of Berengaria, in whom Richard appeared to show little interest. Richard had not organised the wedding while the party remained in Sicily, though it was the liturgical season of Lent, so that was a plausible excuse.

We have no information on whether Joanna was once again afflicted by the sort of seasickness that had laid her low on the way to her wedding as a child, but the journey would certainly not have been one of great comfort, and there was worse to come. Some three days after their departure from Sicily, the fleet was hit by a fierce storm, resulting in the destruction of several ships and many others being widely scattered. This must have been a terrifying experience for Joanna and Berengaria, who are extremely unlikely to have been able to swim and who would be facing certain death if their ship went down. They were in a different vessel from Richard; his weathered the storm and landed safely in Crete, but they ended up stranded near Cyprus along with several other ships. Wary of the ruler of Cyprus, Isaac Komnenos, the two women 'did not go ashore but dropped anchor and remained stationary far out at sea'. It would appear that their suspicions were well founded, as Isaac, upon hearing of their plight, resolved not to help but rather 'to seize and hold captive all those who were on board and plunder their money'.[17] Three of the other ships were driven aground and plundered, their crew and passengers either drowned or taken captive; Joanna and Berengaria are likely to have witnessed the action.

Once again Joanna, unable to take military action on her own behalf, was reliant on her brother to challenge a male antagonist. And once again Richard obliged, arriving in the nick of time with the gathered remains of his fleet to attack and rout Isaac's forces.[18] The two women were safe once more, but Isaac had eluded capture and Richard, sensing another opportunity for gain, decided on a complete conquest of Cyprus. After various skirmishes, he forced Isaac to surrender via the simple expedient of capturing his young daughter, whom Isaac 'loved more than any other creature', and threatening her safety. Isaac, genuinely terrified for his little girl, as well he might be given Richard's reputation and the way he had allowed his troops to behave at Messina the previous year, duly surrendered.* He was cast into a dungeon, tethered there in silver chains as Richard had promised not to put him in irons.[19] With Cyprus firmly under his control and with substantially more wealth at his disposal, Richard married Berengaria in Limassol on 12 May 1191. She was crowned queen of England, and then the whole party could set off again.

Joanna found herself at sea once again, and now with an additional female companion: the daughter of Isaac Komnenos, taken along as a hostage to ensure her father's good behaviour. Her exact age at this point is unknown, but she is described by an eye-witness as 'a little child' and was almost certainly still pre-teen.[20] Her name is also unknown to us: not one contemporary thought it important enough to record, so she is only ever referred to as 'the daughter of Isaac Komnenos' or sometimes 'the Damsel of Cyprus', a convention that has perforce continued in modern scholarship. Being a noble hostage at this time

---

* The concept of 'chivalry' was very much in the eye of the beholder, and none of the English king's tame chroniclers saw anything to criticise in his actions with regard to Isaac's daughter, who (due to her age, sex and rank) might have been classed among those a good knight would seek to protect, rather than to threaten.

did not necessarily involve close captivity, and the evidence suggests that the girl was welcomed as a member of Queen Berengaria's entourage and educated according to her rank.

The rest of the journey was thankfully made without incident and the fleet docked at Acre in June 1191. Philip Augustus had arrived a couple of months earlier; he had left Sicily before Richard did and then moved further ahead while Richard was in Cyprus. Crusading forces had been besieging the great city of Acre since August 1189 with little success, but the combined might of the armies of the kings of France and England offered new impetus and the city surrendered in July 1191.[21] We do not know exactly where Joanna and the other women were lodged during this time; Richard would not have wanted them too near the actual combat, but equally he would not have wanted them sent too far away from him. The crusaders' siege camp had been in place for so long that it was virtually a town in its own right, so perhaps the women were lodged in some part of it that was away from the front line; or perhaps a safe stronghold was located in which they could be housed. In either case their stay was hardly likely to be luxurious, and it would have been fraught with danger, not just from enemy action but also from disease. Various epidemics outside the walls of Acre contributed to a grim mortality rate among the crusaders, with the casualties including Queen Sybilla of Jerusalem and both of her daughters.*

Once the city had fallen – and presumably after some of the spilled blood had been cleaned up and the corpses removed –

---

* Sybilla's husband, Guy de Lusignan, was king only in right of his wife, so (despite his attempts to hold on to it) the crown passed to Sybilla's younger half-sister, Isabelle, whom we met in Chapter 1. As a condition of her accession Isabelle was obliged to put aside her husband, Humphrey of Toron, and marry the battle-hardened Conrad of Montferrat, who was assassinated less than two years later; it was at that point that she was obliged to marry Henry II of Champagne, Joanna's nephew.

Joanna and the other women were brought inside the walls and housed in the palace. They might have felt themselves safe, for the time being at least, but the horror was not yet over. In the middle of August 1191 Richard had 2,700 Muslim prisoners taken to the plain outside the city and beheaded.[22] It is very improbable that the noble ladies were obliged to witness the mass execution, but no atrocity of that scale – not to mention the practical aspects of arranging it and clearing up afterwards – could possibly have gone unnoticed even if they did not see it at first hand.

It was a couple of months after this, in October 1191, that Joanna was involved in perhaps the strangest episode of her eventful life. At that time Richard was embroiled in complex negotiations with the Muslim leader Saladin and, astonishingly, he seems to have suggested the possibility of Joanna marrying Saladin's brother al-Adil (also sometimes known as Saphadin). As part of the proposed deal, Saladin would cede Palestine to his brother and Richard would give up the coastal cities that he held as Joanna's dowry. The couple would live in Jerusalem, to which Christians would be given free access, and all prisoners on both sides would be released.

There were several problems with this plan. The first was that Richard might have been insincere in offering it – that it was some sort of trick. This seems to have been Saladin's opinion, as he did not take the offer seriously at all, waiting six weeks to give Richard an answer and then calling his bluff by saying that the wedding must take place immediately. Richard then stalled by saying that only the pope could supply the dispensation necessary for a king's widow to marry again, and that it would take six months to obtain it, so a stalemate seemed inevitable.

The second issue was that Richard had made this offer without actually consulting Joanna. She, according to contemporaries, flew into an absolute rage at the idea of being asked to marry a Muslim – something almost unthinkable given the religious conflicts of the time (and we must remember to view her actions through the lens of the twelfth century, not the twenty-first). Given her family's status and her own position, she would, of course, expect her brother to be the primary mover in arranging any second marriage for her, but this particular match was unacceptable. She stood her ground, with the backing of various churchmen, and Richard was obliged to alter his offer from the hand in marriage of his adult sister to that of his 7-year-old niece, Eleanor of Brittany, at which point Saladin broke off the negotiations entirely.[23]

Joanna was safe from the threat of the inter-cultural, inter-religious marriage that she had found so objectionable, but she was still not the mistress of her own fate. As the only eligible sister of a childless king of England, she was a valuable asset for Richard, so he kept her near him; and, she might have asked herself, where else could she go?

She was still in Richard's keeping when he decided to leave the Holy Land in late September 1192. As he had done before, he sent the women ahead of him in a separate ship – Joanna, Berengaria and the Damsel of Cyprus, who had been with them throughout. His own route would have to be planned carefully (something we will explore in greater depth in Chapter 6), and he was in any case blown off course. The ship carrying the ladies made landfall safely in Brindisi, a port on Italy's southern peninsula, but they had no idea what had happened to Richard. As it transpired, he had been blown off course and ended up landing between Aquileia and Venice in north-east Italy. Attempting to ride through the Empire incognito, he was recognised and arrested in Vienna by men loyal to Leopold, the duke of Austria, with whom he had been in dispute while they were both at Acre. Leopold informed Emperor Henry, who paid him a fee to transfer Richard to his own custody. Richard was imprisoned at Trifels castle in south-west Germany, and there the king of England would stay until a substantial ransom had been paid.

Joanna and her companions could not have been aware of this for quite some time, so it was in uncertain circumstances that they made their way to Rome, where they were welcomed by Pope Celestine III and where they remained several months. It was sometime during this stay that news reached them of Richard's capture and imprisonment, which would have made their own position ambiguous and possibly dangerous. They left Rome and spent late 1193 travelling through western Europe, via Pisa, Genoa and Marseille; they were then escorted across the county of Toulouse by its count, Raymond V, and his son (the future Raymond VI) until they reached the safety of Poitiers.[24]

Eleanor of Aquitaine, meanwhile, had been busy organising her son's ransom, and she travelled to Germany to deliver it in person, making her way through France and leaving that kingdom more or less as Joanna was arriving in it.[25] As it happens, and as Joanna would no doubt be interested to learn, this situation had profound implications for her former kingdom of Sicily: Emperor Henry used some of the ransom money he received to launch an immediate campaign there in his wife's name, and succeeded in gaining the crown.[*]

Richard was released in February 1194 and headed immediately to England, the realm he had not seen for over four years.

---

[*] By this point both Tancred of Lecce and his eldest son and co-ruler were dead (apparently of natural causes), and the crown had passed to Tancred's second son, William III, then aged somewhere between 4 and 8. After deposing William, Emperor Henry had him sent into captivity in Germany, where the poor boy may have been blinded and/or castrated before dying just four years later. The twelfth century was not a good time to be a child ruler, especially one with a disputable claim to the throne.

Joanna appears to have remained in France, but Richard had not forgotten about her or her value to him on the marriage market.

The counts of Toulouse, as we mentioned briefly earlier in this chapter, had long been at loggerheads with the dukes of Aquitaine over the question of overlordship of the county. The background to this is complex, covering several generations of the intertwined Aquitanian and Toulousian family trees, but Eleanor of Aquitaine's claims had been sufficient for Louis VII, Henry II and Richard I all to press them in her name at various times.[26]

In 1194 Count Raymond V died, to be succeeded by his son Raymond VI, who could claim some powerful family connections of his own: he was a first cousin of King Philip Augustus, as his mother had been Constance of France, Louis VII's sister. Richard, who could not be everywhere in his vast domains at once, sought to solve the Toulousian problem once and for all by arranging a marriage between Raymond and Joanna, and agreeing that he would renounce his hereditary claim to overlordship of the county as part of the deal. Raymond agreed, and he and Joanna were married in Rouen in October 1196. From Richard's point of view, this solved a long-standing problem on his southern border while also making use of his sister, who was by now in her early thirties and thus starting to lose some of her remarriage value. Raymond, meanwhile, got what he wanted in terms of control of his county, plus an additional royal connection to boot.

And what of Joanna's point of view? Again, we have no insight into her personal feelings, but she might not have objected to a match that would give her a permanent home and base to replace her peripatetic existence of the previous decade. Raymond was an astute politician of around 40, an age gap that would have been considered entirely reasonable, and although only a count, he ruled a wide area and could claim descent from the ducal house of Aquitaine as well as the Capetian royal family. The couple had previously spent some time in each other's company as Raymond and his father, Raymond V, had escorted Joanna, Berengaria and their entourage across the county of Toulouse three years earlier on the final stretch of their journey home from the crusade via Rome. Joanna would be Raymond's third wife: he was once widowed and once divorced. It is unclear whether his second wife was still living at this time (we do not know the exact date of her death), but as she had retired to a convent and taken holy orders after her repudiation in 1193, there were no issues to contend with and Joanna's wedding could proceed.

Raymond's two previous marriages had left him with one surviving daughter, Constance, but no sons, so he would naturally have been keen to father a male heir, one who would be related to the ruling houses of both France and England as well as having an unencumbered claim to Toulouse. After the possible barrenness of her first marriage, and the certainty of it having produced no surviving child, Joanna might also have looked forward to the possibility of parenthood. The couple conceived successfully straight away, and their son (the future Raymond VII of Toulouse) was born in July 1197. He was followed in 1198 by a daughter, Joan, and Joanna fell pregnant for a third time in 1199.

By this time, however, the situation in Toulouse had deteriorated. The county was the scene of almost constant rebellion against Raymond's authority as well as unrest caused by a religious movement called Catharism, which would later result in the conflict now known as the Albigensian Crusade. Raymond was not himself a Cathar, but there were suspicions that he might be sympathetic to their cause and accusations that he did not make enough effort to stamp out the movement.[27]

In March 1199 events took a strange turn, the exact course of which is obscure in the sources. Raymond was at this time in the neighbouring county of Provence, where he was engaged in litigation, and while he was away another of his vassals revolted. Joanna, despite being in the early stages of pregnancy, led a force in person to besiege the rebellious castle. Her attempt was unsuccessful as a raiding party managed to set fire to her siege camp and she was forced to withdraw. However, rather than heading back to Toulouse or sending word to Raymond, she fled into Aquitaine with the apparent intention of finding her brother Richard, who was at that time engaged in conflict with rebellious vassals of his own.

One chronicler thought that Joanna was going to seek Richard's help on Raymond's behalf, but although this writer was local to the area, he was composing his text decades later; Joanna's escapade occurred before he was born, so he can only have been basing his account on hearsay and it might have become confused in the retelling. The general consensus otherwise seems to be that the matrimonial relationship had broken down and that Joanna was fleeing her husband's court for the safety of her own family's lands. Given the undeniable fact of her pregnancy, we may infer that she considered her journey urgent, whatever the reason behind it, or she would not have risked her own and her baby's health by travelling. A couple of months previous to the siege, Joanna had ceased receiving any money from Raymond, which indicates that the theory of a marital rift may be the more likely of the two.[28]

After what must have been an uncomfortable journey, Joanna reached Poitou in April 1199, but it was only to find that Richard was dead. He had been killed at the siege of Châlus, throwing the question of the succession to the English crown, and to Normandy, Anjou, Maine and Aquitaine, into disarray. Eleanor of Aquitaine was in her duchy at this time, drumming up support for her youngest son, John, whose accession was threatened by the claims of Arthur of Brittany. Joanna reached her and they were able to comfort each other as best they could.

Joanna next headed for Fontevraud abbey, where she visited her brother's grave and rested for some weeks before setting off again. By July she was in Rouen with Eleanor and John, appealing for financial support. John – now accepted as the king of England – gave her 3,000 silver marks as compensation for the Sicilian dower that Richard had taken from her and never repaid.[29] Her pregnancy being now further advanced, Joanna returned to Fontevraud where, in an extraordinary move for a married, pregnant woman with two young children (and a move that adds additional weight to the idea that she was estranged from Raymond), she asked to be admitted as a nun. With her time of confinement approaching, Joanna made the will that we mentioned earlier in this chapter, a common action for a woman with assets to bequeath at a time when maternal mortality was rife. In the will she left an endowment to Fontevraud along with a request to be buried there, next to Richard, if she did not survive; she also left bequests for faithful servants and retainers, and Masses to mark 'the anniversary of the king of Sicily and herself'. There is no mention of Raymond.[30]

Having given birth to two healthy children in the two previous years, Joanna might have approached her confinement with a degree of optimism, but this time she was not to be so lucky. Perhaps the hardships of her recent travel and anxiety had taken their toll, or perhaps the labour was a complicated one, but in either case she died during the course of it on 4 September 1199, at the age of just 33. There was some hope that the baby might survive, so a Caesarean section was performed after her death. Such operations were not unknown in the Middle Ages, but they were carried out only when the mother had died and there was a reasonable hope that the child might survive. In this case a son was delivered, apparently alive. He may have been called Richard, although we do not know whether the name was stipulated by Joanna before she died or given to him by her attendants. Tragically, however, he lived only long enough to be baptised, and he was buried along with his mother.[31]

Even by the standards of royal women of the age, Joanna led an amazingly action-packed and well-travelled life. Other than her own mother, there can be few women who made homes and lives for themselves in so many different realms so many miles apart, and who experienced such extreme variations in fortune – and even Eleanor did not find herself faced with the prospect of marriage to an enemy in the Holy Land.

Like many of her peers and contemporaries, Joanna's life was superficially one in which she did not experience a great deal of personal autonomy: her father and her brother organised her marriages, and her first husband gave her a crown. But this is to simplify the way in which royal women's lives functioned; their success or otherwise can be judged by how they exercised authority in the life that had been presented to them. Joanna did not choose William of Sicily as a husband, but she made the most of the relationship once it was formed. When he died, it would have been easy to accept the political reality of the situation and recognise Tancred as the new king of Sicily, but Joanna did not. This came at a short-term personal cost, but she was aware that her network of family connections would be to her advantage, and the gamble, if it was one, paid off.

To experience personally the glory and the danger of the Holy Land in the late twelfth century was an honour shared by few western European women, and here again Joanna was able to use her autonomy and personal authority to refuse a marriage that she found distasteful.[32] Of course, her objections seem prejudiced now, but we must view them with a contemporary eye – Saladin and his brother were enemies of her family and her religion, and even in a world in which the happiness of royal women and girls was routinely sacrificed to peace treaties, the proposed alliance was a step too far.

Joanna might or might not have had more of a say in the choice of her second husband, but in either case she certainly took autonomous action when she left Raymond and their children in order to make the perilous (given her pregnancy) journey to Aquitaine. It was there that her life ended and there that she chose to be interred among members of her natal family rather than having her body conveyed to the lands of either of her husbands. Despite her almost total disconnect from all of its members except Richard throughout her adult life, the ties of her birth family – that political and strategic unit – were the ones she felt most strongly in life and in death.

Raymond VI of Toulouse would later go on to marry for a fourth time, to none other than the daughter of Isaac Komnenos, she who had experienced so much and travelled widely throughout Europe and the Holy Land without anyone bothering to record her name. However, he subsequently found the marriage either personally or politically inconvenient and it was dissolved only a couple of years later, after which he married for a fifth time.*

---

* The Damsel of Cyprus continued her extraordinary and peripatetic life after separating from Raymond. In 1202 or 1203 she married Thierry of Flanders, one of the commanders of the Flemish fleet of the Fourth Crusade, probably in order to have his help in claiming Cyprus (her father, Isaac Komnenos, having died in 1196). This is indeed what they attempted: the Flemish fleet stopped in Cyprus on the way to the crusade and Thierry claimed it in his wife's name. However, the conquest was unsuccessful and the couple headed for Armenia, at which point the Damsel disappears completely from the historical record.

Neither of these marriages produced any children, so he was survived only by Constance, the daughter of his second marriage, and Raymond and Joan, Joanna's children. Raymond VI died in 1222, embroiled for much of the later part of his life in the Albigensian conflict and having seen his lands confiscated. He would eventually be succeeded by his and Joanna's son, Raymond VII, after the war was brought to an end. This younger Raymond had been little more than a toddler when he lost his mother, but he evidently retained a sense of family feeling (or at least family pride), incorporating 'son of Queen Joanna' in his style. When he died in 1249, half a century after his mother, he chose to be buried at Fontevraud alongside her.

PART III

DAUGHTERS-IN-LAW

MARGARET

On 2 November 1160 a royal wedding took place at Neubourg in Normandy. The bride was Margaret, the third daughter of King Louis VII of France, and the groom was Henry, the eldest son of King Henry II of England. The ceremony was performed by the archbishop of Rouen in the presence of two papal legates. Normally such a high-profile wedding would be a glittering occasion with representatives of many royal and noble families in attendance, but this one was rather more low-key because it was, in a number of respects, an outrage.

One of the problems with the union was the rather unorthodox spiritual connection between the bride and the groom. Young Henry's mother, Eleanor of Aquitaine, had once been the wife of Margaret's father, Louis VII of France, and the daughters of that union (Marie and Alix) were half-sisters to both of them. A second issue was that Young Henry and Margaret were related within the prohibited degrees to each other – distantly, it was true, but given that Louis and Eleanor had separated supposedly on the grounds of consanguinity, this meant that the issue of the blood relationship was public and could not be completely ignored. A third difficulty was that the bride's father, the king of France, had no idea that the wedding was taking place and would not have given his permission for it if he had known. And a fourth was that neither groom nor bride could in any meaningful sense have consented to the marriage, as he was 5 and she a toddler of just 2 years of age.

Margaret had been born sometime in 1158, the first child of Louis VII and his second wife, Constance of Castile.[1] Her arrival was a severe disappointment to Louis, who had been hoping for a son and heir following a fifteen-year marriage to Eleanor of Aquitaine that had produced only two daughters. Still, he made the best of it; girls were always useful as bargaining chips, and little Margaret was just 6 months old when a marriage was arranged for her.

The Vexin, an area that straddled the Norman–French border, had long been a bone of contention between the two ruling houses. It was divided into two, the Norman Vexin and the French Vexin, with the traditional border being the River Epte that ran down the middle. However, thanks to the gains made by Louis VI of France (Louis VII's father and Margaret's grandfather) against Henry I of England (Henry II's grandfather), the territory controlled by the French now crossed the river and encompassed the important castles of Gisors, Neufle and Châteauneuf. This did not please Henry II, who wanted them back.

The birth of a son to Henry in 1155 and a daughter to Louis in 1158 provided an opportunity, and Margaret was not even out of swaddling bands before the negotiations for a match were underway in that same year. A delegation sent to Paris and led by Henry's chancellor, Thomas Becket, was deliberately sumptuous in order to impress the locals:

The chancellor prepared to display and lavish the wealth and resources of England, so that in all things and before all men the person of his liege lord might be honoured in his envoy [...] He had about two hundred of his own household mounted on horseback, including knights, clerks, stewards, serjeants, squires and sons of nobles [...] Twelve pack-horses and eight chests carried the chancellor's gold and silver plate, his cups, platters, goblets, pitchers, basins, saltcellars, salvers and dishes. Other coffers and packing-cases contained his money [...] Some Frenchmen rushed out of their houses when they heard the din, asking who it was and whose the equipage. They were told it was the chancellor of the English king going on embassy to the king of France. Then said the French, 'What a marvellous man the king of England must be, if his chancellor travels thus, in great state!'[2]

Louis was perhaps not quite so easily impressed by the ostentatious display, but he agreed to the match and offered the Norman Vexin and the three castles west of the river as Margaret's dowry. In return, Henry II put forward as her dower the city of Lincoln, £1,000 and 300 knights' fees in England, and the city of Avranches, two castles, another £1,000 and another 200 knights' fees in Normandy.

The attractions of the match were clear for both kings. Louis would have a daughter married to the eldest son and heir of the king of England; she would be his queen consort and in due course her children would rule that kingdom. Henry would gain control of the Norman Vexin, and there was the possibility of an even greater prize: if Louis were to die without a male heir, Young Henry would be a plausible candidate for the throne of France. In such a situation he would no doubt face challenges both from Robert of Dreux, Louis's younger brother, and from Counts Henry of Champagne and Theobald of Blois on behalf of their wives (Louis's elder daughters), but as none of these could hope to match the resources available to the king of England, Henry might well win the crown for his son and thereby add France to the wider family empire. The stakes could hardly be higher.

That the marriage was entirely a political arrangement is obvious both from the ages of the parties involved – neither of them were, or could possibly be, consulted about it – and from the clause that stated that if Young Henry were to die before the wedding could take place, Margaret would marry one of his brothers and the Norman Vexin would still form the same part of the deal.[3]

King Louis's assent to the betrothal came with two specific conditions, both of which were agreed. The first was political: that the parts of the Vexin that were to form Margaret's dowry would not pass into Henry II's control until the actual wedding had taken place – Louis assuming, naturally, that this would not be for at least ten or a dozen years. It was not uncommon for a betrothal to take place while the parties were still very young (although few were as young as 6 months), and such engagements could be and were sometimes broken when the political situation changed or if a better offer appeared. A wedding, however, was – supposedly, at least – permanent, and did not take place until the parties were of the canonical age, which was widely interpreted as 14 for boys and 12 for girls. As we have seen in earlier chapters, Henry II was later happy to ignore this when it suited him, his three daughters marrying at the ages of 11, 9 and 11, but that was all in the future, and at this point Louis had no reason to suspect that Henry would override Church rules. In the meantime the French king could look forward to a decade or more of uncontested rule over the whole Vexin. At least one chronicler saw it the same way, noting that 'the children, who because of their youth could not yet wed, should be joined in marriage when the time came'.[4] The delay was not a problem for King Henry either at this stage, in 1158, as he was looking to secure the future of his family in the long term.

Louis's second proviso sounds as though it might have had more of a personal motivation behind it: he was happy to pass custody of his infant daughter to Henry II, but he insisted that she should not be brought up in the personal household of

Eleanor of Aquitaine, who was Henry's queen but also Louis's ex-wife. Thus little Margaret, not yet out of her cradle, was taken away from her mother – whose opinions on the matter nobody thought to record – and placed in the household of Robert of Neubourg, seneschal of Normandy.[5] She would remain there, it was assumed, until she was old enough to be married and cohabit with her husband.

The faces that Margaret would henceforward see from her cradle, the people who would watch over her as she learned to walk, as she spoke her first words and laughed and began to interact with the world, would not be her own family; indeed, she would never see her mother again, nor even remember her. Margaret's intended fate had nothing to do with her own wellbeing or happiness and everything to do with her status as a political pawn in a game played by powerful men. All that could be hoped in the meantime was that she might be allowed the space to grow up in peace surrounded by people who, although not her relatives, cared for her.

But even this was not to be, because it was not long after these arrangements were made that the political situation took a drastic turn. Margaret's mother, Constance of Castile, queen of France, died in childbirth in 1160 while giving Louis a fourth daughter and Margaret a full sister. The baby survived and was named Alice. Louis, at the age of 40, found himself again single and still without a male heir. He needed to take action quickly, and he immediately made plans to marry for a third time. The problem for Henry II – and, as it turned out, for Margaret – was not Louis's decision to remarry, but his choice of bride.

Adela of Blois was in her teens, an age gap objectionable now but one that was not unusual at the time and was practical in terms of providing the best chance of the birth of an heir. But if her youth was not an issue, her family background was. She was the sister of Henry I of Champagne and Theobald V of Blois, meaning that Louis was making himself the brother-in-law of his sons-in-law. Meanwhile, Henry II of England was disadvantaged by this arrangement twice over: any match that gave Louis another shot at fathering a son would endanger Young Henry's chances of eventually sitting on the French throne, and this specific choice might even endanger the English crown as well. The Champagne–Blois faction was exceedingly powerful in France and also had a potential claim across the Channel because Henry, Theobald and Adela were the nephews and niece of the late King Stephen, against whom Henry II and his mother had fought an almighty campaign for the throne. While we know now, in hindsight, that Henry II was never challenged for the crown of England by the remaining members of the house of Blois, this was far from certain at the time and the events of the war known as the Anarchy were still very recent. Henry and Theobald were ambitious young men and their other uncle, Henry of Blois (King Stephen's brother), was still bishop of Winchester and could have exercised considerable influence on their behalf in England. Henry II was thus right to be suspicious.

He retaliated immediately with the means at his disposal; having both children to hand, he arranged for the wedding of Margaret and Young Henry to be celebrated straight away. So quickly did this happen, in fact, that it actually took place two weeks before Louis's, on 2 November 1160 (Louis and Adela were married on 13 November). That the wedding could be allowed to happen at all is an illustration of how much power and influence Henry II wielded on the international stage at this time. The Church could – and perhaps should – have forbidden it, but Henry gained the approval of the two papal legates by promising his support in turn for the newly elected Alexander III against the putative antipope who was opposing him. The legates therefore sanctioned the union and, as we saw at the beginning of the chapter, attended the wedding themselves.

Contemporaries were shocked. One chronicler wrote that Henry II had pressed ahead with the ceremony 'although they were as yet but little children, crying in the cradle', and Young Henry and Margaret can barely have been aware of what they were doing as they walked down the aisle, never mind consenting to a lifelong union.[6] But once it was done it was done, and under the terms of the marriage settlement, the castles of the Vexin were handed over to Henry's control, giving him a foothold rather closer to Paris – and rather sooner – than Louis was anticipating. Louis and his brothers-/sons-in-law were 'much incensed', but they were caught in a trap of their own making.[7] They found themselves unable to dissolve the marriage on the usual grounds of consanguinity, as Young Henry and Margaret were related in exactly the same degree as Louis and Adela, so any claim on those grounds would be putting the French king's own new union in jeopardy.

Henry II quickly re-fortified and re-garrisoned the great stronghold of Gisors, but his triumph came at a price: 'It is known,' wrote one chronicler of the episode, 'that the two kings mentioned were never at peace with each other for long, and the peoples on each side became inured to suffering whatever madness the kings perpetrated in their arrogance.'[8]

All of this had personal consequences for Margaret as well as implications for her political future. Now that she was married, her father had no say at all in her placement or upbringing, and she was moved into Queen Eleanor's household. Her little husband was also there with her for a short while, before he was removed at the age of 7 in 1162 to be brought up in the household of England's chancellor, Thomas Becket. Margaret would have seen others come and go from the royal nursery, including her three sisters-in-law Matilda, Leonor and Joanna. They, of course, were to be sent away for marriages of their own before they reached puberty, but more future brides arrived: the 5-year-old Constance of Brittany, intended for Henry and Eleanor's son Geoffrey, was brought to live at the English royal court in 1166; and Margaret's own full sister Alice of France, who was betrothed to Richard, arrived in 1169 at the age of 9.

The future daughters-in-law of the king and queen therefore had more opportunity to get to know each other than the daughters, as they accompanied Eleanor in England, Normandy or the family's other continental lands. This was the way things worked and the experience was valuable: the brothers would (it was assumed) work together to further the interests of the family firm, so their wives would need to play their part while the daughters of the family took on new roles abroad. In Margaret's case, living at the Anglo-Norman court and building ties to her husband's family were particularly important; as far as anyone was concerned at this time, Young Henry was going to be the next king of England and she his queen consort (and, in due course, the mother of the king after that). However, their ambitions would be restricted to that realm rather than France: Henry II's designs on the Capetian crown were thwarted in 1165 when Adela of Blois gave birth to a long-awaited son and male heir, Philip. There was, of course, frequent correspondence between the two courts and the 7-year-old Margaret would have received the news that she had a brother soon after the event. This altered the prospects of her future political role quite considerably: she would now lose any chance of being queen of two realms simultaneously, but would instead be a queen who was the wife of one king and the sister of another – kings who were sure to be at odds with each other at some point. Margaret would therefore be expected to play an intercessory, mediating role between them.

In 1170, the year Margaret turned 12, it looked as though she might be on the verge of an unusual promotion.

Once again, the catalyst for this change in her life was political, rather than personal. To summarise briefly, in France it had always been the custom of the Capetians for a king to have his heir crowned as 'junior king' during his own lifetime, and this had been one of the factors behind the successive smooth transfers of power in that realm. The dynasty had passed the throne from father to eldest surviving son since before the turn of the millennium, and when each king died, there was already another crowned king to take his place, whose rights could not be contested.

The situation in England could hardly have been more different: since 1066 the Anglo-Norman succession had been tangled in itself, and it had been preceded by decades of contested Anglo-Saxon and Danish claims, most of them resulting in violence. Henry II was only on the throne at all because his mother, the only surviving legitimate child of Henry I, had fought a bloody and dogged campaign to restore the right of succession to her own line from that of her cousin Stephen of Blois. There were, of course, more complicated issues at play here involving the question of female succession and/or transmission of the crown, but one of the most important factors in Empress Matilda's failure to gain the English throne for herself was that she was never crowned. Before he died, Henry I had made his barons and bishops swear an oath to uphold his daughter's rights, but this was very different from a sacred coronation, and the noblemen and churchmen of the land had reneged on their promise once he was dead.[9]

Henry II might at this time still have felt insecure about the future of his dynasty, so he took the decision to institute a new custom: he would have his eldest son crowned during his own lifetime so that nobody could dispute Young Henry's right to succeed. There were, however, problems to be overcome before this could take place, not least that the coronation ceremony was normally carried out by the archbishop of Canterbury and that the present incumbent, Thomas Becket (who had been appointed rather unexpectedly in 1163, having previously been the chancellor, a secular position), had fled into exile following his disagreements with the king. He was at this time living in France under Louis VII's protection. But Henry pressed ahead, and in June 1170 the crown was set on Young Henry's head by the archbishop of York in a magnificent ceremony attended by most of the nobility, 'to the great joy of the clergy and people'.[10] England now had two kings.

It did not, however, have two queens, because Margaret had not been at the coronation at all. In the months leading up to the ceremony, she had been with Queen Eleanor in Normandy. Knowing that the coronation was planned, she had headed for Caen and was ready and awaiting her summons to cross the Channel, but it never came. Henry II's rule and governance arrangements were so well organised that it seems very doubtful that this can have been an accidental oversight, so the only conclusion we can come to is that her omission from the ceremony was deliberate.[11] This opinion was shared by King Louis, who was enraged when he heard the news. He took it to mean that Margaret had been 'repudiated [...] to the disgrace and contempt of her father', and his immediate response was to mount an attack on the Norman border.[12]

It was in December of the same year that Becket was murdered in Canterbury cathedral, having returned from France, and Henry II found himself a pariah in western Europe and particularly with Louis, who claimed to be *rex christianissimus* (a most Christian king) and who had publicly backed the archbishop and the Church against the king. Henry needed to take steps and at Easter 1171 Margaret (who had returned to England in the meantime but who had still not been crowned) was dispatched across the Channel once more. The precise reasons for this trip are unclear, but it may well have been to see her father and to persuade him of Henry II's innocence in the murder. Once again she was being used for political purposes, and this time bearing a great responsibility, despite being still only 12 or 13 years of age. The trip did give her one taste of the future, however: for the first time she was travelling as the head of her own household, and not as part of Eleanor's, so she might have enjoyed the sense of independence. Henry II promised that he would have Margaret crowned, in a second ceremony, and Louis was to some extent placated.

Margaret returned to England in August 1172 and was crowned on 27 August. The ceremony had to be something of a compromise in several respects. The see of Canterbury was still vacant following Becket's death and the archbishop of York had been excommunicated for performing the 1170 coronation, so the celebrant this time around was the archbishop of Rouen. Westminster – associated with coronations by the archbishop of Canterbury – was avoided as the venue, so Margaret was crowned at Winchester, a city with ancient royal connections and the site of crown-wearings by previous kings who had already had their official coronations. This was to be the case here: in order to emphasise his superior status, Young Henry had a crown placed on his head first, before Margaret was consecrated and crowned.[13] At the age of 13 or 14, Margaret was a queen, set apart from other mortals, chosen and approved by God.

Of course, the title 'queen of England' was already held by Eleanor of Aquitaine, and although the two of them were now technically equal, in practice they were nothing of the sort. Margaret could no more take Eleanor's place on the national or international stage than Young Henry could take Henry II's, although sensibly Margaret did not even try. While the two men were referred to in convoluted terms ('the king of England, the father, leaving the king his son behind in England, crossed over into Normandy' and 'Henry, king of England, the son of

King Henry' are just two examples of the sort of knots in which contemporaries had to tie themselves), we find Margaret styled more simply and directly as 'junior queen' (*Regina Juniora*) in a Pipe Roll of 1174. She did later make something of an effort to assert her status in the only charter of hers that survives from the time when she was married to Henry; in it she styles herself 'queen of the English and sister of Philip, king of France' (*Dei gratia regina Anglorum, soror Philippi regis Francie*), though in the absence of any further evidence we have no way of knowing whether this was a one-off or the style she normally used.[14]

Following her coronation Margaret made another visit to France, this time in the company of her husband. It would appear that it was about this time that they began to cohabit; she was by now 13 or 14 while he was 17. King Louis was mollified by his daughter's new status and by Henry II keeping his promise, so it was a good time for a diplomatic mission and he welcomed the young couple 'most joyfully, as he would his children'.[15] Everything passed off very smoothly: Margaret was obviously in her father's good books, and Young Henry – known to be affable – got on well with his father-in-law and might actually have preferred him to his authoritarian father. He was not particularly shrewd, however; Louis was a master at exploiting divisions in Henry II's family, so his welcome to the Young King may not have been all that it seemed. He encouraged Young Henry to expand his aspirations and expectations and to demand more of Henry II, emphasising that he was the king of England just as much as his father was.

Young Henry certainly enjoyed the prestige of being a crowned king, but he had none of the power or authority associated with the position, and very little of the money. This was a potentially dangerous situation, for, as a contemporary observed, 'a king without a realm is at a loss for something to do'.[16] It was probably at Louis's instigation that Young Henry asked his father outright for control of one of England or

Normandy, and it seems certain that it was the French king who suggested that if this request were not successful, the young couple should return to France and make their home there, and Louis would support them.[17] We can assume that Margaret approved of this idea; in England and the other Angevin lands she was merely the 'junior queen', while in Paris she was treated with due respect as the wife of the king of England *and* the daughter of the king of France.

Henry II refused point blank to cede any power, and events reached their logical conclusion when Young Henry rebelled against him, supported by his brothers Richard and Geoffrey. This was to have serious consequences for Margaret. Her husband made it safely to Paris, but he had left her behind and she, along with Queen Eleanor, fell into Henry II's hands. Both of them, along with Eleanor's two youngest children Joanna and John (and also Alice of France and Constance of Brittany), were transported from Normandy to England in the summer of 1174 to await Henry's decision on their fate.

This must have been a hugely worrying time for Margaret. She was the king's daughter-in-law, but what did that signify when the king's son, her husband, was a rebel? She was effectively a hostage for Young Henry's good behaviour and could expect to be treated accordingly. She would have had some confidence that her relationship to the king of France would have stopped the worst happening, but it still must have been incredibly nerve-wracking. As it transpired, she was separated from her mother-in-law; Eleanor was sent to Salisbury and Margaret to Devizes, one of the king's strongest fortresses.[18]

Henry II was too powerful for his sons and they were eventually forced to submit. Young Henry still had no real authority but for now he accepted a large cash allowance, and Margaret was released and was able to travel to France to join him. He preferred to spend his time in that realm for now, a decision of which Margaret no doubt approved. England might be her future, but at present she was better off in her father's kingdom with her husband, rather than remaining under the watchful eye of her father-in-law. The couple began to cohabit again; with Margaret by now in her late teens, the pressure to conceive and bear a son would soon start to mount. There is, unfortunately, little evidence to shed light on Margaret and Henry's personal relationship, although such information as we can glean is positive. As we will see later, she remembered him with great affection after he died; no contemporary mentions him having a mistress and he is not known to have fathered any illegitimate children.[19]

Despite his moral and practical victory over his rebellious sons, Henry II was still not satisfied with his gains, and nor was he happy with the closeness of the relationship between his eldest son and the king of France. In the spring of 1177 he made two demands that were so unreasonable that they must have been deliberately framed to provoke confrontation. As a start, he insisted that Louis should cede the whole of the Vexin (and not just the Norman part, as originally agreed) as part of the marriage settlement between Young Henry and Margaret, something Louis was certainly not about to agree to. The second demand involved Alice, Margaret's sister. She had now been betrothed to Richard for almost ten years and was 17, more than old enough by the standards of the age to be married. For political reasons of his own, King Henry had been stalling, and he now told Louis that he should additionally hand over Bourges (in central France) and other territories as Alice's dowry before the wedding could proceed. This had never been agreed to at all – it having been specified in the original arrangement that the match should take place without a dowry – and Louis could not assent without losing face.

So irritated was the French king with these demands that he retaliated with a counter-demand of his own, that Alice's marriage to Richard should take place, as promised, now, without any dowry. He considered it an insult that the wedding had not already taken place, and was supported by Pope Alexander III, who now threatened Henry with interdict if he did not comply and arrange the wedding straight away.[20]

Margaret's feelings about the plight of her younger sister are unrecorded. She had other concerns at this time, for at the end of 1176 or early in 1177 she had discovered that she was pregnant. Pregnancy was, of course, a physically dangerous state, but Margaret was also in a precarious political position, sensing or knowing that more conflict was on the way and no doubt keen not to get stuck in the middle of it again at a time when she was particularly vulnerable. In the spring of 1177 she and her husband were in Plantagenet-controlled lands, but as Henry II made the demands outlined above, she fled his territories for Paris, pregnant as she was.

Henry II had certainly not given his permission for his heir's wife to do such a thing. We do not know whether Margaret undertook her journey with the consent of her husband or not, though the former is perhaps more likely – he had left her to be captured as a hostage once before and would presumably be keen to make sure that this did not happen again, either to his wife or to his soon-to-be-born heir.[21] Henry II was angry, not wanting the direct heir to the English throne to be born in Paris, and he added another demand: that Louis should send back his daughter forthwith. There was a danger of the pendulum swinging in completely the opposite direction from what the situation had been when Henry had arranged the match: not only had he lost any hope of his son inheriting Louis's crown, but Louis would soon be celebrating the birth of a grandchild who, if male, would one day sit on the English throne.

As it transpired, the child *was* born in Paris, but Margaret's labour in June 1177 was a premature one, perhaps brought on by the stress of her journey and her situation. The celebrations attending the arrival of a boy, who was named William, soon turned to sadness as he died just three days later.

Infant mortality, as we know, was frighteningly common at this time, and Margaret surely knew it was a possibility, but to lose her firstborn and much-anticipated son in such circumstances must have been heartbreaking. There is no information on the details of the labour or on what Margaret suffered, but she would never bear another child. Whether or not this was known to her and to her husband at the time, or whether it only became apparent later when she failed to conceive again, is debatable. One clue that it may have been the former is that she and Henry ceased cohabiting, at least for a while; he left her behind as he turned his attention to the tournament circuit in northern France.

On the one hand, this was a useful distraction exercise; it gave Young Henry something to do while he was kicking his heels and waiting for power and authority to come his way. He enjoyed being treated with deference by the knights and nobles who travelled around to participate, which was partly due to his rank but also a consequence of the enormous amount of money he expended. The object of a tournament was to capture as many opposing knights as possible, in order to confiscate their arms and horses and to collect ransom money, but there were no rules on how many men could attack another simultaneously. One of the best ways to win was therefore to pay to employ a substantial number of retainers, which is what Young Henry did with lavish and spendthrift generosity. One notable disadvantage to the heir to a throne engaging in tournaments, however, is that they were dangerous: large groups of armed men fought against each other in an unregulated melee, ranging over a wide area, and real weapons were used. Although the aim was to capture, rather than kill, opponents, fatalities were not uncommon and serious, crippling injury was a constant threat.[22]

Ladies did sometimes watch tournaments, but the whole enterprise was very much an elite boys' club, so while Young Henry was thus engaged, Margaret elected to travel to Troyes to take up residence with her elder half-sister Marie, the countess of Champagne, as we saw in Chapter 1. This happened at some point between late 1177 and May 1179, when Margaret is known to have been present at the birth of Marie's second son, Theobald, who was born in that month.[23] Margaret stayed there for some time, no doubt enjoying the unfamiliar sense of peace and the luxurious surroundings. While she was there she would have had plenty of opportunity to meet and get to know her eldest nephew, the future Henry II of Champagne, who was just coming up for 13 at the time of his brother's birth. Margaret and Henry would meet again later in their lives, in circumstances that neither of them could possibly have predicted at this time.

In September 1180 Margaret's father, Louis VII, died. The new king of France – acceding uncontested as a king who had already been crowned – was her 15-year-old half-brother Philip Augustus. Margaret no doubt grieved for the loss of a father who had, by the standards of the day at least, been kind to her once she had helped him to achieve his political ambitions. But his death and Philip's accession otherwise had little effect on the life she was now living.

At some point before 1182 Margaret rejoined Young Henry, who was still on the tournament circuit, and it was in that year that a curious and possibly even fictional episode occurred.

The senior knight in the Young King's entourage was William Marshal. He had started life as the fourth son of a minor baron but had risen to prominence by loyal service to Queen Eleanor and King Henry before being placed by Henry II in his eldest son's household in order to keep an eye on him. Marshal was an extremely skilled tournament fighter and had by now made a tidy profit, which naturally made him less popular with the other knights in Young Henry's entourage. Marshal, who would go on to have a long life and a distinguished career, was the subject of a biography written just after his death – one that was rather embellished and verging on the hagiographic – and it is this text that now mentioned Margaret in less than ideal circumstances.

Other household knights (who use the terms 'the king' and 'the queen' to refer to Young Henry and Margaret rather than his parents) are depicted as complaining among themselves about Marshal and his selfish behaviour in tournaments, when suddenly the accusations take a much more serious turn:

> But this is not the provocation which most incites our anger. The fact of the matter is that he is fornicating with the queen, and that is a great sorrow and does great harm to the land. If only the king knew about this wild affair, we would certainly take our revenge on the Marshal.[24]

Such an affair, if real, would have been treason as well as adultery, with serious repercussions for both parties. But the denouement and anti-climax arrive almost straight away when the allegations reach Young Henry's ears: 'The king said: "By Saint Denis! I will not believe what you say on this; don't give me those fabrications."'[25] Margaret is not mentioned again and the only outcome is an estrangement between Henry and William Marshal that goes on for some time.

If this episode had been real, we might expect either more suspicion on Henry's part about Margaret's actions, or, conversely, a more heated defence of his wife's morality. But as we examine the incident, we can see that Margaret is no more than a plot device: the subject of the narrative is the causing of a rift between the two men by other men who are jealous and who thus make false allegations. Given that this whole episode appears only in William Marshal's biography and in no other text, it is possible that the author may have invented it entirely in order to explain the estrangement that really did occur between Young Henry and William Marshal at this point.[26] This would be very cruel and ungallant towards Margaret, but as the biography was not written until the 1220s when all parties were dead, perhaps the author thought it was excusable. There is no suggestion anywhere else that Margaret was ever unfaithful to her husband, so it seems more sensible to give her the benefit of any doubt.

It was not long before more conflict reared its head, this time between Henry II's sons, with Henry and Geoffrey allying themselves against Richard, who was by now the duke of Aquitaine, Eleanor having ceded the title to him when he reached his teens.

Having learned his lesson previously, Young Henry took the precaution of sending Margaret to Paris, where she would be out of danger under the protection of King Philip. After that, he and Geoffrey invaded Aquitaine, but they were no military match for Richard and their campaign was a disaster. Worse, Young Henry fell dangerously ill, and before long it was clear that he was dying. Margaret was in his thoughts as he lay on his deathbed: 'As he drew near his end [...] he sent a letter to his father, requesting that [...] he would deal mercifully with his mother, the queen of England, and his wife, the sister of Philip, the king of the French.'[27] Margaret would never see him again: he died on 11 June 1183, at the age of just 28.

Margaret had lost the man to whom she had been married for almost the whole of her life, and she had also lost her status as queen before she could ever enter into it fully and properly. The whole experience must have been disorientating and traumatic, and she needed some time to come to terms with it. Once again she took refuge with Marie in Troyes, rather than at the royal court in Paris, but she was not to be left to grieve in peace: as a childless widow in her mid-twenties, she was of use to Philip Augustus on the marriage market. She was also, as ever, a political football, as Philip used Young Henry's death as an excuse to demand the return of the Norman Vexin from Henry II:

> Philip asked for the return of the castle of Gisors and the other neighbouring castles, which his sister Margaret had received as a dowry from her father King Louis when she married the illustrious Henry, son of Henry [II]. These are the conditions that were stipulated. [Young] King Henry would possess the dowry during his lifetime and transmit it to his heirs, if the queen gave him any. If, on the other hand, Margaret left no children, the dowry would return uncontested to the French king on [Young] King Henry's death. The English king had already been reminded more than once on this subject, but he had always managed to invent some difficulty [...] But Philip was not fooled by the sharp practice of the king of England and, seeing that his own interests were thereby jeopardised, he decided to enter [Henry II's] territory under arms.[28]

Henry II disputed Philip's claim, saying that Louis had ceded all rights to the Norman Vexin when he gave it as Margaret's dowry. However, he was at the disadvantage of not having Margaret in his custody and was thus forced to negotiate. At a meeting of the two kings in March 1186, Philip agreed to transfer the dowry to the long-suffering Alice – who had now been in Henry's custody, unmarried, for seventeen years – on the condition that her long-awaited marriage to Richard should take place immediately.[29] Henry swore that it would be done and the kings parted, but the wedding still did not take place and Alice remained in limbo, betrothed and unfree but never married.

The pause in political hostility did at least give Margaret a short breathing space in which she could grieve and make arrangements to commemorate her late husband in an appropriate style. In a charter, she promised to use some of the income that she was to receive from her second husband for chaplains at Rouen cathedral (where Young Henry was buried) to say Masses for his soul. She did this because, 'ever preserving the memory of her lord and husband, King Henry the Younger, [she was] anxious to maintain the same union of minds when dead as when alive'.[30]

As implied by the terms of the bequest, Margaret already had a second husband lined up; Philip had wasted little time in organising a new match that would be beneficial to his own interests. This would open a new and very different chapter in Margaret's life as she was now to be sent not west, but east.

Béla III, king of Hungary, was a forward-thinking and outward-looking monarch who had been on his throne for sixteen years. He was a widower with four children (two sons and two daughters), his first queen having died a couple of years previously. He had already made unsuccessful overtures for the hands of a Byzantine princess and of Richenza, the only daughter of Henry the Lion, duke of Saxony, and his wife Matilda of England. Marriages between Hungarian kings and Byzantium or the Empire were relatively common, but as his quest for a second wife continued, Béla decided to spread his net a little wider and cast it further west. He had already shown an interest in French architecture and culture (at his invitation, a group of Cistercian monks had arrived from France to set up new abbeys in Hungary between 1179 and 1184), and now he took an interest in a French princess. His application to Philip for Margaret's hand was successful, and she travelled to Hungary in the summer of 1186 for her second wedding.[31] She appears to have had little choice in her new partner, but at least she might hope to understand her vows and give her own consent at the altar this time.

In some respects, of course, this second marriage involved a huge uprooting of Margaret's life: travelling further than she had ever done before, learning a new language and getting used to a new realm, a new court, a new culture. But we should not necessarily see this as negative; Margaret may well have welcomed it. The alternative was a long and dull life as a widow at her younger brother's court, a relatively confined existence with a status well below the one she had been used to and the ever-present possibility that she would become embroiled in the never-ending wrangling between the English and French kingdoms. The union with Béla got her away from all that, and it would also mean that she was a queen once more, able to influence her new surroundings rather than simply assimilating into them. Few widowed queens had such an opportunity, and there were two other distinct advantages: Margaret would no longer be simply a 'junior' queen but rather the wife of the reigning monarch, and she had no powerful mother-in-law to contend with. Béla's mother, Euphrosyne of Kiev, had at the time of his accession attempted to put his younger brother on the throne in his stead, but Béla had defeated the coup and captured them both. Euphrosyne was imprisoned and would soon be exiled from the kingdom to live out the rest of her life as a nun in the Holy Land.

This left Margaret as very much the pre-eminent woman at the Hungarian court, and she undertook many of the usual duties of a queen, including cultural patronage and overseeing building work. The royal palace and cathedral built in Béla's capital, Esztergom, during the 1180s and 1190s was the first example of Gothic architecture (which was popular in France) in central Europe, and French culture began to permeate in other ways. One interesting example is that forenames from the courtly and chivalric literature popular in western Europe became more widely used alongside more traditionally Hungarian names.[32]

Margaret also appears to have encouraged the cult of Thomas Becket in Hungary, although her reasons for doing so were very different from those of her sisters-in-law Matilda and Leonor. Margaret had no cause to love Henry II or to promote his interests, but Young Henry had been happy in Becket's household as a boy and Margaret would have known the archbishop herself. And, of course, it was her own father, Louis VII, who had sheltered and supported Becket during his exile from England. The French king had in 1179 made a pilgrimage to pray at Becket's shrine in Canterbury for the health of his only son and heir, Philip, who was at that time dangerously ill, and his prayers had been answered.[33]

Other aspects of royal life were similar regardless of the location, such as welcoming visiting international leaders. In 1189 German crusaders led by Emperor Frederick Barbarossa marched through Hungary on their overland route to the Third Crusade. They were welcomed by Béla and Margaret at the palace of Esztergom.[34]

Perhaps inspired by the emperor – and feeling secure in the knowledge that his realm was safe from any further potential rebellion by his mother and brother – Béla later took a crusading vow himself. Unfortunately for him he did not live to fulfil it: he fell ill and died in April 1196, aged somewhere in his late forties. He was succeeded on the throne by his elder son, Emeric, and – in an attempt to avoid Emeric experiencing the same sort of rebellion that he had – he left land and castles to his younger son, Andrew, but only on the condition that Andrew led a crusade to the Holy Land.*[35]

As Emeric was in his twenties and had no need for a regent or for a widowed stepmother to advise him, and Margaret had no children of her own, this left her free to pursue her own agenda. She evidently had no desire to return to France or to marry again, so she decided on a more radical course of action: she would make a pilgrimage to the Holy Land. This was an extremely ambitious undertaking for a single woman, even a royal one, and it demonstrates both that she had faith in her own abilities and that her religious conviction was strong. That her intention was to spend the rest of her life in the east is indicated by the letter she wrote to her half-sister Marie of Champagne, explaining her wish to 'end her days' there.[36] She cut her ties to Hungary, selling her dower rights and revenues to Emeric, and then took the cross and set off with a party of German knights.

Margaret was sure of a warm welcome upon her arrival in the Holy Land in late August 1197, for the king of Jerusalem at this point was none other than her nephew Henry II of Champagne, whom she knew of old. Alas, the reunion was to be tragically short-lived:

> Count Henry went to Tyre to see his aunt, and he greeted her with the greatest honour. But within eight days of her arrival she died and was buried in the choir of the church at Tyre. She gave all her wealth to Count Henry because he was her nephew, the son of her sister.[37]

---

* Andrew rebelled anyway, and would eventually seize the Hungarian crown when his brother died. He overthrew Emeric's 4-year-old son and successor, Ladislaus III, in 1204, and the boy rather conveniently died a few months later.

We cannot be sure of the cause of Margaret's death, but the implication is that it must have been from illness; if it had been the result of any kind of hostile action then contemporaries would have remarked upon it. Her nephew Henry was himself killed in an accident only days afterwards, and the double news of both deaths, when it reached her back in France, was enough to send Marie of Champagne into a depression from which she never recovered.

Margaret of France led a thrilling (though not always happy or comfortable) life, but she has left a curiously slight personal impression. Her appearances in contemporary narrative are fleeting, and almost all relate to someone else – father, father-in-law, brother, husband – meaning that her personal thoughts and feelings are all but unknowable. We can speculate, perhaps, that she was determined to make the best of the life that was allocated to her: she had no say in the choice of either of her husbands, but we can see that she worked at her duties and her relationships and that both Young Henry and Béla came to esteem and perhaps even love her. She played an intercessory role as well as anyone could have done, given the extremely difficult family circumstances with which she was often faced. At the very end of her life, when Margaret finally found herself free of the shackles of marriage that had been placed on her when she was just 2 years old, we can see that she took very decided action on her own behalf and in pursuit of her own desires, uprooting herself once again to travel – without husband, father or brother – to achieve a fervent ambition that was all her own.

BERENGARIA

Berengaria of Navarre is probably best known as the answer to the quiz question 'Who was the only queen of England never to visit England?' While this depiction of her needs to be nuanced (she never set foot in England during her tenure as queen, but there is some evidence she might have visited later), it is true that she is one of the more shadowy figures in English royal history.[1]

Berengaria first comes to prominence in contemporary sources at the time of her marriage to Richard the Lionheart in 1191, but of course her story starts much earlier than that, in the Spanish kingdom of Navarre. As we try to discover and reconstruct her childhood there, we encounter the first of many frustrating lacunae: we do not know when or where she was born. Contemporaries often did not bother to record such information for girls, even royal ones, so all we can do is hazard a best guess of 'around 1165' and speculate that a likely location was Tudela, a favourite residence of her parents. We do know who they were, at least: Sancho VI the Wise of Navarre and his queen, Sancha of Castile. The royal couple had five children, of whom Berengaria was the eldest of the three daughters and probably the eldest of all. Queen Sancha was the sister of, among others, Constance of Castile, queen of France (the mother of Margaret and Alice), and Sancho III, king of Castile (the father of Leonor's husband, Alfonso VIII). As Sancho the Wise's siblings included Margaret of Navarre (the mother of Joanna's first husband, William II of Sicily), this meant that Berengaria could number among her first cousins a group of international royal figures who were connected to the Plantagenet family by marriage.

Berengaria would have received an education suitable for a girl of her rank, and may have helped to educate her younger siblings following the death of their mother in 1179. The Navarrese court was a pious one and Berengaria appears to have been deeply religious, perhaps even to the point of considering taking holy orders.[2]

There are a couple of vague references in chronicles of the Third Crusade that imply that Berengaria might have met Richard when she was in her teens – one says that 'since the time when he was count of Poitiers she had been his heart's desire', and the other notes that 'attracted by her graceful manner and high birth, he had desired her very much for a long time' – but these are unlikely to be based on any substantive information.[3] There are plausible reasons why Richard might have encountered Berengaria's father, Sancho the Wise: firstly, as we saw in Chapter 3, during the 1170s the Navarrese king was embroiled in a territorial dispute with Alfonso VIII of Castile, and both kings agreed to submit their claims to Henry II of England to arbitrate, meaning that that Sancho was in frequent contact with Henry's court. Secondly, Richard was the duke of Aquitaine and thus ruled lands that bordered Navarre, so they may have had occasion to meet to discuss matters of mutual interest. In both cases, however, it is difficult to imagine that Sancho would have brought his unmarried daughter to a political meeting.

He might, however, have brought his elder son; heirs to thrones were often introduced to political life at an early age and we do know for certain that this son, also called Sancho, was a close ally and friend of Richard's later on. The future Sancho VII of Navarre was in all probability a number of years younger than Richard, but he was a renowned warrior and they would have had interests in common. We will meet him again later in this chapter, but of interest at this point is that he was known as Sancho the Strong, and analysis of his exhumed bones indicates that he stood a startling 2m 20cm (7ft 3in) tall.[4] Richard was of no insignificant stature himself, but the sight of a boy who was probably taller than he was even in his early teens would no doubt have caught his attention. In sum, then, Richard's initial interest in Navarre and in Berengaria would seem to be political and military rather than romantic.

As the years went by, this interest became all the more important. Following the death of Henry the Young King in 1183, Richard became heir to all his father's lands as well as his mother's. Rather than remaining only the duke of Aquitaine, he would now expect in due course to rule territories that ran all the way from the north of England to the south, across the Channel to Normandy and then down through Anjou, Maine and Aquitaine to the Pyrenees.[*] Nobody could be in all those places at once and Richard would need strong allies on his southern border, which in practice meant the Spanish kingdoms. The political acumen of Sancho the Wise and the military prowess of Sancho the Strong were probably both factors in his choice of Navarre rather than its larger neighbour Aragon for the purpose. Richard already had an alliance with Castile, of course, as his sister Leonor was the queen there; any further intermarriage with that kingdom would be not only unnecessary but also impossible, as the available princesses were his nieces.

---

[*] There was some thought (on Henry II's part, at least) that Richard should make over Aquitaine to his youngest brother, John, now that he was the heir to the patrimony, and this was the cause of more family conflict. However, this dispute does not form part of our story here.

Technically, of course, Richard should not have been thinking of a marriage alliance with anybody as he was betrothed to Alice of France, and had been since 1169. However, the longer they remained unmarried, the less likely that union became, and neither he nor his father Henry II demonstrated any urgency to arrange a wedding. We have no firm evidence that Richard began to think of the idea of a Navarrese marriage alliance as early as 1183, but it is certainly an idea to consider – and one that is lent weight by Sancho the Wise keeping Berengaria unmarried far beyond the normal age for royal daughters. It would have been a great and prestigious coup for the king of the smallest of the Spanish realms to see his daughter as queen of England, and he made no move to secure any other alliance for her.

The first solid evidence that we have of Richard entering into negotiations for a marriage with Berengaria comes in 1190, the year after he acceded to the English throne. By this time Berengaria was probably in her mid-twenties, and unfortunately we know nothing of how she had spent the last decade except that she remained in Navarre and attracted no controversy. Richard's need for her (or rather, for her father and brother) was by now an urgent one: not only did he rule extensive lands but he was about to set off on crusade, his mother would be busy on his behalf in England and thus have little time to spare for Aquitaine, and he was still in dispute with Raymond V, count of Toulouse, on the subject of overlordship there.

With his political need being so acute, Richard was happy to accept that Berengaria would come with a small dowry of only two castles on the Navarrese–Aquitanian border. In return he needed to offer her a dower, but there was a problem: the traditional dower of the queen of England (comprising lands in England, Normandy, Touraine and Maine) was currently in the possession of his mother. As Eleanor was by now in her late sixties it was probably – although mistakenly, as it turns out –

assumed that she would not live much longer, so Richard made Berengaria a temporary grant of lands he held in Gascony, with the intention that she would be endowed with the traditional dower upon his mother's death.[5]

Eleanor of Aquitaine, as her son's closest confidante, was involved in the arrangements for the union, and it was she who would escort the bride to meet her husband. She was also tasked with convincing Sancho the Wise that Richard's betrothal to Alice of France, which was still standing at this point, could be put aside; whatever the enticement of the crown of England, Sancho would not want to send his daughter halfway across Europe on a wild goose chase that might result in a catastrophic loss of face for both of them.

Eleanor arrived in Navarre in the autumn of 1190, and was evidently persuasive, as King Sancho agreed to Berengaria's departure. The question of where they were departing *to* was uncertain; by this time Richard had already set off on crusade and they would need to catch up with him somewhere in the Mediterranean.

The two women had an arduous journey ahead of them. Although we can extrapolate their route, it is frustrating (a word that crops up frequently in studies on Berengaria) that we have absolutely no information at all on what they might have talked about on the way as they spent the long and uncomfortable hours in each other's company. We can speculate, of course, and it is probable that they spoke of the duties of queenship and of Richard himself – Eleanor perhaps advancing a positive depiction of her favourite child despite his public reputation for being both unpredictable and violent.[6] Their language of conversation is also a moot point. It is conceivable that Berengaria's knowledge of Occitan (which was used along the Spanish pilgrim route as well as in Languedoc) was better than Eleanor's of Navarro-Aragonese, and if all else failed they would have had some Latin in common. Perhaps Berengaria was even able to take the opportunity to learn the Anglo-Norman dialect that she would need in Normandy and England in due course. Whatever languages they conversed in, we may hope for Berengaria's sake that her mother-in-law-to-be warned her of the tense political situation she was about to walk into.

Richard was at this time in Sicily, together with his newly rescued sister Joanna and with Philip Augustus, the French king. Philip was still under the impression that Richard intended to marry the unfortunate Alice, who had now been in Plantagenet custody for more than twenty years. He was Richard's ally on the present crusade and Richard would not have wanted to jeopardise this military relationship, but with Berengaria actually on the way it was now time for him to grasp the nettle and break the news, however unpleasant the consequences might be.

How the French king would react would depend upon the reasons given for the repudiation, and Richard apparently decided to go for the personal rather than the political, making a shocking allegation: 'The king of England made answer, that he would on no account whatever take his [Philip's] sister to wife; inasmuch as the king of England, his own father [Henry II], had been intimate with her, and had had a son by her.' He added that he could produce 'many witnesses to prove the same, who were ready by all manner of proof to establish that fact'.[7] Whether or not Richard actually made such an accusation, and if so, whether the substance of it contained any truth, has never been proved one way or the other, but the fact of the matter was that Philip agreed to the dissolution of the betrothal. His sister – and the castles of the Vexin, which had become her dowry when her sister Margaret was widowed

– were to be returned to Philip, and 'he gave to the king of England leave to marry whomsoever he should choose'.[8] Then he left Sicily to continue his journey to the Holy Land.

Meanwhile, Berengaria and Eleanor's journey had taken them on an exhausting overland route – during the winter – across the Pyrenees, through the southern part of France, into the Empire, across the Alps and down through Italy. When they reached Naples, Richard sent ships to meet them, but they preferred to continue overland. As it happened, this worked in Berengaria's favour: the journey took them longer than travelling by sea, meaning that Philip Augustus had already left Sicily by the time she arrived and she did not have to face the awkwardness of meeting him face to face. It was close, though: she arrived in Messina on 30 March 1191, the same day on which he had departed only hours earlier.[9]

Berengaria's appearance in Sicily was the first chance for the English crusade chroniclers to write properly about their future queen, but their depictions vary considerably. One dismisses her rather brusquely as 'a maiden more prudent than pretty'; a second calls her 'a wise maiden, a fine lady, both noble and beautiful, with no falseness or treachery in her'; while a third eschews any physical description at all, only noting tersely that she was 'the daughter of Sancho, king of Navarre', which was presumably to him the main point of interest in the union.[10]

The indefatigable Eleanor of Aquitaine stayed only a few days before setting off again for England, leaving Berengaria with her fiancé and his sister. This was convenient as Joanna, as a widow, could act as her chaperone – and Berengaria still needed one when the party left Sicily on 10 April 1191.

---

* Alice's story did end a little more happily than might have been expected. In 1195, when she was 35, Philip arranged a marriage for her with William Talvas, count of Ponthieu, and she went on to bear him two children and to live peacefully for another twenty years.

The chronicler who earlier called her 'more prudent than pretty' notes snidely that she left the island 'perhaps still a virgin', but this was hardly surprising given that the wedding had not yet taken place. It was the liturgical season of Lent, which was either the reason for the delay or Richard's excuse for it.[11]

As we saw in Chapter 4, Berengaria and Joanna experienced danger upon their arrival in Cypriot waters. When Isaac Komnenos arrived near to where they were anchored, he made several efforts to entice them to land:

> [Isaac] sent a message to the queens couched in amicable but fraudulent words. He informed them that they could come ashore safely, and by his unconditional decision they could be assured of suffering no difficulty from any of his people. They refused. The next day [Isaac] sent many presents to the queens, on the pretext of honouring them [...] he tried to get round the queens with flattery and deceit. The queens were in a tight spot. They began to waver, anxious that if they submitted to the emperor's persuasions they would be taken captive. On the other hand, they were afraid that he would attack them if they persisted in their refusals.[12]

Of interest here is that the chronicler refers to Joanna and Berengaria as 'the queens', even though Berengaria was at this point only betrothed to Richard rather than married, and that his neutral 'they' implies that they took their decisions in concert, rather than one being in charge of the other.

Richard arrived just in time and all was well, which must have been a relief to Berengaria – her career as queen had been in danger of ending before it had even started. As it was, the two women were finally escorted off their ship and taken to Limassol, 'where after all the hardships and unpleasantness of the sea they relaxed in peace and security'.[13]

Then, finally, it was time for the ceremony that would comprise both wedding and coronation. This took place on 12 May 1191, and again our accounts vary in quality and detail. The chronicler who earlier described Berengaria only as Sancho's daughter and gave no description of her is again rather dry and official:

> Berengaria, daughter of the king of Navarre, was married to Richard, king of England [...] Nicholas, the king's chaplain, performing the services of that sacrament; and on the same day the king caused her to be crowned and consecrated queen by John, bishop of Évreux.[14]

Another at least bothers to note that Berengaria was 'very wise and of good character', while a third gives a little more detail:

> The next morning the young woman was married and crowned at Limassol. [She was] beautiful, with a bright countenance, the wisest woman, indeed, that one could hope to find anywhere. There was the king in great glory, rejoicing in his victory and in his marriage to the woman to whom he had pledged his troth.[15]

By virtue of her coronation and anointing, Berengaria was now the queen of England, a realm she had never even come close to visiting.

Following her marriage and coronation, a queen would normally have many duties to keep her busy. She might hear petitions, the supplicants hoping that she would intercede with the king on their behalf. She could engage in cultural, literary or religious patronage or acts of charity. She would be required to welcome diplomatic or international visitors to her husband's court when he was present, and might supervise his estates or act as regent in his absence. At the very least, she would have a household to run. But Berengaria, far away from England, Normandy or Aquitaine and with no settled abode, had none of these. She had nothing to keep her busy and no immediate duties beyond following Richard. She would be available if he wanted her presence but would need to acquiesce quietly if he preferred to place her somewhere away from him.

'Away from him' is more or less where Berengaria remained for the duration of the crusade, shifted from location to location as the campaign continued, protected but never consulted. The language used by the chroniclers reflects her powerlessness and Joanna's: following the capture of Acre, Richard appropriated the royal palace 'in which he placed his queens'; later 'he had the queens brought back and installed in Jaffa', and when it was time to leave 'he put his wife and sister and the daughter of the duke [*sic*] of Cyprus in the ships' – the sort of phraseology that might also be applied to goods and chattels.[16]

We should sound a small note of caution here: although there is little evidence to suggest that Berengaria and Richard spent much time in each other's company, this does not necessarily mean that they did not – it might just be that the contemporary observers did not remark upon it as they preferred to concentrate their efforts on the military and political aspects of the crusade. We can never know for sure either way.

Berengaria was, at least, not alone: she had her sister-in-law Joanna for company as well as the young Damsel of Cyprus, who had been placed with her 'to be cared for and educated'.[17] This last was the one duty that bore any resemblance to the normal responsibilities of a queen, who would expect to have young royal or noble girls about her and to supervise their education. There are also some vague references to the queens moving 'with their ladies', so they must have had other attendants as well.[18]

Regardless of Berengaria and Richard's personal relationship, their marriage was bearing fruit in other ways. In 1192 there was a revolt in Aquitaine involving not only some of the Gascon lords who owed allegiance to Richard, but also the dangerous Raymond V, count of Toulouse. Richard was still in the Holy Land, but the rebellion was put down on his behalf by Sancho the Strong, who – with the approval of his father – swept into the region with a large force of knights, defeated the rebels and ravaged the lands around Toulouse.[19]

After some fifteen months in the Holy Land, during which time he was not able to capitalise on his initial success at Acre, Richard decided to head home. When Berengaria heard the news, she must have been excited at the thought of travelling to England, the realm of which she had been queen for some time already. She might have hoped that once their lives were a little more stable, she could finally take on the full range of queenly duties – including falling pregnant, which she had not yet done in the year and a half of her marriage, although this is not surprising given that she appears to have had little opportunity to conceive. Once again, she and Joanna were to travel separately from Richard. They sailed from Acre on 29 September 1192, and he followed on 9 October.

The problem for Richard was that he had, over the years, managed to provoke or upset so many European rulers that there were very few safe routes or places to stop. After his marriage to Berengaria and his treatment of Alice of France, he could hardly expect to be welcomed if he landed in any territory controlled by Philip Augustus; this by extension ruled out Hungary, where Béla III was Philip's brother-in-law and ally thanks to his marriage to Margaret of France. North-western Italy was dominated by the Montferrat family, who suspected that Richard might have had a hand in the assassination of Conrad of Montferrat in the Holy Land, so landing there would be risky. Finally, Richard's support for and deal with Tancred in Sicily meant that he had made an enemy of Emperor Henry VI, the husband of Constance, Sicily's rightful heir.

Richard's only allies were those gifted to him by the marriages of his sisters. The widowed Joanna, of course, had no kingdom of her own; the conflicts following the death of her husband did mean that Richard could make safe landfall in Cyprus or Sicily, but they were still a long way from his own domains and he would need a further stopping point. Leonor and Alfonso VIII would no doubt have welcomed him in Castile, but that was too far away to reach in a single journey. So that left Matilda. She, of course, had died in 1189 but her widower and sons were firm allies, so Richard might well have been attempting to make it to the safety of Bavaria and Henry the Lion's protection when he set sail. However, his ship was blown off course and he ended up in north-east Italy, from where he travelled overland into the territory of Leopold of Austria, another ruler he had managed to antagonise. Leopold imprisoned Richard in the castle of Dürnstein and then informed Emperor Henry, who was delighted to buy the English king's custody. He transferred Richard to Trifels castle, in south-west Germany, and then wrote to Philip Augustus to apprise him of the news that 'will afford most abundant joy to your own feelings'.[20]

Berengaria would not, at first, have been aware of any of this. She and Joanna (still with the young Damsel of Cyprus in their entourage) reached Rome and it was there that the news eventually reached her. She remained there for six months 'through fear of the emperor', but despite her uncertain situation, she did not forget her rank or try to dissociate herself from her position: in a charter drawn up in Rome in 1193 she styles herself 'B[erengaria], queen of the English, duchess of the Normans and Aquitanians, countess of the Angevins'.[21]

Richard, however, does not seem to have seen things in quite the same way. It was not an uncommon circumstance for a nobleman to be held for ransom, and it had also happened to a few previous kings. In such a situation it would normally be his wife – his 'other half' in the eyes of God and the law – who took the lead in negotiating for his release, but Richard made no move to contact Berengaria, writing instead to his mother, Eleanor of Aquitaine, whom at least one English chronicler was still referring to at this point as 'our lady the queen'.[22] Richard also wrote to his half-sister Marie, but as far as we can see he did not communicate with Berengaria at all. She could justifiably feel aggrieved about this: whatever the nature of their personal relationship, it was an insult to her position as queen.

Throughout all these events, we continue to see Berengaria as essentially a passive character. As a newly-wed in the unfamiliar and dangerous surroundings of the Holy Land, this was entirely understandable – actions and decisions were best left to the military experts. But now, having arrived in Poitou, a territory over which her husband ruled, she could count herself safe; it is therefore difficult to see why she did not make more of an effort to improve her own situation. She seems to have made no attempt, for example, to travel to England. Did she think that somehow she was not entitled to do this unless Richard was with her? Did she simply not want to? Or was there a combination of factors at work?

Berengaria was still in France in 1194 when Richard was released from captivity. Strangely, although she does not seem to have been involved in the process, her family was: one of the hostages left with the emperor until the balance of the ransom could be paid, along with Otto of Brunswick, was Ferdinand of Navarre, the younger of Berengaria's two brothers.[23]

Upon his release, Richard travelled straight to England, making no move to see his wife first or to summon her to join him. In April 1194 he engaged in a crown-wearing at

Winchester, alone, despite the fact that this would have been the ideal opportunity to introduce his queen to his English subjects and for her to wear her own crown before them for the first time. This neglect of Berengaria and the insult to her position is all the more inexplicable given that her family continued to act on his behalf; in addition to the sacrifice of Ferdinand's freedom, Sancho the Strong was still performing his role as an ally, having entered Aquitaine in the spring of 1194 to quell another revolt there. He did eventually have to withdraw when news reached him that Sancho the Wise had died on 27 June; the younger man returned to Navarre to be crowned Sancho VII and would be busy there for the foreseeable future, which would have implications for the alliance and for Berengaria personally. We do not know how she reacted to the news of the death of her father, but without his support, her position as a neglected queen became even more precarious. Richard, keen to quell the trouble that had arisen while he was away, was by this time already in Aquitaine himself, where he and Sancho besieged the fortress of Loches together. After the new king of Navarre left, Richard turned to Touraine, where he fought an engagement with Philip Augustus at Fréteval on 4 July 1194. Despite now being much nearer geographically to his wife, he still made no move to summon or to visit her.

The question of *why* Richard should have neglected Berengaria throughout almost the entire eight years of their marriage is one that has been much discussed. There might, perhaps, have been some excuse for keeping her at arm's length while they were in the Holy Land (although the dangers of crusade did not stop later kings such as Edward I of England or Louis IX of France from seeing their wives, both of whom gave birth to children while they were in the east), but the continuation of such behaviour once they returned to western Europe requires some sort of explanation. What follows will necessarily be speculative, but it covers some of the major themes and theories.

The first idea is that a marriage that had been undertaken for purely political purposes had outlived its usefulness. However, this seems unlikely as we can clearly see that the couple were already distanced both while and before Navarrese military assistance was forthcoming. This leads us on to the suggestion that there must have been some personal element to the estrangement, the most commonly cited reason for which is that Richard might have been homosexual. A debate has raged over this since around the middle of the twentieth century and has been well summarised elsewhere; in short, the view that he was either homosexual or bisexual first gained and then lost ground, with scholarly opinion now veering towards the opinion that he was not, although there is no absolute consensus.[24] The two contemporary passages most commonly discussed in support of the theory are one that tells of Richard sharing a bed with Philip Augustus and one in which he is told to put aside the sins of Sodom, but both are open to interpretation: sharing a bed could be a political as well as a personal act (sleeping in someone else's presence, at a time when all men carried knives, showed that they could be trusted), and in the late twelfth century 'the sins of Sodom' could be taken as referring to a range of sins, mainly sexual in nature but not necessarily homosexual.[25]

What does seem plausible, and even likely, is that – for whatever reason – Richard and Berengaria became aware fairly early in their relationship that they were not going to have children. In the summer of 1194 he was 36 and she probably still on the right side of 30, so age cannot have been the reason, or at least not entirely. Whether this was due to sexuality or to some physical problem of either or both could be discussed ad infinitum, but if the fact of there being no prospect of an heir were known, then it does make more sense of the course of their marriage.

To continue in a speculative vein, it is the opinion of this author that a close personal relationship with Berengaria was simply never one of Richard's priorities. He certainly had the best of both worlds when it came to the political alliance: both Sancho the Wise and Sancho the Strong seemed to be happy enough with the *fact* of the marriage (rather than with any interpersonal relationship contained within it) to act in Richard's interest. He did not, therefore, need to engage in any performative concern for his wife in order to continue to enjoy their support. He does not appear to have actively disliked her – not in the way that Philip Augustus continued a vendetta against his own repudiated wife, Ingeborg of Denmark, for example, which was happening at this very time – but, rather, he was simply not interested. If, as suggested above, we add to this the idea or the knowledge that their relationship was not going to result in the birth of an heir, there can have been no real reason for them to live together.

In all this talk of Richard's neglect of Berengaria, we should not discount the possibility that she might have been happy with the situation herself. Richard does not appear to have been a particularly pleasant individual, so it may well have been the case that she was content with the title of queen and a quiet life away from him. In this we can once more use the comparator of Ingeborg of Denmark, who never ceased petitioning either King Philip, her brothers Cnut VI and Valdemar II, or various popes in order to have her rights restored to her. There is no evidence to suggest that Berengaria ever did anything similar, either by correspondence or by travelling to see any authority in person.

In 1195 there was a curious episode in which Berengaria was briefly reunited with Richard. This came about due to one of the incidents we mentioned above, Richard being chastised for his sins. Apparently a holy hermit approached Richard, telling him to 'be mindful of the destruction of Sodom, and abstain from what is unlawful'. Richard at first took no notice, but when he fell ill shortly afterwards, he had a change of heart:

> The Lord scourged him with a severe attack of illness, so that, calling before him religious men, he was not ashamed to confess the guiltiness of his life, and, after receiving absolution, took back his wife, whom for a long time he had not known: and, putting away all illicit intercourse, he remained constant to his wife, and they two became one flesh, and the Lord gave him health both of body and of soul.[26]

This happened at Easter 1195, and the reconciliation lasted at least a few months, as Berengaria is known to have been at Richard's Christmas court at Poitiers that year. However, after that Richard's interest waned once more – perhaps as a result of his bout of dangerous illness being now safely consigned to the past – and there is no evidence to suggest that he and Berengaria ever met again.

Richard went about his business; Berengaria remained living in Anjou. Given that the king was still in his thirties, she probably expected the situation to continue for many years, but in fact Richard died just four years later, in April 1199, aged 41. Once again his lack of interest in her (or possibly their mutual lack of interest in each other) meant that she was not summoned; as he lay on his deathbed, Richard wanted his mother, not his wife, by his side. However, once news of his death and burial reached Berengaria, she must have set out straight away – we can see from a charter of Eleanor's issued at Fontevraud that they were both there on 21 April.[27]

As we will see in the next two chapters, Richard's death prompted a succession crisis, as there were two heirs with competing claims: his brother John and his nephew Arthur of Brittany. Armed conflict ensued in Anjou and Maine, which did not affect Berengaria directly as she took no public side in the dispute and had no resources at her disposal to support either candidate. However, the violence would have come geographically close to her, and the possibility existed that she might become the target of any opportunist who wanted to capture her for ransom, so she needed to be careful.

Richard's death, of course, made Berengaria a(nother) dowager queen of England, and the question of her rights would soon arise and come to dominate much of the rest of her life. In the short term, however, she had a family reunion and more pleasant matters to attend to. Blanca of Navarre, her youngest sibling, arrived in France for her wedding to Theobald III, count of Champagne (the younger son of Marie of Champagne, he who had succeeded his elder brother after the latter's death in the Holy Land), which took place on 1 July 1199. Theobald had a permanent court in Troyes, so as Berengaria escorted Blanca there, she might have envied her sister. At first everything went according to plan: a daughter was born to the couple within a year of the wedding and then Blanca fell pregnant again very quickly. But tragedy struck as Theobald died unexpectedly in May 1201, aged just 22. Blanca gave birth to a son, Theobald IV, just a week later, and she would be his regent in Champagne for the entire twenty-one years of his minority.

The two sisters were now both widows, and Berengaria seems to have stayed with Blanca for some while before moving the 180 miles west to Le Mans in 1204. This was to be her home for the remainder of her life, and it was from here that she embarked on a programme of good works while simultaneously engaging in what was to be a very long struggle over her dower payments. Although she was the dowager queen of England, at the time of Richard's death the previous dowager, Eleanor of Aquitaine, was still very much alive and in possession of the traditional dower lands and their incomes. Berengaria should therefore have been awarded the temporary grant of lands in Gascony, but this never materialised either.

In August 1201 King John, unwilling to cede lands, promised Berengaria a cash allowance in lieu of her dower. He was seemingly serious about this and had written specific instructions to his exchequer:

> John, by the grace of God, etc., to the justiciary and barons of the exchequer of London, etc.
>
> Know that it has been agreed between us and Berengaria, once queen of England, wife of king Richard our brother, about her dower, which she asked for; namely that we have assigned her, for her dower, a thousand marks of silver per year; 13 shilling and 4 pence computed for the mark.
>
> And of those thousand marks she will receive 150 Angevin pounds from the income of Segreio which we assigned to her; and of the rest, beyond those 150 pounds, she will receive half at our exchequer at Caen on the feast of St. Michael, within eight days after the feast, the other half at Easter, within eight days after Easter.
>
> And thus we order you to make that remaining payment of said half at said time, without delay or interference to her or her representative who carries these letters to you.
>
> As witness, W. Count Marshall, at Chinon, 2nd day of August.[28]

However, no money ever arrived. Berengaria could do little but wait for Eleanor's death; however, by the time this occurred in 1204, John was married to Isabella of Angoulême, and he had assigned the English royal dower to her. An additional complication was that by this time he had lost Normandy and many of his ancestral French lands to Philip Augustus, so some of the properties that Berengaria was seeking were actually now under the control of the French king. Undeterred, Berengaria addressed herself to him, and – perhaps surprisingly – received a favourable answer. It is tempting to think that Philip, as a long-time antagonist of Richard, took pity on Berengaria as he felt sorry for her neglect at Richard's hands. But Philip never did anything that was not to his own political profit; it is thus more likely that he saw Berengaria as no threat and thought it would be good for his image to aid a helpless widow who had the sympathy of the pope, while at the same time weakening the English position further.

The French king and the former queen of England made an arrangement whereby Berengaria would cede the properties she claimed in Normandy (Falaise, Domfront and Bonneville-sur-Toque) and in return she would receive 1,000 marks (£667 sterling) and the city of Le Mans from Philip. This was not just the right to reside in Le Mans, but authority over it and its surrounding area, including the right to name her own seneschal and to receive the income from the various tithes and rents owed by the inhabitants.[29] Berengaria thus moved herself and her household to become 'the Lady of Le Mans', a title she would retain for the rest of her life in lieu of any claim to be dowager duchess of Normandy or countess of Anjou.

In December 1207 Berengaria's life took another unexpected turn when she became, at least technically, the heir to the Navarrese crown. Sancho VII had been married twice but had no children from either union, so his heir was his younger brother Ferdinand, who had eventually been released from his position as hostage in the Empire once King Richard's ransom had been paid in full. However, Ferdinand died childless at the end of 1207, meaning that the eldest sister of the family was next in line.* In practical terms it is difficult to see that the Navarrese nobles would have taken seriously the claims to the throne of a childless widow who was past childbearing age, but in the event Berengaria's theoretical right was never tested, as Sancho the Strong outlived all his siblings. He had one great campaign left in him, joining the kings of Castile and Aragon to win a great victory at the Battle of Las Navas de Tolosa in 1212 (as we saw in Chapter 3), but in later life he suffered from ill health and retired to live as a recluse in Tudela. Of all his siblings, the only one to produce children was Blanca, the youngest, so when Sancho eventually died in 1234, he was succeeded by his nephew, Count Theobald IV of Blois, who became King Theobald I of Navarre.

It is unlikely that Berengaria ever made serious plans to return to Navarre and take up residence there in the expectation of the crown, and she remained in Le Mans. The next we hear of her is in 1215, by which time King John had spent sixteen years evading his responsibilities towards his brother's widow. Berengaria, who was now styling herself 'Berengaria by the grace of God once humble queen of England' – although the 'humble' seems a little over-emphasised under the circumstances – wrote to him again in 1215 to reiterate the agreement they had made and to ask again for her rights.[30] John was by now in deep trouble in England, and by 1216 half his realm was under the control of Louis, Philip Augustus's son and heir

---

* This was a situation similar to that which later occurred in Castile (as we saw in Chapter 3) when Leonor's eldest daughter, Berenguela, succeeded her young brother after his untimely death. In a further example of the intermarriages between the royal and noble families of southern France and the Spanish kingdoms, Sancho VII's first wife had been Joanna's stepdaughter Constance, the daughter of Raymond VI of Toulouse by his earlier marriage.

(who was married to Leonor's daughter Blanche of Castile). John used this as an excuse to avoid payment once again:

> Since at the instigation of the enemy of mankind, and the connivance of our barons whom he incited against us, our kingdom of England is already troubled, and now more so from the advent of Louis, the firstborn of the king of France, who not fearing to offend God or the Church, endeavours to take our kingdom from us, we have already poured out the largest part of the money which we had determined to spend in seizing the Holy Land from the hands of the enemies of the cross and each day we must spend more and more.
>
> We beg your love, in which we have confidence, most assiduously, asking that you have compassion on us in this time of such adversity, and patiently bear for the present [a delay] of the payment of money by which we are bound to you. Until with the mediation of him who disposes the soul as he wishes, this dark cloud is cleared from us and our kingdom rejoices with full tranquillity. And we will then answer you fully for the money we owe you with the greatest thanks.[31]

One cannot help thinking that the excuse of 'exceptional circumstances' might have carried more weight had John not been stalling for seventeen years already.

John's own death in October 1216 complicated matters, as it resulted in yet another dowager queen, but still Berengaria was determined. She now addressed herself to John's successor (once Louis had withdrawn from England in the autumn of 1217), the young Henry III. As he was just 9 years old at the time of his accession, all government business was in the hands of a regency council, and they had much to deal with, so – once again – Berengaria's concerns were not an immediate priority.

In 1220, nearly thirty years after being crowned its queen, Berengaria seems to have visited England. The occasion was the translation of the relics of St Thomas Becket in Canterbury, which drew a high-profile crowd; one chronicler noted in passing that among the attendees was 'Queen Berengaria, who was King Richard's wife'.[32] It was in that same year that the members of Henry III's council realised that paying Berengaria – who was now asking for not only the promised £1,000 per year but also £4,500 in arrears – would be the best way to avoid the young king becoming embroiled in any financial scandal. Given all their other problems, they might also have been wary of any potential incursion by Sancho the Strong on the southern borders of Gascony, one of the few French lands Henry III still held; Berengaria's 1219 request for a safe-conduct to travel through Gascony to Navarre to see her brother might have reinforced this suspicion. A document was drawn up and the first payment made. Berengaria had been a widow for over two decades, but she had finally received what was hers by right.[33]

By this time Berengaria was probably in her mid-fifties. Finally financially secure, she could devote herself properly to good works, and she engaged in a number of projects of religious patronage, financially assisting a new Franciscan friary in Le Mans, founding a Cistercian abbey nearby at L'Épau, donating land to the Dominican order and funding major building works at Le Mans' cathedral. As these religious orders in their turn offered support to the poor and the sick, Berengaria's generosity made her popular with the local people.[34]

The upheavals that took place in the French royal line during the 1220s touched Berengaria only slightly. Philip Augustus died in 1223, to be succeeded by his son Louis VIII (he who had invaded England during John's reign), but Louis, although only in his thirties, reigned for just three years before dying prematurely. He was succeeded in turn by his son Louis IX, who was only 12 years old when he was crowned in November 1226, and who was subject to the regency of his widowed mother, Blanche of Castile. As Alfonso VIII of Castile, Blanche's father, had been Berengaria's first cousin, this meant that the two queens were closely related, and this in turn meant that Berengaria was secure and certain of respect as she entered her declining years. Indeed, Louis IX referred to her as 'our dearest relative and liegewoman, Queen Berengaria'.[35] It is perhaps ironic that, thanks to Louis and his grandfather, Berengaria received more respect and recognition in France than she ever did in England.

Berengaria lived quietly in Le Mans for more than two decades, dying peacefully there in 1230. She was buried in the Cistercian abbey of L'Épau that she had founded, and a beautiful stone effigy was produced at some point in the thirteenth century. She was not to rest in peace, however; the tomb was later vandalised and looted (probably during the Hundred Years War), her crown forcibly removed and her remains lost. They were discovered in the mid-twentieth century when the then-disused abbey was being restored; she was re-buried in the refurbished chapter house under the intact effigy.[36]

Berengaria was remembered with affection by the people of Le Mans and by those who knew her. A Navarrese chronicler, writing about ten years after her death, said of her:

> Berengaria was the wife of King Richard of England. When he died without issue, she lived on as a most praiseworthy widow and stayed for the most part in the city of Le Mans, which she held as part of her marriage dower, devoting herself to almsgiving, prayer and good works, witnessing as an example to all women of chastity and religion.[37]

Berengaria is often considered only through the prism of her marriage, a marriage that lasted for a mere eight of the approximately sixty-five years of her life and one that illustrates that not all arranged marriages resulted in the development of mutual affection. However, it served its political purpose at the time, in that Richard did not lose Aquitaine while he was on crusade in 1192 or while he was in captivity in 1194; and it also served Berengaria in that it gave her the status of queen and dowager queen, resulting (eventually) in her gaining the authority and wealth that enabled her to pursue her own interests.

If events had turned out differently, Berengaria would probably have made a very good queen consort of England. She demonstrated many of the feminine qualities that were admired at the time, such as piety, chastity and loyalty, as well as some others that male contemporaries found not quite so endearing but were nevertheless very useful: tenacity and a great strength of purpose. But she and Richard never had a settled home and she was deprived of both her duties and her entitlements. However, following his death she was able – by virtue of her own efforts – to secure her rights and to live the second half of her life on her own terms. In this she was fortunate, because a long and peaceful retirement was not to be granted to all of Eleanor of Aquitaine's daughters-in-law.

2

2

CONSTANCE

Constance of Brittany's life began just like that of many other noble girls. Born in 1161, she was the first child of her parents, arriving about a year after their wedding; they celebrated her safe arrival, assumed she would be useful in forming a marriage alliance later on, and probably hoped for a boy next time around.[1] Constance's father was Conan IV, duke of Brittany, and her mother was his duchess, Margaret, who was the sister of the Scottish kings Malcolm IV and William I and the second cousin of Henry II of England. Despite the early success of their marriage in childbearing terms, Conan and Margaret were to have no other surviving children, so from a young age Constance was recognised as heiress to the duchy in her own right, as well as to the earldom of Richmond in England, which was also held by Conan.[*] This, of course, made her a great marriage prize and it was to be expected that the planning for her future would begin while she was still young. So far, so normal, but it was not to be long before the little girl's life took the first of many unusual turns.

The Breton succession had been complex during the previous half-century, mired in deathbed claims of illegitimacy, disinheritance and family in-fighting.[2] Henry II, who as duke of

---

[*] Conan IV had inherited Brittany from his mother, Bertha. His father had been Alan the Black, earl of Richmond in England, so after the deaths of his parents Conan held both titles.

Normandy claimed overlordship of Brittany, had taken advantage of the turmoil and in 1156 he had managed to install his younger brother, Geoffrey fitzEmpress, as count of Nantes, one of Brittany's subsidiary titles. It was perhaps Henry's intention to see Geoffrey eventually take over the whole of Brittany – it would have been a great advantage to have his brother holding from him the duchy that bordered Normandy – but Geoffrey died childless just two years later, in 1158. At that stage Henry II had only two surviving sons, Henry and Richard, who were already provided for in the traditional way as heirs to their paternal and maternal inheritances respectively. But just a few weeks after Geoffrey fitzEmpress's death, Queen Eleanor gave birth to a third son. He was (probably not coincidentally) named Geoffrey, and his arrival gave King Henry a chance to continue with his plans for Brittany.[3]

In 1166, when Constance was 5 and Geoffrey 8, Henry compelled Conan to agree to the betrothal of the two children, and a high-profile ceremony took place in Rennes cathedral. This course of events was not unusual, but the aftermath was: Henry forced Conan – who was only in his twenties – to abdicate his position as duke in his daughter's favour. In order to arrange all of this, the king had to seek a dispensation, as the children were related in a prohibited degree twice over, both being descendants of Henry I of England *and* Malcolm III of Scotland.* However, the effort was worth it as the combined betrothal and abdication gave Henry direct control of Brittany

---

* Geoffrey was the great-grandson of Henry I via Empress Matilda and Henry II; Constance was Henry I's great-great-granddaughter via one of his illegitimate daughters (confusingly also called Matilda), who had married Duke Conan III of Brittany. In this line Geoffrey and Constance were thus second cousins once removed to each other. Additionally, both were great-great-grandchildren of Malcolm III of Scotland (Constance via her mother's family and Geoffrey via Empress Matilda's mother), making them third cousins in that line, so they were related within prohibited degrees twice over.

in Constance's name until such time as the children were old enough to be properly married.[4] Henry appointed his own men to all the major administrative posts in Brittany and took Constance into his custody, thus lessening the chances of any potential rebellion by Conan, who would have been concerned for his daughter's safety. Any danger from the ex-duke disappeared completely when Conan died in 1171; Henry arranged for the widow, Margaret, to marry one of his own loyal men in England and she was soon busy bringing up a second family.

All of this, of course, resulted in huge upheaval for little Constance personally. At 5 years of age, she would have been well able to walk and talk at the time of her betrothal, but she cannot really have understood the import of the ceremony, nor given her consent in any meaningful way. After the service she was taken away from her mother and father, away from Brittany and all that was familiar, in order to be placed in the household of Eleanor of Aquitaine. At this time the other children in Eleanor's care would have included her own daughters by Henry (Matilda, aged 10; Leonor, 5; and baby Joanna) as well as the 8-year-old Margaret of France, whose sister Alice would join them a few years later. Eleanor would have been pregnant as Constance arrived, giving birth to her youngest son, John, at Christmas 1166. The older boys of the family were unlikely to have been with them: young Henry was already in the household of Thomas Becket, and Richard and Geoffrey were 9 and 8 respectively and thus had been removed from the female-dominated nursery to the world of men.

From what we know of Constance's later life and actions, we can infer that she was by no means happy about being wrenched away from her native land and forced to live under Plantagenet authority. As a powerless young girl, there was little she could do in the way of rebellion, but she certainly made no attempt to assimilate or to align herself with Henry II's family ambitions.[5] Meanwhile, her Breton duchy and her English county were being ruled by men appointed by Henry II; Geoffrey was dispatched to Brittany a few times in order to learn about the territory over which he would rule in the future, but very little reference was made to Constance at all, and she took no part in the governance of her lands.[6]

The years went by; we know virtually nothing of how Constance passed her time, though we may assume that she received an education appropriate to her sex and rank.[7] As she entered her teens, she would no doubt have considered the prospect of her forthcoming marriage and how she might best use it to her advantage. One point in her favour here was that Geoffrey was of a similar age to herself; once they were married and he became duke in her name, she might hope to have more influence on him as a wife than she could ever hope to have on Henry II as a daughter-in-law and ward, or on a husband who was much older. As she grew up, she might even have looked forward to the marriage as being the opportunity to escape from under the royal thumb and return to her homeland with a certain degree of independence. But Constance was to be frustrated in her ambitions for some years: the status quo suited King Henry very well, and he delayed the wedding as long as he could. The ceremony did not take place until 1181, at which point Constance was 20 and her husband 23, far older than might be expected under the circumstances.

Following the wedding, the details and exact date of which have not come down to us, Constance's status changed. As envisaged, she moved back to Brittany to take up residence there, thus ensuring that she was visible to the people who had not seen her – the living representative of their ruling dynasty – since she was a little girl. Her position and her authority were soon established: Geoffrey was the ruler of Brittany, having styled himself duke since his own majority, but as his wife and duchess in her own right, Constance's assent was sought (at least in principle) for various acts. The earliest extant charter of

Geoffrey's as duke of Brittany, dating from late 1181, notes that he grants it with the consent of 'Constance my wife, duchess of Brittany'. Indeed, there is evidence that Constance exercised authority under her own name, such as a charter in which she (alone) confirms the grants made by her ducal predecessors to the abbey of Sainte-Croix de Quimperlé.[8]

There are a number of different possible explanations for the way in which the couple chose to conduct themselves, none of which are necessarily mutually exclusive. Geoffrey appears to have accepted with good grace the fact that he derived his right to the duchy from Constance, and he sought her assent for his actions in order to appease the Breton nobles, whose loyalty lay with her. This was a sensible course of action, and Geoffrey may also have been using it to further his personal and familial ambitions: in consciously identifying himself with Brittany in order to gain the nobles' support, he could dissociate himself from his father. He was now a lord who held lands and titles by right of his own marriage, rather than as a gift from Henry II that could be rescinded at any time. Geoffrey, along with his brothers, had been in sporadic conflict with Henry II for many years, and it is likely that Constance was not averse to this state of affairs.[9]

It seems to have been generally recognised that Geoffrey could be duplicitous, and this is something Constance would have to deal with and perhaps use to her own and Brittany's advantage. One contemporary does not hesitate to call him a 'son of iniquity', while another says scathingly that Geoffrey was 'pouring out words smoother than oil [...] able to unknit whatever has been joined together and with a tongue powerful enough to ruin two kingdoms [...] an unreliable hypocrite and dissembler in all things'.[10] Not content with rebelling against his father, Geoffrey and his eldest brother Henry later teamed up to make war on Richard, and he also spent time at the court of Philip Augustus in Paris, where he talked himself into such popularity that he was named seneschal of France.[11] Geoffrey's military and political activities meant that he was frequently absent from Brittany, leaving Constance to rule in his stead, and this suited Constance and her loyal nobles very well.

Henry the Young King died in June 1183. This had significant consequences for Geoffrey and Constance, as Geoffrey was now second in line to the English throne (and the duchy of Normandy and the other family lands in France) after his brother Richard – who was unmarried and childless and who was often involved in dangerous military pursuits that might result in his sudden death at any time. It is entirely possible that the couple began to form ambitions that encompassed more than Brittany. But in order for any enduring dynastic plans to be made, they would need an heir.

The late age (by contemporary royal standards) at which Constance married meant that she had passed through her teenage years before she became pregnant, which was an advantage for her health. She gave birth to two daughters during the first few years of her marriage to Geoffrey: Eleanor, in 1184, and Matilda, whose date of birth is uncertain and may have been either before or after Eleanor's. There is no indication in any of our sources that either of the pregnancies or labours were life-threatening for Constance, and she appears to have recovered quickly each time. The names given to the two girls reflected their Plantagenet, rather than their Breton, ancestry. They were Henry II's only grandchildren in the male line, but as they were both girls, they might have been less favoured in any potential succession dispute than the sons of King Henry's daughter Matilda, duchess of Saxony, of whom there were four by this time, the three eldest having already survived the perils of early childhood.

Having experienced little difficulty in conceiving and in surviving her labours, Constance would have been confident that she could soon produce a son and heir for Brittany and for any other opportunities that might arise. In the meantime, her relationship with her husband and their rule over Brittany seemed set fair. However, in another of the twists that were to characterise Constance's life, tragedy struck. In August 1186 Geoffrey was at the court of Philip Augustus in Paris when he died suddenly at the age of just 27. Reports vary as to whether this was due to illness or a tournament accident (fatalities at such events were not uncommon), or possibly a combination of both.[12] His body was never returned to Constance; King Philip had Geoffrey buried in Paris.

The shock that Constance experienced, upon hearing the news, must have been great, and all the more so given that she found herself once more in the early stages of pregnancy. Precisely how much actual grief she felt must remain a matter for conjecture. On the one hand, she had been forced to marry Geoffrey without consultation, the decision made for her as a child, and she may have resented him for that reason and for being the son of Henry II and Eleanor of Aquitaine who was to control Brittany, her own birthright. However, on the other hand, she must have known that rule of Brittany would pass into the hands of anyone she married, and Geoffrey was a better option in this regard than some others. The two of them had been on the same side in conflict against his father, and the available evidence seems to indicate that they worked together at least amicably, if not necessarily with a great deal of personal affection. Constance also suffered a second loss at around this time, as her young daughter Matilda died either shortly before or shortly after Geoffrey.

As duchess of Brittany in her own right, Constance could not be pushed aside or shunted off to dower lands in the way that some other young widows were. However, she was still vulnerable: she was a pregnant widow in her mid-twenties in charge of a duchy that was perennially threatened by the interests of its larger neighbours Normandy, France and England. She would need to find a way to walk the tightrope between the competing claims and ambitions of Henry II and Philip Augustus while keeping Brittany safe. She emphasised her own hereditary right in her style, calling herself 'Constance, daughter of Count Conan, duchess of Brittany and countess of Richmond' with no reference to her late husband or his family.[13]

Constance's immediate concern, however, would be to survive another pregnancy and labour. The course of Brittany's future and her own would be determined by the sex of the infant, and the events that would ultimately lead to tragedy were set in motion when she gave birth to a boy on the feast of Easter Sunday, 29 March 1187. As we noted above, Constance's two daughters had – probably at Geoffrey's instigation – been given the names of his mother and grandmother, and Henry II now pushed for the new baby, his only grandson in the male line, to be named after him. But this is where we can see palpable evidence of Constance's wish for independence from Henry's family, of the rebellious streak that had perhaps been developing since she was a powerless young girl in the Plantagenet nursery. In a gesture of defiance that should not be underestimated, given the situation in which she found herself, Constance refused to bow to Henry's wishes: she called her son Arthur, a name of Breton significance.[14]

Once she and Arthur had survived the birth and the lying-in period, Constance's next challenge was to retain custody of him. The tiny figure in the cradle represented Brittany's future, but he also posed a threat to – and provided an opportunity for – Henry II and Philip Augustus. If Arthur were to be taken away by King Henry to be raised in the Plantagenet court, it was possible that Constance could be forced to abdicate in his favour (as her own father had been), leaving her bereft of both child and duchy, and Henry free to exercise power on Arthur's behalf for many years. However, to go too far the other way would also be dangerous; Constance needed to be wary of the motives of King Philip, who might use any uncertainty in Brittany as an excuse to further his own designs. Additionally, the fate of Constance's surviving daughter, the 3-year-old Eleanor, had to be considered: she would be a pawn in the marriage market, with her paternal grandfather claiming the right to decide upon her future union and the timing of it. Constance was going to have her work cut out if her children were to survive and thrive, and their interests would become the exclusive focus of the rest of her life.

It was inevitable that Constance would, at some point, be pressured to marry again. Having the duchy of Brittany in the hands of a single woman – and an independently minded one, at that – served the interests of neither king, and each would prefer to see Constance wed to a man of their choosing. But it was Henry II, as Brittany's overlord, who was able to force her hand, and his choice of husband was Ranulf de Blundeville, the earl of Chester.* Geographically and administratively, this made sense: Ranulf's Norman lands bordered Brittany and his English ones were close to the holdings of the earldom of Richmond. The wedding took place in the spring of 1189 and Henry hoped the arrangement would keep Brittany – and Constance – on a tight rein.

---

* Ranulf was, as it happened, another direct descendant of Henry I (via Henry's eldest illegitimate son, Robert, earl of Gloucester), but it does not appear that a dispensation was sought for his marriage to Constance.

However, as was so often the case in twelfth-century unions, no consideration had been given at all to personal feelings, and in this case neither Constance nor Ranulf seems to have been particularly keen on the match. The age difference did not help – he was about ten years younger than her and still in his teens – but there is no sign of any personal connection at all. This may have been partly due to Constance's increased age and experience this time round, and thus the greater determination she was able to exhibit in keeping her own rights, and she was helped by the Breton nobles: they took her part and never recognised Ranulf as their lord. He, in turn, made only intermittent use of the title 'duke of Brittany' but seemed otherwise uninterested, continuing to reside in England or Normandy while Constance lived in Brittany.[15]

Constance was thus able to concentrate her energies on continuing to govern Brittany herself, as she had been doing since Geoffrey's death, while also planning for the future of her children, and particularly her son. A change in their circumstances occurred in July 1189 when Henry II died, to be succeeded as king of England and duke of Normandy by his eldest surviving son, Richard. Richard was still, at this point, unmarried and childless, meaning that Arthur, as the only son of Richard's next brother, had a good case to be considered his heir. The situation was a delicate one, however, due to Arthur's age: Geoffrey might once have wished for his brother's early death so he could assume the throne himself, but Constance was now, if anything, hoping that Richard would *not* die any time soon. Regardless of hereditary principle, the claims of a child to the English throne would be overlooked if there was an adult male available – and at the time of Richard's accession Arthur was only 2, while Richard's surviving brother, John, was a grown man.

Richard set off on crusade soon after his coronation, stopping in Sicily on the way to deal with the situation enveloping his sister Joanna. This left Constance to rule her duchy with a greater degree of autonomy, but she was to be affected by the faraway events. As we saw in Chapter 4, as part of his agreement with Tancred of Sicily, Richard proposed that his nephew Arthur should marry one of Tancred's daughters. This news, when it reached Constance (probably in early 1191), would have been a shock to her, and it would not be surprising if she resented Richard's high-handed offering of her son in this way without consulting her. However, like any sensible ambitious twelfth-century mother, she would also have seen the advantages. Arthur was the male half of the marriage arrangement, so he would not be the one sent abroad: he would remain in his own lands while the bride was dispatched to him. A royal match was also a prestigious step in his fledgling career, and the icing on the cake was Richard referring to Arthur in the agreement as 'our nephew, and, if we shall chance to die without issue, our heir'.[16]

As it transpired, the betrothal was never formalised, and expectations had to be further reined in when Richard married Berengaria in May 1191; as soon as he had children of his own, Arthur would lose his place in the direct line of succession. During the first half of the 1190s, therefore, Constance was right to remain circumspect about Arthur's prospects and to concentrate on his future as the duke of a Brittany that was in constant danger from its larger neighbours.

Philip Augustus had also gone on crusade, but he was back in France by the end of 1191 and intent, as ever, on expanding his royal authority. He was already the ultimate overlord of Brittany – which owed allegiance to the duke of Normandy, who in turn gave homage to the French king – but it would be to his advantage if the relationship were more direct. Philip had made an initial move in this direction back in 1186, seeking wardship of the young Eleanor (who was at that time Brittany's heir, Arthur having not yet been born) at the time of Geoffrey's death. However, this was 'a thing which the king of England would on no account comply with', and the idea was dropped.[17] Philip, however, had not given up on his ambitions, and the replacement of Henry by Richard on the English throne and in the duchy of Normandy provided new opportunities. The situation was further complicated by the opinions of the Breton nobles themselves, some of whom would have preferred Capetian overlordship to Plantagenet, and others who favoured neither.[18]

It was events involving King Richard that were to cause the next upheaval in the lives of Constance and her children. When he was captured during his journey home from the crusade, the arrangements for his ransom involved several members of his extended family, as we have seen in previous chapters. Once again it was with no reference to Constance that Richard organised a marriage for one of her children: the 9-year-old Eleanor was not only to be a hostage, like Otto of Brunswick and Ferdinand of Navarre, but was to wed Frederick, the son of Duke Leopold V of Austria. Constance was obliged to part with her young daughter, probably thinking that it would be for the last time (the distances involved meant that future visits were unlikely), but Eleanor would return unmarried when the arrangement fell through on Leopold's sudden death in a gruesome accident.[*19]

Constance had to endure further struggles over the custody of her children. Eleanor's exact whereabouts before and after

---

* Leopold fell from his horse while out riding, and the horse rolled over his foot, crushing it. The injury was so bad that broken and splintered bones projected through the skin, and Leopold realised that amputation would be necessary if his life were to be saved. There was no time to find a skilled surgeon so he ended up holding an axe against his leg himself while a servant struck it with a hammer to sever the foot. Leopold died the following day, either from shock or from blood poisoning.

her return from the Empire are uncertain: there was some talk of her marrying Louis, the son and heir of Philip Augustus, but this came to nothing, and there is also evidence that she had been at Richard's court soon after his accession in 1189, though it is not clear how long she stayed there.[20]

The situation with Arthur was even more acute, as maternal control of a son became more difficult as he grew older. Once Richard returned from his captivity in 1194, he demanded that the now 7-year-old Arthur be handed over to him to be brought up at his court. Constance refused, perhaps due to the continuing fear that she might be forced to abdicate in her son's name, a danger that would be increased if *both* her children ended up in Richard's custody. She managed to hold out for some while as Richard was busy in the short term re-imposing his kingship on England, but it was inevitable that he would turn his attention to Brittany as soon as he had the chance. In the spring of 1196 he summoned Constance to appear in person at his court in Normandy.

Constance could not refuse: to do so would be tantamount to a declaration of rebellion against her overlord, which would be foolish in the extreme. However, she was politically aware enough to go on her own, leaving Arthur safe in the care of some of her loyal Breton advisors. Her caution proved to be well founded: no sooner had she crossed the Breton–Norman border than she was kidnapped, by none other than her estranged husband Ranulf, the earl of Chester. Richard claimed in public that this was simply a matrimonial dispute and nothing to do with him, but it seems highly unlikely that Ranulf would have taken such action without Richard's knowledge – it was well known that Constance was travelling to meet the king. Indeed, it is entirely possible that Ranulf might have been acting at Richard's direct order, though there are unsurprisingly no official documents that could prove this either way.[21]

Constance was detained in Ranulf's castle at St James de Beuvron, near the border. As was the case for other noblewomen who were imprisoned, this was not the sort of incarceration that involved being kept in a dark, damp dungeon, but it was captivity nonetheless. The idea was presumably that Constance would agree to give up custody of Arthur in return for her own freedom, but if Richard had expected this, he was sorely mistaken in her character. She happily traded her own liberty for her son's, even when Richard launched an invasion of Brittany in the spring of 1196.[22]

Constance remained imprisoned for at least a year, issuing instructions to her loyal nobles by letter. In the autumn of 1196 they renounced their fealty to Richard, swore allegiance to Arthur and appealed to the French king for assistance.[23] Under Constance's direction, they were able to spirit Arthur away into hiding and then get him to the (comparative) safety of King Philip's court in Paris. Philip was only too glad to stir up rebellion against Richard, and he welcomed Arthur, who spent a couple of years in Paris in the household of Philip's son, Louis, who was the same age.

Richard realised that even he could not break Arthur out of Paris, and Constance was eventually released from Ranulf's custody; we do not know the exact date, but she was certainly back in Brittany in July 1198.[24] Their marriage was annulled, which must have been a great relief to both parties.

Constance and Arthur continued under the protection of King Philip for a short while, but she was as wary of falling under his complete control as she was of falling under Richard's. Moreover, the political situation in England had developed: by 1198 Richard was into his forties, had no children and was living entirely separately from his wife. This meant that the position of heir to the English throne was there for the taking, so it made sense for Constance to switch her and Arthur's allegiance. He was now 11; she was associating his name with hers in her charters, and he was of an age where she could begin to push him forward to act independently.²⁵ This might have been a first step towards having him invested as duke once he reached his majority, as other ruling women (including Eleanor of Aquitaine) had done for their sons. It was thus in his own name – though undoubtedly on his mother's advice – that Arthur in 1198 renounced his fealty to Philip and agreed to be guided by Richard in his dealings with the French king.²⁶ Richard accepted the overture, and Arthur, having left Paris, was permitted to remain in Brittany with his mother and sister for the present. Eleanor was now 14, but no further betrothal arrangements had been put forward for her; it seems likely that all parties were waiting to see whether she would end up as the sister of a duke or the sister of a king.

Constance might have thought that she and her children could now enjoy something of a breathing space, a chance for the children to grow up and for Arthur to gain more governmental experience before staking a claim to be Richard's heir when he was an adult (and one who could be trusted more than the other principal claimant, John, who was not popular). However, in what was to be a crushing and dangerous blow, the news reached her in early April 1199 that Richard had been killed at a minor siege in Châlus in his own duchy of Aquitaine.²⁷ Constance would undoubtedly have wanted Richard to live long enough so that Arthur was an adult when the time came for him to press his claims to the throne, but as it was, he was only 12 and his rights were immediately disputed by the 32-year-old John, Arthur's paternal uncle.

Here we need to step back a little from Constance's story to explain the competing claims of Arthur and John to the English crown, and why matters were not quite as clear-cut as they might seem to us now. If primogeniture were to be applied strictly, Arthur's claim was superior; he was the son of John's elder brother. However, primogeniture was not the only concern at the time, and nor was it as rigidly applied as it would be later. In the late twelfth century, there was an equally valid idea that a man who was the son of a king (i.e., John, the son of Henry II) should take precedence over a king's grandson whose father had never ruled (i.e., Arthur, the son of Geoffrey), even if that grandson descended from the senior line. Added to this was the fact that the wishes of the previous king in designating his heir were usually taken into account, and here there was confusion. Richard had so designated Arthur back in October 1190, in Sicily, but there was also evidence that he might subsequently have changed his mind to favour John, given that the two of them had been reconciled following Richard's return from captivity.[28]

The whole situation was a mess, and it was one that Constance would have to deal with, given that her son was still underage. There was, unfortunately, no possibility of simply walking away from the issue, of Arthur resigning his claims in favour of John. All the nobles in England, Normandy, Anjou, Maine and Touraine, as well as in Brittany, would know that Arthur had a superior hereditary claim to John, and if ever they were dissatisfied with John's rule (which seemed likely, given his previous record), they would raise banners of rebellion in Arthur's name even if he had no wish to join them. Arthur would therefore always be a threat to John, however much he tried to restrict his activities to Brittany. His life would always be in danger, and so the best way to protect him was to attack: to make sure it was he, and not John, who sat on the English throne. This was the cause to which Constance would now devote herself.

John, who was on the Continent at the time of Richard's death, reacted quickly and moved to secure the all-important royal treasury at Chinon; having the wealth of the crown at his disposal was a big step in seizing the crown itself. Constance could not hope to match this level of resource and thus took the only option open to her: she appealed to King Philip. She also began to raise troops, and before long her army entered Angers, the capital of Anjou. So swift had her actions been that when a group of barons there declared Arthur their lord on Easter day (18 April) 1199, it was just two weeks after Richard's death.[29] Constance and Arthur then moved to Le Mans, where the nobles of Maine declared their support for his cause.

Victory was not to be swift, however, for other players now entered the fray. The barons of Normandy had no wish to be ruled by a Breton, and they in their turn proclaimed John as duke in Rouen on 25 April. King Philip, meanwhile, turned matters to his own advantage by seizing the person of Arthur: he 'at once sent him [Arthur] to Paris under charge of a guard, and received into his care all the cities and castles which belonged to Arthur'.[30] There he knighted the boy and accepted his homage for Anjou, Maine, Touraine, Brittany and Normandy, thus technically making himself the overlord of all of those places and legally entitling him to seize them from John on behalf of Arthur, his vassal.[31] Philip moved in with his troops and took control of the towns and fortifications in those areas while keeping Arthur in Paris. John countered by crossing the Channel and having himself crowned and consecrated as king of England at Westminster on 27 May 1199.

This was the decisive blow: coronation was the all-important factor in making a monarch. It did not matter who a man had been beforehand, or what his nominal place in the succession had been; once he had been crowned and anointed in an official ceremony, he was the king – for good or for ill.[32] This made Constance's task all the harder: picking up a vacant crown for her son was a much more straightforward task than wresting it off the head of an incumbent. But there was no stopping now, because Arthur's life (and potentially Eleanor of Brittany's as well) would be in danger whatever happened.

In the meantime, another formidable opponent had taken to the stage: the dowager Queen Eleanor. She had previously withdrawn from the world to live at Fontevraud abbey, but now she came out of retirement in order to engage with the great political controversy of the time. Eleanor, of course, was duchess of Aquitaine in her own right, even though she had ceded the title to Richard when he was a teenager, so she simply picked it back up with no opposition. She had a great deal of influence and resource to place at the disposal of whichever candidate she favoured, and she chose to favour John – which may have had something to do with her mutual antipathy with Constance.[33] Despite now being in her late seventies, she made a tour through Poitou, the northern part of Aquitaine, securing for John the support of the nobles and the Church as she went.

England was firmly in John's hands, but the continental possessions associated with the crown were still very much in dispute through the spring and summer of 1199. In August the two parties met for negotiations, Philip asking John to cede Poitou to Arthur on top of the other territories for which Philip had accepted Arthur's homage. This was an arrangement that would suit the French king; he had no designs (yet) on England itself, but large parts of France would now come under his direct overlordship. It might also have suited Constance, in the short to medium term at least, because having the continental lands and titles would provide Arthur with sufficient resource to mount a greater challenge for the throne in the future, when he was older and had consolidated his gains.

However, both Philip and Constance were aware that by now the momentum was with John. England and Normandy held for him and he had the support of Aquitaine, which meant that the lands under his control surrounded Arthur and Constance geographically – a dangerous situation. Constance, with her family's survival at stake, might have been prepared to fight on, but Philip's priorities were France and his own interests, so continued support for Arthur was becoming risky and counter-productive. He therefore agreed to conciliate, and the outcome was the Treaty of Le Goulet, sealed in May 1200.[34]

By the terms of this treaty, Philip recognised John as Richard's lawful heir in all his territories, which meant that Arthur was to lose Anjou, Maine and Touraine. He could not be deprived of Brittany so easily, as it was his own birthright, but he would hold it from John (as duke of Normandy), who would in turn recognise Philip as his overlord there. Arthur, 'with the sanction and advice of the king of France', gave homage to John, and the deal was completed by a marriage.[35] John, of course, had no children so he needed a suitable niece, and as the daughter of a brother (rather than the daughter of a sister), Eleanor of Brittany might have been considered the obvious choice. However, this was problematic due to the very fact that had been under dispute: Eleanor and Arthur's technically better claim to the English crown than John. A marriage alliance between Eleanor and the French royal house might give young Louis rights on behalf of his wife that King Philip would be able to exploit, and John was naturally unwilling to risk this, so he decided to call on the family of his sister Leonor: the bride would be her daughter Blanche of Castile. As Blanche had the added cachet of being the daughter of a king, Philip was satisfied and the wedding went ahead once she arrived after her long journey.*

---

* As it happens, even a marriage with the daughter of Henry II's daughter proved sufficient for Louis and Philip to make a claim for England; we will explore this further in Chapter 8.

This new state of affairs might have suited John and Philip, but it was not good enough for Constance. She would have to continue the fight without Philip, and that inevitably meant armed conflict. Constance was a firm and popular ruler in her duchy, and the nobles there respected her for it regardless of her sex. However, there was one thing she could not really do for her son, and that was ride at the head of his troops and lead his forces into battle. His age meant that he could not, either, at least for the time being. What Constance needed was a grown man to help her – and preferably one who would be wholeheartedly on their side, rather than simply pushing his own agenda, as Philip Augustus clearly was.

This need was doubtless one of the factors behind Constance's decision to marry again in October 1199. Her choice of husband, however, was unexpected: he was Guy de Thouars, the brother of Aimery VII, viscount of Thouars (a region in Poitou), heir to his brother's lands but currently a landless younger son.* There were some political dimensions to the match: it meant an alliance that reached into Poitou, plus a husband who at this point would rely on Constance for lands and title and would thus have a vested interest in supporting her and Arthur. However, in purely political terms there were certainly better candidates, and the general consensus seems to be that Constance chose her new husband at least in part because of personal preference.[36] And, we might well ask, why shouldn't she, following two forced marriages, at least one of which had brought her no contentment at all?

---

* The viscounty of Thouars had an unusual system of inheritance whereby all the sons of the previous ruling lord held the title in turn before the inheritance passed to the next generation, in the persons of the sons of the eldest son. Guy, as the second brother, was therefore heir to the title despite Aimery having six or seven children – although as it happened he would never inherit as Aimery outlived him.

If the purpose of Constance's third marriage was personal happiness, then it was a success, but if the motive was to support Arthur's cause, it backfired spectacularly. In the late twelfth century, marriage nearly always meant pregnancy, and Constance's fertility, even in her late thirties and thirteen years after the birth of her last child, was still evident. She spent most of her marriage to Guy either pregnant or recovering from lyings-in, remaining in Nantes and thus putting herself out of action for long periods during this crucial phase of her son's campaign.[37]

A combination of the paucity of surviving evidence and of contemporaries not being particularly careful about recording the births of girls means that there is confusion over the dates of birth of Constance's children with Guy, and even over how many of them there were. They certainly had an eldest daughter who was named Alix, probably born within a year of the marriage. They then had a second daughter called Catherine, whose date of birth is uncertain but cannot feasibly have been before mid-1201. Some sources also claim that they had a third daughter called Margaret, but looking at the length of the marriage, it seems implausible that Constance would have had time to go through three pregnancies. This led to subsequent speculation that Catherine and Margaret (if she existed) were twins, and that a difficult twin birth may have been what killed Constance. This must remain uncertain.[38]

Constance died in September 1201, at the age of 40. Her cause of death is not known: it might have been due to childbirth complications – whether with twins or not – though other theories have been put forward and one contemporary even claims that she was afflicted with leprosy. We should note, however, that at this time leprosy was sometimes considered a punishment for sins, so the one (clerical) chronicler who mentions it might have been indicating his disapproval of a woman who acted so independently throughout her life.[39]

Constance was buried in the Cistercian abbey of Villeneuve in Nantes, to which she had been a generous benefactor.

Constance was mourned throughout Brittany, but not by either King John or Eleanor of Aquitaine, for whom she had been a perennial thorn in the side. Guy was left as a widower with two (or three) tiny daughters, though he did not have to act as regent in Brittany: Arthur, now 14, was proclaimed duke in his own right despite not having attained his official majority.* Constance's early death meant that her younger children would hardly remember her, but her two eldest must have missed her terribly – both on a personal level and because, without her strong hand guiding and leading their cause, their lives went horribly, tragically wrong.

Arthur, unsurprisingly given his age and inexperience, found himself unequal to the task of dealing with both Philip Augustus and King John. John summoned him to do homage for Brittany now that he had acceded to the duchy in his own right, but Arthur, fearing a trap, instead went to Philip and threw himself on the French king's mercy. John was by now facing discontent with his rule in both Normandy and Poitou, so when a revolt broke out in Arthur's name in Poitou, Philip sent Arthur there while he himself invaded Normandy. Arthur was welcomed by the leading Poitevin nobles, but was soon captured by John's forces and imprisoned. He was sent into captivity at Falaise, then transferred to Rouen, and then never

---

* As we saw in Chapter 1, the official age at which young nobles in France attained their majority and could take control of their inheritances was 21. However, some exceptions were made: Philip Augustus had ruled without a regent after the death of his father, although he was only 15, and Richard the Lionheart had been invested as duke of Aquitaine at 13 when Eleanor ceded her rights to him.

seen or heard of again. There is little doubt that he was murdered at John's order, at the age of just 15.[40]

This left any residual family claim to the English throne resting with Eleanor, Constance's eldest daughter, and she too was taken into John's custody. By now she was 18, so there was a danger that anyone who married her would be able to launch a campaign for the English throne; John therefore kept her in close confinement in a series of well-defended English castles. Eleanor's captivity did not cease with John's death, and by the time she eventually died in 1241, she had been imprisoned for all thirty-nine years of her adult life.

Constance's line did survive in Brittany, where, after Arthur's assumed death and Eleanor's imprisonment, the barons recognised Alix, the eldest of Constance's daughters by Guy de Thouars, as their duchess. It is perhaps almost a mercy that, after fighting so hard for her children for so much of her life, Constance did not survive long enough to know what happened to them. Of course, if she *had* lived longer, then things might have turned out differently – but, as it was, the new and now undisputed king of England was to be not Constance's son Arthur but Eleanor of Aquitaine's youngest child, John.

ISABELLE AND ISABELLA

If there is one medieval queen consort of England even less well known than Berengaria of Navarre, then it is surely Isabelle of Gloucester.[*][1] Isabelle was of royal stock herself, albeit through an illegitimate line: her paternal grandfather was Robert, earl of Gloucester, the eldest illegitimate son of Henry I, who was a great supporter of his half-sister Empress Matilda and his nephew Henry II in their battle for the English crown. Robert died in 1148, leaving the rich earldom of Gloucester to his eldest son, William. William had one son, Robert, and three daughters: Mabel, Amice and Isabelle. Tragically, young Robert died in 1166 at the age of 15, which had a significant effect on the prospects of the girls, who became co-heirs to the earldom and its vast lands.

This, of course, made them great marriage prizes. Mabel was matched with Amaury V de Montfort, the count of Évreux in Normandy, and Amice with Richard de Clare, the earl of Hertford in England. That left young Isabelle, who in the mid-1170s was identified by Henry II as the means by which his youngest and landless son, John, would be provided for. Henry arranged for the two young people to be betrothed, but this was not enough for him and, just as he had a decade earlier when

---

* Although both names are often used for both women, I have chosen to use 'Isabelle' for John's first wife and 'Isabella' for his second, in order to avoid confusion.

he pushed through the marriage of Constance of Brittany, he now rode roughshod over the accepted conventions. When a lord had no sons but a number of daughters, it was customary for all of them to share in the inheritance equally, but King Henry obliged Earl William to name John his sole heir.[2] Shockingly, he even forced William to agree that if he should go on to father another legitimate son, that son would not inherit the earldom and its lands outright but would share them with John. The prospective bride and groom were, of course, related to each other well within the prohibited degree as they were second cousins (both being great-grandchildren of Henry I), but the king simply ignored this and no papal dispensation was sought.

We do not know exactly when Isabelle was born but the likeliest date seems to be around 1160, meaning that she would have been 16 or thereabouts at the time of the betrothal in 1176. This was more than old enough by contemporary standards to be married, but – in an unusual reverse of the common age gap, and one that showed just how desirable Isabelle's riches were – John was only 9, so the wedding could not be celebrated just yet. At this point in her life, Isabelle was perhaps expecting a reasonably quiet existence: she would remain on her own family lands rather than be sent away as her sisters had been; as the countess through whom her husband derived his rights, she would expect to be involved at least to some extent in the governing of those lands; and she would be connected to the crown to a degree that was sufficient for prestige but not enough to be dangerous. As a fourth son, John would have no expectation of ever sitting on the throne – particularly as his eldest brother, Henry the Young King, and his wife Margaret of France were at this time expecting their first child.

However, as was the case for all the women featured in this book, events elsewhere and outside of Isabelle's control were to exert a considerable influence on her life. The first of these took place within a year of her betrothal, when the baby of Young Henry and Margaret died shortly after birth. They would never have another child, meaning that Henry's younger brothers were not ousted from their places in the succession. The next event was that in 1183 Isabelle's father died, at which point she would naturally have expected to be married so that John, now 16, could come into the vast Gloucester inheritance. However, it suited Henry II to keep the income from the estates in his own hands, so instead of heading for the altar, Isabelle found herself taken into royal wardship and denied any access to her birthright: she was 'in the hand of God, and in the power of the king', as one contemporary put it.[3] She was left in this limbo throughout the 1180s as two more significant deaths – those of the king's first and third sons, Young Henry and Geoffrey – altered John's prospects for the better. By the end of 1186 he found himself second in line to the throne after the unmarried Richard.*

As it happens, this made John markedly *less* keen to press his father to allow the wedding to take place, even though he was now 20 and Isabelle probably some six years older. A rich domestic heiress might be a suitable match for a fourth son, but a second son with a childless elder brother was within touching distance of the crown and could cast his net a little wider. John was thus in no hurry to tie himself down until he had a clearer idea of what Richard's family situation would be, and poor Isabelle was left to kick her heels throughout her twenties – her prime childbearing years – while she waited in vain to become anyone's priority.

The moment finally arrived in 1189, but it was hardly a glorious occasion nor one that offered Isabelle much honour.

---

* This was before the birth of Arthur (who arrived in March 1187), so there were no other claimants to the English throne who were both male and born in the male line.

In that year Henry II died, to be succeeded unopposed on the English throne by Richard. Richard was still unmarried and (rightly, as it would turn out) suspicious of John. The new king therefore pushed through John's wedding to Isabelle specifically in order to *limit* the extent of his ambitions – John would no longer be able to consider a prestigious international match but would be tied to his English lands. Isabelle was conveniently close at hand: as a royal ward and the fiancée of a royal son, she was in Eleanor of Aquitaine's household, along with Richard's betrothed, Alice of France. They were both grown women but still very much under Eleanor's control. Isabelle was summoned and married to John at Marlborough on 29 August 1189.[4]

The marriage was not a success in either personal or political terms. Isabelle would no doubt have been keen to get her adult life started after such a long wait, and there may have been some initial attempt on John's part to make the best of what he saw as a bad situation; having a son would bolster his dynastic position and Isabelle was probably still on the right side of 30, so all hope was not lost. However, no pregnancy resulted within the first few years and the couple soon drifted apart, probably ceasing to cohabit in around 1193/4.[5] Meanwhile Baldwin of Forde, the archbishop of Canterbury, had summoned John to appear before him to explain why he had married a woman so closely related to him without seeking Church approval. The situation got very messy for a while – Baldwin laid an interdict on John's lands that was later quashed by a papal legate – but it eventually settled and Isabelle might have thought that her position was safe.[6] However, the dispute had only served to remind John that he had a ready-made excuse whenever he decided that his union with Isabelle was no longer his best bet.

Richard's marriage to Berengaria in May 1191 was a dent to John's ambitions but, conversely, a brief moment of hope for Isabelle. If Richard and his Navarrese bride were to produce a brood of children, then John would be moved further down the line of succession and might come to appreciate the Gloucester estates that his wife had brought him. However, Richard's capture during his return from the crusade, and the long-term incarceration that seemed likely to result, meant that the writing was on the wall for the union. John entered into negotiations with King Philip Augustus of France about a marriage to the latter's sister Alice, who had been in English custody for more than two decades before her betrothal to Richard was finally formally dropped.[7] The fact that he already had a wife did not seem to bother John at all.

Richard was released, upon payment of the ransom collected by his mother and the handing over of hostages from various other members of his extended family. John's plans to wed Alice came to nothing and he remained married to Isabelle, though – as far as we can tell from the scanty evidence – they now lived entirely separately.

When Richard died in 1199 and John succeeded in overcoming the claims of his nephew Arthur, Isabelle unexpectedly found herself, in name at least, queen of England. This could have been an opportunity for her to take a place on the national stage and to carry out the duties associated with the position, even if she and John were not living together as man and wife. It could have given her the respect and the dignity that had been stolen from her during the long, powerless years of her youth. However, this was not to be. Isabelle was pointedly not invited to John's coronation, and one of his first actions after it was to arrange for the annulment of his marriage on the well-worn and obvious grounds of consanguinity. This was swiftly achieved and contemporary observers dismiss the event airily in a couple of sentences, with no mention of Isabelle's point of view. Indeed, the chronicler whose account is generally the most detailed of the period even fails to get her name right, calling her Hawisa, which was her mother's name.[8]

Isabelle found herself, at the age of around 40, single once more. However, if she thought that this was at last going to be the opportunity to take more control of her destiny and her lands, she was sadly mistaken. In the first instance, John took a leaf from his father's book and moved his ex-wife – in her position as an unmarried heiress – into his wardship, which meant that he could still enjoy the revenues from her lands without the inconvenience of being married to her. He even took Isabelle's title away, naming her nephew Amaury VI de Montfort (the son of her sister Mabel) earl of Gloucester in order to make reparations for the lands Amaury was forced to give up in France as part of the Treaty of Le Goulet in 1200.[9]

Isabelle, despite being one of the richest heiresses in the land and not subject to a husband's authority, had nothing. The most she could look forward to was a life of quiet retirement, trapped in a childlike existence in which she had no control of her lands or income, and no household of her own to run. She was certainly not kept in poverty – as a royal ward her expenses were met and we can see that John sent her gifts of wine and cloth – but she was simply marking time. It is also possible that, during 1205–06 and perhaps at other times, she was subject to the humiliation of being obliged to reside in the same household as John's second and much younger wife, Isabella of Angoulême, when both were at Winchester. This arrangement, if it existed, had ceased by 1207; Isabella remained at Winchester but Isabelle had been moved to Sherborne and then Bristol.[10]

Isabelle's peripatetic yet aimless existence appears to have continued for the next decade, but fate – or, rather, John – had another twist in store. In 1213 Amaury VI de Montfort died, childless and brotherless, meaning that the earldom of Gloucester reverted to Isabelle once more. John was by this time embroiled in disputes with his barons and desperately in need of money, so he sold Isabelle's marriage to Geoffrey de

Mandeville, who was already the earl of Essex and who became earl of Gloucester in right of his wife when the wedding took place in early 1214. The impetus for the match does not seem to have been Geoffrey's, and indeed he might even have tried to resist it, as it was rather disadvantageous to him. He was forced to pay the enormous sum of 20,000 marks (£13,333) for the privilege, more than twenty times the annual income he might expect from the earldom, so he would be hugely and dangerously in John's debt. Moreover, the castle and profitable manor of Bristol were specifically excluded from the deal, and he found himself with a wife some thirty years his senior who could not possibly give him heirs.[11]

Isabelle's feelings on being compelled into this match are, predictably, unrecorded. However, there is some evidence that through it she attained at least a modicum of independence and authority, acting jointly with her new husband in some respects.[12] Any feelings of joy were not to last, however, for John set such a swift schedule of payments for the fee that Geoffrey owed for the marriage that he could not keep up; when he fell into arrears John confiscated the Gloucester estates, as had perhaps been the plan all along. Both Geoffrey and Isabelle joined the rebellion against the king, and in 1215 Geoffrey was one of the twenty-five 'Magna Carta barons' tasked with ensuring that John kept to the terms of the charter.[13] When John reneged on the agreement, Louis of France, the son and heir of Philip Augustus, was invited to come and take the English crown (we will hear more of his campaign later in this chapter). It would take him some time to organise matters and set sail himself, but in the interim he sent over an advance party of French barons to show his support. These were welcomed by Geoffrey and his compatriots, and a tournament was organised in London in February 1216 as a kind of team-building exercise. As we know, however, tournaments were dangerous affairs and this one was to be fatal: Geoffrey de Mandeville, having apparently failed to arm himself properly, was accidentally killed by a French knight.[14]

This news would have come as a great shock to Isabelle, who had no doubt been expecting her much younger husband to outlive her. We do not know what sort of personal bond – if any – they had formed, so it is difficult to make any assessment of the private impact this loss had on her. What we do know is that as a widow she could now finally take more control of her own estates, and she issued a number of charters in 1216–17, in which she styled herself 'Countess of Gloucester and Essex in my free widowhood', sometimes adding 'and in my full power'.[15]

Inevitably, though, a woman who was rich and titled in her own right would not be allowed to stay unmarried for long, no matter how old she was. Following John's death in October 1216, the accession of the 9-year-old Henry III and Louis's eventual withdrawal in September 1217, Isabelle made her peace with the crown along with the other rebels. She was almost immediately obliged to marry Hubert de Burgh, a senior figure in the new administration who was a long-time adherent of John (he had at one time been the gaoler of Arthur of Brittany before the latter's mysterious disappearance) and was now England's justiciar and a member of little Henry III's regency council. The wedding took place in September or early October 1217, but how this new marriage might have functioned will never be known, for Isabelle died just a few weeks later, on 14 October, aged somewhere in her late fifties.

Sadly, Isabelle appears to have been little missed and her death elicited virtually no attention from contemporaries except a passing mention in a couple of monastic chronicles, one of which manages to call her Joanna.[16] She had no children to mourn her. One of her sisters, Amice, was still alive but it is unclear how much contact they had enjoyed with each other during the decades since the separation caused by Amice's marriage when Isabelle was still a young girl. The only interest raised by Isabelle's death was not personal but concerned the future of her title and estates: these would not go to Hubert de Burgh, whose brief tenure as earl of Gloucester was ended by Isabelle's demise, so they passed by default to Amice and thence to her elder son, Gilbert de Clare, who was already the earl of Hertford.

Isabelle was, at least, accorded the dignity of a burial in Canterbury cathedral. There are no contemporary images of her (other than a stylised, conventional depiction on her seal), no descriptions of either her appearance or her character, and no record of her thoughts or feelings. She is a shadowy figure whose life story can only be partially constructed, and even then only at second hand by finding her in the background of other people's lives. She was – in name, at least – briefly a queen, but her significance in contemporary events was more due to her bloodline and position than her independent actions. Within the unbreakable constraints that bound her, we can just about discern that Isabelle made the most of the life that she was permitted to lead, but it is her fate to be forever overshadowed by her successor as queen of England.

After annulling his marriage to Isabelle of Gloucester in 1199, John found himself in need of a new wife, one who could provide him with heirs and who would preferably also bring him a significant international political advantage. He found one, but the manner in which he went about the business caused upset and outrage that would have far-reaching effects.

Isabella was the only child and heiress of Aymer, count of Angoulême, and she was also a close relative of Philip Augustus as her mother was Philip's first cousin.[17] We do not know the exact year of Isabella's birth. The date most commonly suggested is 'around 1188', but this is counted backwards from the date of her marriage to John in 1200, when various commentators noted that she looked about 12. However, this might have been a polite fiction as 12 was the minimum canonical age for marriage and it is possible that contemporaries were glossing over a hasty marriage between John and an underage girl (of which more shortly). Isabella may thus have been born sometime between 1188 and the early 1190s; it is very unlikely that her date of birth was before 1188 for the reasons we will discuss below and also because she was still healthily and regularly bearing children into the 1230s.[18]

In late 1199 or early 1200, when Isabella was probably 11 at most, she was informed that she was to be the means of forming a beneficial alliance for her father – a situation that was entirely normal and that was presumably not too much of a surprise to her. In this case the happy news was that she would be able to remain in the local region: the man seeking an alliance with Aymer was Hugh IX de Lusignan, lord of Lusignan and count of La Marche, which bordered Angoulême. The union of these territories via marriage would provide Hugh and Isabella, and their heirs, with a significant power base.

The obvious candidate to marry Isabella would seem to have been Hugh's eldest son and heir, Hugh X de Lusignan, who was 17 and unwed. However, Hugh IX's own marriage had been annulled so he was also available; he decided to marry Isabella himself, despite the fact that he was more than old enough to be her father. This is unpleasant to modern sensibilities but, as we have seen, large age gaps (particularly between an older husband and a younger wife) were not uncommon among nobility and royalty at this time. Isabella was given no choice in the matter herself, so all she could do was prepare herself for a wedding and a new life.

It is at this point that doubts about Isabella's date of birth arise. As she and Hugh IX were both single and there were no objections to the match, there was no reason for the wedding not to take place immediately ... unless the bride were under-age. One contemporary certainly believes this to be the case:

> The said count had acknowledged her as his wife, by promise made as pledge for the future, and she had taken him for her husband by promise made for the future; for because she had not yet attained marriageable years, the said Hugh declined to be united to her in presence of the church.[19]

The wedding proper might not have taken place, but the young Isabella knew what the future held and it seemed secure. However, events outside her control were conspiring to change her fate. King John was on the lookout for a new bride who would bring him an advantage, and the heiress to Angoulême – a county that was of strategic significance as it lay between his strongholds of Poitiers and Bordeaux – was a very suitable match. Moreover, John was alarmed by the prospect of a union of the Lusignan–La Marche–Angoulême lands, something that would give Hugh IX far too much power in Aquitaine, in the absence of a resident duke. Taking Isabella away from Hugh would thus be a way to prevent the amalgamation, so in territorial terms, John marrying Isabella himself was a win–win situation. Aymer of Angoulême was not averse to the idea, as it meant that his daughter would be a queen rather than a countess and this would be of great advantage to himself. He therefore put up no opposition as John intervened in the situation, forbade Hugh's wedding before it could take place and announced that he would marry Isabella himself.[20]

Isabella, probably taken aback by the speed with which her life had been turned upside down, found herself at the altar of Bordeaux cathedral on 24 August 1200, married to a very different older man (John was by this time 33) from the one she had anticipated. The whirl was to continue as she was almost immediately transported north to Chinon and then to England, a place she had never visited before, where she was crowned queen at Westminster on 8 October.[21]

As Isabella stopped to draw breath and consider her dizzying promotion, John might have been congratulating himself. However, although he had made territorial gains, politically he had made a blunder of the highest order. His family, of course, had previously had little compunction about ignoring the accepted conventions surrounding marriage, but here the aggravating factors piled up: Hugh and Isabella were formally betrothed, and Hugh was one of John's vassals (in John's position as duke of Aquitaine) and should thus expect to be treated fairly and with honour. Not only had John acted in an unprincipled manner, but instead of apologising or trying to make amends by offering Hugh lands, money or an alternative match, he had simply dismissed Hugh's complaints with disdain and even seized some of his property.

John's greatest mistake, however, was to have chosen the wrong target: unlike some of the others who had been trampled by Plantagenet family interests in the past, Hugh was in a position to fight back. In 1201 he renounced his allegiance to John and defected to Philip Augustus, appealing to him as their joint and ultimate overlord. In April 1202 Philip, having summoned John to answer for his actions and received no reply, used a combination of this and his concurrent support for the claims of Arthur of Brittany as a pretext to pronounce against John a sentence of the forfeiture of his estates in France. This, in turn, gave the French king an excuse to launch a military campaign against John.[22] He invaded Normandy while Arthur moved into Poitou, where Hugh IX de Lusignan was one of those who had rebelled against John in the young duke's name.

None of this would have been immediately apparent to the girl of no more than 12 who found herself queen of England. We do not have a great deal of information about Isabella's early years in the kingdom, though it is clear that she did not enjoy anything like the privileges of some of her predecessors: she did not, for example, receive as of right the incomes either from her own inheritance in Angoulême (which should have been hers following the death of Count Aymer in 1202) or from her dower estates. The English royal dower, as we saw in Chapter 6, was at this time a subject of some dispute. When Eleanor of Aquitaine died in 1204, it should have passed to Berengaria, rather than Isabella, and Berengaria made every effort to claim it; she was supported by King Philip of France, which further inflamed the already strained Plantagenet–Capetian relations. Isabella had no say in this dispute, but what is clear is that rather than having an income that was hers by right and could be used to run her own household, she was kept dependent on John for her day-to-day expenses. As we saw earlier in this chapter, she may even have been housed with Isabelle of Gloucester, her husband's ex-wife, for accounting purposes.

Isabella was also deprived of advisors from her homeland, as John had not allowed any to accompany her to England (this was in marked contrast to Eleanor of Aquitaine, her mother-in-law, and Eleanor of Provence, her later daughter-in-law, both of whom brought large retinues from their home territories). The young queen took no part in the politics of the court, seems to have had very little patronage to dispense and did not issue any charters in her own name. John was well known for wanting to keep his subordinates completely in his power, and it would seem that this extended to Isabella.[23]

The personal relationship between Isabella and John has been the subject of much speculation over the years. The sudden nature of their betrothal and wedding, combined with the circumstances of her previous betrothal, led some rather fanciful commentators to suggest that John lusted after her at first sight, and even that he actually kidnapped her from the altar. In the thirteenth century there was some speculation about John and his very young bride (one commentator wrote that, from quite early in the marriage, John 'feasted sumptuously with his queen daily, and prolonged his sleep in the morning'), but this was written several decades later, with the hindsight of the disaster of the later part of John's reign and when the reputation of 'Bad King John' was already firmly established, so it may simply have been another criticism to level at him.[24]

John's motives for the match were undoubtedly political, and indeed it would appear that he did not actually cohabit with Isabella until she was in her mid- to late teens. There are sporadic references to her being in his company at various points, for example in the spring of 1201 at York, but otherwise she was lodged separately from him, as accounts show.[25] Isabella did not give birth to her first child until October 1207, seven years after the wedding, at which point she was probably around 18 or 19, young to be a parent now but a respectable age for a thirteenth-century queen. Given how easily she appears to have conceived thereafter, for all of the rest of her fertile years, the most likely explanation for a lack of children before 1207 is the absence of a sexual relationship.

Happily for Isabella, for John and for the stability of the succession, the child she bore in 1207 was a son and heir, Henry. A second son, Richard, was born just fifteen months later, and three daughters (Joan, Isabelle and Eleanor) would follow. We might choose to note that the children's names very much foregrounded John's dynasty and immediate family while relegating Isabella's to the background: other than her namesake second daughter, the royal children were named after his mother, father, brother and sister.*

On a dynastic level, then, Isabella could count the first decade of her marriage as a success: she had produced the required male heir and spare, plus daughters who would be useful in forming alliances. She could perhaps also congratulate herself on a personal level, as she had not antagonised the English nobles (or chroniclers) with an excessively lavish lifestyle and had managed – as far as we can tell – to remain on relatively good terms with a husband of notoriously difficult temperament. However, as we might have predicted, it was wider political concerns, not Isabella's personal behaviour, that were to affect the next phase of her life.

Following the events of 1200, Hugh IX de Lusignan defected from John's allegiance to Philip's, giving the French king an excuse to attack John and invade his territories. Philip enjoyed great success and ultimately conquered the whole of Normandy in 1204, as well as taking control of the Plantagenet ancestral heartlands of Anjou and Maine. This was an absolute catastrophe for John; the duchy had been linked to the English throne since 1066 and the other lands had been in his family for many generations.

This affected Isabella in several ways. There was some attempt in the thirteenth century to make a link between her and the losses: instead of responding with vigorous military might to Philip's invasion, said one writer, John 'was staying inactive at Rouen with his queen, so that it was said that he

---

* 'Joan' and 'Joanna' were used interchangeably at this time (much like the variant spellings Isabel, Isabelle and Isabella), and John's sister Joanna appears in some contemporary records as Joan.

was infatuated by sorcery or witchcraft'. Bad news of his losses reached John, but this did not bother him unduly because 'when this was told to the English king, he was enjoying all the pleasures of life with his queen, in whose company he believed that he possessed everything he wanted'.[26] This was written by the same later chronicler who accused John of languishing in bed with his bride, but a more exact contemporary says almost the same ('he paid attention to nothing but dogs and birds and to enjoying himself with the queen his wife') and actually has John himself blaming Isabella: 'He said to the queen, "Listen, lady, I have lost all this for you!"'[27]

Following the loss of Normandy, Anjou and Maine, Isabella's family and dynastic position became more important to John: his only remaining territory in France was Aquitaine, of which Angoulême formed a pivotal element – and parts of Aquitaine were now under threat as well. Isabella had not been the only 12-year-old to have made a royal marriage in 1200; in that same year, following the Treaty of Le Goulet, the wedding had taken place of King Philip's son and heir, Louis, with Blanche of Castile, who was Leonor's daughter and John's niece. A decade later, Louis was in his twenties and eager for action, at which point he and his father began to make plans to bring more of the Plantagenet-held lands under French royal control and to attempt the conquest of England itself.

An initial plan to launch an invasion was thwarted in 1213, when the French fleet was attacked and burned in the harbour at Damme before it could set sail. This gave John some false hope, and he set about making alliances with rebel French lords and also with the Holy Roman Emperor – who happened to be his nephew Otto, the son of his sister Matilda. This coalition was to attack France from the north while John concentrated on Poitou, bringing Isabella with him across the Channel in an attempt to negotiate with the Poitevin nobles. One of the agreements that was reached was the possibly awkward one that Hugh X de Lusignan (the son and heir of Isabella's original intended husband, now around 30 and still unmarried) was betrothed to John and Isabella's daughter Joan, then aged 4.

This bought Lusignan loyalty for John – for a while, at least – but otherwise the campaign was a disaster. John was defeated at La-Roche-aux-Moines by Louis; or, to be more specific, he ran away when Louis approached, leaving Louis to gain a significant victory over the army he left behind. John's allies were defeated on 27 July 1214 at the Battle of Bouvines by King Philip himself.[28] Otto fled the field, never lived the humiliation down and went into a kind of internal exile in Germany until his death four years later. John, now in a worse position than he had been to start with, was forced to retreat to England and would never leave it again. Isabella travelled with him, possibly regretting the fact that she could not stay longer in her homeland and wondering when or if she might come back.

The details of the ensuing baronial rebellion that led to the creation of Magna Carta do not form part of our story of Isabella, except to note that it resulted in further restrictions on her freedom and in her losing the companionship of her children even earlier than she might have expected. Henry, the heir to the throne, had already been removed from her at the age of just 4, and she does not appear to have seen him often thereafter. Joan had also been taken away, sent to France to be brought up in the household of her future husband. But now Isabella lost the others as well: for a combination of political and safety reasons Richard, Isabelle and Eleanor (who must have been only a very tiny baby at the time) were placed in separate households in different parts of the realm, while Isabella was moved to the well-defended castle of Corfe.[29]

More danger was to threaten Isabella when John reneged on the terms of Magna Carta and the barons responded by offering the English throne to Louis of France. Their choice fell on him partly due to his availability and readiness, and the probability of his success in any consequent war, but it was also due to his family connections and the international network that the Plantagenet women had created. 'They chose Louis as their lord,' explains one chronicler, 'by reason of his wife, whose mother, namely, the queen of Castile, was the only survivor of all the brothers and sisters of the said king of England.'[30] The imminent threat of a French invasion of England had repercussions for Isabella – who was, after all, French herself as well as being a relative of Louis's. The surviving evidence now indicates that she was put under guard, her household composed entirely of men chosen by John and headed by one Terric the Teuton (who, as his name implies, was a German who had first come to England as a representative of John's nephew Otto).[31] It is open to interpretation whether this confinement of Isabella was due to John's concern for her safety, or whether he did not entirely trust her. Her blood relationship to some of the protagonists was certainly closer than John might like; Robert de Courtenay, who would command a fleet of reinforcements later sent to Louis, was Isabella's uncle.

Isabella was not at her husband's side when he died at Newark on the night of 18–19 October 1216. John's long-standing denial of her queenly authority was in evidence again, as was a possible lack of trust: he did not mention her at all in his will, and neither was she named among his executors. The war continued for another year after John's death (during which time Thomas, the count of Perche who was Matilda Plantagenet's grandson and John's great-nephew, was killed fighting for Louis), but the all-male group of nobles who now took charge of the kingdom and of the new 9-year-old king seemed intent on sidelining the widowed queen. Mothers were often named as regents for underage sons at this time, but this was not the case here and Isabella, after attending her son's hastily arranged coronation, was to have no role at all to play in the new regime.

It is perhaps not surprising, then, that the call of Isabella's homeland – where she could exercise authority in her own right – was strong and that she decided to leave England. It has often been said of her at this point that she 'abandoned' her children, but what else could she do, if she were not to be allowed to see them anyway? The decision to remove little Henry from her care and place him in the household of one of John's most fervent supporters when he was just 4 can hardly have been Isabella's choice, and all her children were taken away one after the other as toddlers or even babies. She was treated almost as a brood mare, conceiving and birthing off-spring but never allowed the chance to get to know them. She certainly did not have the opportunity to form the sort of relationships or networks that Eleanor of Aquitaine had done with her own daughters and daughters-in-law.

All of this being the case, it does not seem surprising that Isabella should want to leave England, even though she would receive a bad press for it. She was still in her twenties and had most of her life in front of her – a life she must have felt entitled to live in a place and a manner of her own choosing. She was, after all, countess of Angoulême in her own right and could throw herself into that role with enthusiasm. This was exactly what she did, travelling back to Poitou in 1217. She retained the style of 'queen' (as was her right, because the anointed status was for life) and set about establishing her authority after the long absence of any resident count. This was all undertaken very much on her own behalf; there was no pretence that Isabella was merely acting in the name of her son.

Isabella might, thereafter, have faded into the sort of obscurity enjoyed by Berengaria, but in 1220 she shocked the whole of England and France by deciding to marry again. That a young widow, and especially one who had lands and a title of her own, should wish to make a second match was not surprising, but her choice of husband was: 'She [had previously] arranged the marriage of her daughter and Hugh de Lusignan, son of Hugh Le Brun, count of La Marche, so as to get his help, then undid that marriage and married him herself, which caused much talk.'[32] This succinct and rather bland summary by a contemporary does not convey the scandal and uproar that the match caused. Isabella married, of her own free will, the man who was her daughter's fiancé, and who was, moreover, the son of the man to whom she had previously been formally betrothed. They were not closely related to each other by blood, so the union was not consanguineous in that respect, but the two previous betrothals made the situation dubious, to say the least, and the marriage also deprived young Joan of the future she had been brought up to expect.* Moreover, as Hugh X de Lusignan was now count of La Marche following Hugh IX's death in 1219, his marriage to Isabella created exactly the same power bloc in Poitou that John had been trying to avoid two decades previously, and which Isabella knew would not be pleasing to her son and his regency council.

Isabella made an attempt to justify her marriage in a letter to Henry III, rather tenuously trying to make out that it was in his own interest:

> We make known to you that when the counts of La Marche and Angoulême died, lord Hugh of Lusignan remained alone and without heir in the region of Poitou, and his friends did not permit our daughter to be married to him, because she is so young; but they counselled him to take a wife from whom he might quickly have heirs, and it was suggested that he take a wife in France. If he had done so, all your land in Poitou and

---

* Joan, who was at this time resident in Hugh X de Lusignan's lands, became the subject of a brief custody dispute between Isabella and her son Henry III, who demanded the return of his sister so she could be used elsewhere on the marriage market. Joan was married in 1221, shortly before her eleventh birthday, to Alexander II, king of Scots.

Gascony and ours would have been lost. But we, seeing the great danger that might emerge from such a marriage – and your counsellors would give us no counsel in this – took said H[ugh], count of La Marche, as our lord; and God knows that we did this more for your advantage than for ours.[33]

In among the political justifications, is it possible that Isabella and Hugh also felt a personal attraction for each other? It seems likely: nobody was putting pressure on Isabella to marry again, and she could easily have sustained a friendly alliance with Lusignan and La Marche without it. Her second marriage appears to have been one of much more equality and joint enterprise than her first. She and Hugh acted together to a much greater extent than had ever been the case with John (whom, incidentally, Isabella never mentioned again in any of the surviving documents from the rest of her life). She also started a second family, bearing Hugh no fewer than nine children – five sons and four daughters – within twelve or fifteen years. All of them survived infancy, putting Isabella in the extremely unusual position of being a medieval mother of fourteen children who all lived to adulthood.

Philip Augustus died in 1223, leaving the French throne to his adult son Louis (now Louis VIII), who continued his father's long-standing vendetta against the Plantagenet family. Louis did not attempt a further invasion of England, but he was determined to drive the English off the remaining fragments of French soil over which they still ruled. This included Poitou, which in turn included Angoulême and La Marche, and he needed allies in the region. Isabella was faced with choosing between the future interests of her first family and her second, and she elected to favour her second. In 1224 she and Hugh sided with Louis VIII against the English in Poitou, being rewarded for his success with control of the island of Oléron. However, when Louis VIII died in 1226 at the unexpectedly early age of 39, leaving the crown to his 12-year-old son Louis IX, they defected again – no doubt thinking that their interests were best served by England under an adult king who was Isabella's son, rather than a French boy king with a female regent, who might not be strong enough to fight off any threat.

This latest change of allegiance, however, proved to be a mistake. The new king of France (the future St Louis) proved to be strong-minded even at an early age, and his regent was none other than his mother, Blanche of Castile, who had been well schooled as a girl in the exigencies of queenship by her own mother Leonor, had spent some time during her formative years with Eleanor of Aquitaine and was determined to do the best for her son.

With the stark reality of their situation facing them, Isabella and Hugh came to terms with Louis IX and Blanche, agreeing in 1227 to the betrothal of their eldest son, the 6-year-old Hugh XI de Lusignan, to Louis's only sister, the 3-year-old Isabelle of France. As it happened, this match would later fall through (Isabelle being of a religious disposition and electing never to marry at all), but Isabella and Hugh remained loyal to the French crown for the next decade.

Peace was not to last, however, and Isabella was to have more conflict ahead of her as she entered middle age. In 1241 two very different events took place. The first was that King Louis invested his brother Alphonse as count of Poitiers, a title that had traditionally been a subsidiary of the duchy of Aquitaine. This title had already (and somewhat optimistically) been bestowed by Henry III on his brother Richard, and Isabella, despite her lack of contact with either of them, was offended on her second son's behalf. Moreover, having the French king's brother as count – and a count who actually intended to reside in the region –

meant that Hugh and Isabella's joint and almost unchallenged authority in Poitou would be subject to much greater oversight, and they were not keen on this. Secondly, when Isabella met with Louis IX and Blanche (who was no longer regent, the king by now having attained his majority, but who was still one of his closest and most experienced advisors), she felt herself slighted by them. She had retained – as she was entitled to – the style of queen after returning to France, but she did not feel she was treated with the dignity appropriate to this rank.

A letter written by a third party to Blanche of Castile depicts Isabella in a fury after she came away from the meeting, 'seizing the cloths with chests and bedding, even tripods, cauldrons and all domestic utensils and ornaments, large and small'. The particular reason for her ire was the lack of respect with which she had been received, being considered merely countess of Angoulême rather than a former queen:

> She said [to Hugh, who was listening to the diatribe]: 'You worse than anyone living, did you not see at Poitiers, when I waited three days to atone to your king and queen, that when I came before them in the chamber, the king was sitting on one side of the bed and the queen, with the countess of Chartres and her sister the abbess on the other.* They did not call me nor have me sit with them, and they did it so that they would render me vile before the people. And indeed I was vile as a stupid hireling standing among the people before them. They did not rise when I came in nor when I left, not even a little, disparaging me.'[34]

---

* The 'countess of Chartres and her sister the abbess' mentioned were Louis IX's cousins Isabelle and Alix, the two youngest daughters of Alix of France (featured in Chapter 1) and her husband Theobald V, count of Blois (the title was sometimes given as 'of Chartres' after the location of the comital seat). Isabelle was by this time countess in her own right following the death of her sister Margaret and Margaret's children, while Alix was the abbess of Fontevraud.

Depending on which contemporary accounts one reads, this perceived lack of respect might have been one factor in Isabella and Hugh's decision to rebel: Hugh travelled to Alphonse's Christmas court in 1241 and renounced his allegiance.

Once again this proved to be a mistake. All the outrage and the resources that Isabella and Hugh could summon between them were no match for the might of the French crown, as Louis descended with an army to impose his authority and demonstrate his support for his brother. Isabella appealed to Henry III for help, and he and his brother Richard arrived in Poitou in May 1242, meeting their mother in person for the first time since she had left England a quarter of a century earlier. War was declared, but the very un-martial Henry was swiftly and soundly defeated. Hugh and Isabella surrendered to Louis IX in July and were obliged to give up many of the territories they had gained in recent years, although, in a show of leniency, they were permitted to keep their joint ancestral lands of Angoulême, Lusignan and La Marche.[35]

This defeat seems to have finally convinced Isabella that a quiet life might be preferable, and it also seems to have prompted an estrangement from Hugh. We do not have any specific information on her health (either physical or mental), but it was shortly after these events and at the relatively early age of her mid-fifties that Isabella made plans to retire from the world and take holy orders. She left her French lands to Hugh XI de Lusignan, her eldest son by her second marriage (Henry III, her eldest son overall, technically had a claim but was unable to pursue it after his defeats), and retired to Fontevraud, the foundation strongly associated with her first husband's family and the resting place of her erstwhile mother-in-law, Eleanor of Aquitaine. She died there in 1246, a veiled nun probably aged around 58, and was buried in the chapter house.

❧

Hugh X de Lusignan survived Isabella, but not for long. He and their eldest son, Hugh XI, went together on Louis IX's Seventh Crusade in 1248 and both died in Egypt, the elder at the siege of Damietta in 1249 and the younger at the Battle of Fariskur in 1250. Henry III at first seemed little touched by the death of his mother, but later he relented and personally travelled to Fontevraud, where he had her body moved from its relatively humble place so that it lay close to the tombs of his Plantagenet ancestors. Isabella's effigy is the fourth of those still extant today, lying with those of Henry II, Eleanor of Aquitaine and Richard the Lionheart.

After her death, Isabella's name quickly became infamous. She was much maligned and, as the easiest way to slander a woman was to accuse her of being promiscuous, it was not long before a chronicler of the mid-thirteenth century noted that it was common gossip 'that she ought to be called a wicked Jezebel, rather than Isabel, for having sowed the seeds of many crimes'.[36] There is no evidence whatsoever to support the various allegations of adultery and even incest that sprang up over the years with regard to her tenure as queen – and with whom in England could she possibly have been incestuous in any case?

It is, of course, a matter of recorded fact that Isabella left England in 1217 and did not return, but the extent to which this was her 'abandoning' the children from her first marriage, as opposed to being kept away from them, remains a matter for debate.[37] Like all the women in this book, she must have had the desire to have a life of her own, to have some autonomy and control over her own fate. Unlike some of the others, she succeeded: she might have faced defeats as well as victories in her later life, but at least they were her own.

CONCLUSION

It is a common misconception that because royal and noble women were rarely able to choose their own husbands during the twelfth and thirteenth centuries, they must have led lives that were completely powerless. This is to misunderstand the situation: the task these women had to face was to orient themselves to the position in which they found themselves and *then* to work out how to use their authority to best effect and to carve out the life they wanted.

Most of the women featured in this book had their married lives mapped out for them at young ages, and the courses of those lives were, as expected, initially determined by the men to whom they were wed – some happily and some not. They each grew into their roles in different ways and, although none of them had a say in their first marriages, we can see that they acted with greater confidence and autonomy as they grew older. Some, on outliving their husbands, elected to remain independent widows so they could manage their own affairs. Joanna managed to resist the pressure applied by a man who was both her brother and a king in order to turn down a marriage proposal to which she objected. Later, to all appearances, she took proactive steps to escape a relationship she did not like. Constance succeeded in having an unwanted marriage annulled, and she and Isabella both went on to marry men of their own choosing.

But the lives of these ten women were not just about personal relationships; they were also political actors on the national and international stages. All of them eventually found a way to exercise some kind of personal authority, though they took different paths to get there and succeeded in varying degrees. Marie, Alix and Matilda all acted as regents on behalf of husbands or sons; Leonor would have done the same had she lived longer, and even during her life she was a huge influence on her royal husband and children. Constance, Berengaria, Isabelle and Isabella were able to rule estates on their own behalf as widows ('in my free widowhood and in my full power' is a mighty statement to read in a charter), and Margaret and Joanna both took drastic and independent steps towards the ends of their lives.

Of course, the paths of these ten lives were very different. Marie and Alix, for example, never left France, while others, notably Joanna, Berengaria and Margaret, travelled widely; some were anointed queens while others never achieved that exalted rank. But they did all have some things in common. They were all well educated, intelligent and motivated to do the best they could for themselves and their families, no matter what the circumstances, and they were all connected by their ties to Eleanor of Aquitaine. Their links to her and to her two husbands – whether by blood or by marriage, or indeed both – were the major influential factor for all ten women. Some, it is fair to say, were impacted by these ties more positively than others.

As we have discovered over the course of this book, these women led lives that were often geographically distant from each other. Joanna and Berengaria were together for a number of months, as were Marie and Margaret, but none of the others spent a great deal of time as adults in each other's company. However, it is important to stress that despite this, they were all linked in a powerful network and their actions affected the lives of the others and their children, no matter how far apart they were. The lives of noble and especially royal women of this period are often seen in isolation, or dismissed with a simple 'and she was married off at a young age to ...', as though their interest in and impact on family affairs ceased at that moment. But, as we have seen, each of these women continued until the end of her days to represent her birth family, as well as the one into which she had married.

For a hundred years, these women were as much a pivotal part of the politics of the Angevin empire – indeed, of the whole of western Europe and well beyond – as any of their husbands or brothers, and their contributions should not be underestimated.

NOTES

A list of the abbreviations used for primary sources, and full references for all secondary works cited, may be found in the bibliography.

Introduction

1   For more detail on Eleanor's early life, see Turner, *Eleanor of Aquitaine*, pp. 10–37.
2   This is necessarily a brief overview of the situation. For more, see any of the many published biographies of Eleanor. For specific discussion of the quote attributed to her, see Turner, *Eleanor of Aquitaine*, p. 47.
3   *GC*, pp. 67–8; Nangis, pp. 35–6. For more discussion on the divorce, see Turner, *Eleanor of Aquitaine*, pp. 104–7.
4   On the circumstances surrounding Eleanor's second marriage, see RT, p. 66; Gervase, vol. 1, p. 149; *GC*, p. 68; WN, vol. 1, pp. 129–30; Warren, *Henry II*, pp. 44–5; Turner, *Eleanor of Aquitaine*, pp. 107–9.
5   For further discussion on this point, see Turner, 'Eleanor of Aquitaine and Her Children'.
6   Turner believes that it was Henry II, rather than Eleanor, who was the driving force behind the arrangement of the matches: 'For Henry II, the girls were important weapons for winning diplomatic advantage, and like other princes, he always had in mind some goal to achieve through their unions' (*Eleanor of Aquitaine*, p. 144). See also Gillingham, 'Love, Marriage and Politics in the Twelfth Century'.

Chapter 1

1   In the twelfth century, to be 'confined' meant exactly that, and the term has endured. For more on childbirth in the Middle Ages, see Leyser, *Medieval Women*, pp. 126–30; on the specific experiences of royal women, see Bartlett, *Blood Royal*, pp. 55–62.

2   Marie is, unusually for a medieval woman who was neither a saint nor a reigning queen, the subject of a dedicated biography: see Evergates, *Marie of France*.

3   *JS*, p. 61.

4   *GS*, p. 227.

5   Marie's biographer writes of her receiving a 'traditional Latin-based education' (Evergates, *Marie of France*, p. 6), and it was evident from Marie's later career that she had a keen interest in literature. For more on female education, see Kersey, 'Medieval Education of Girls and Women', and on education in the Middle Ages more generally, the relevant chapters in Orme, *Medieval Children*.

6   Margaret will be the subject of Chapter 5. Alice does not have her own chapter in this book, as she was neither a daughter nor a daughter-in-law of Eleanor of Aquitaine, but she will make a number of appearances as we go along. She is a fascinating figure and the archetype of a medieval woman who had many years of her life stolen and wasted due to her family's political interests, with no concern for her own personal welfare. She has attracted relatively little scholarly attention to date, but a forthcoming work that should shed more light on her life is Bassett, 'An Instrument of Diplomacy? The Curious Case of Princess Alice of France'.

7   For discussion of Theobald's presence in Troyes at Christmas 1166 and the logical assumption that Alix accompanied him, see Evergates, *Marie of France*, p. 17. Evergates notes that 'although Marie once referred to her "dearest" sister [Alix], they seem to have led entirely separate lives, both in their formative years as young women and even later as regents and widows' (ibid.).

8   *CT*, p. 207. In his notes to Chrétien's text, Kibler says that Marie and her husband presided over 'the principal literary court of twelfth-century France [...] rivalled in Europe only by that in England of her mother Eleanor and her second husband, Henry II Plantagenet' (ibid., p. 511).

9   *AC*, pp. 167–77. For a discussion on Eleanor and Marie's 'participation' in the court, see McCash, 'Marie de Champagne and Eleanor of Aquitaine'.

10   The full letter is available on the Epistolae site, at epistolae.ctl. columbia.edu/letter/819.html. 'Count/countess of Troyes' was an

alternative title in use at the time for the rulers of Champagne, the city of Troyes being the county's principal seat. For more detail on Marie's early months in charge of the county after her husband's departure on crusade, see Evergates, *Marie of France*, pp. 29–31; Plate 6.

11   This letter may be found on the Epistolae site, at epistolae.ctl. columbia.edu/letter/155.html; the emphasis is mine, to show that the request to protect the lands originally came from Marie.

12   See, for example, the wording in a letter of Marie's from 1186, confirming a gift, which may be found on the Epistolae site, at epistolae.ctl.columbia.edu/letter/818.html. See also Evergates, *Marie of France*, p. 45.

13   Quote from GW, p. 479. We will explore Margaret's life more fully in Chapter 5 and Constance's in Chapter 7.

14   Rigord, pp. 60–1; Rigord notes that Count Theobald was also present at Geoffrey's funeral, but he makes no specific mention of Alix.

15   For a brief overview of the Jerusalemite succession up to this point, and the preponderance of female heirs, see Hanley, *Two Houses, Two Kingdoms*, pp. 118–19; for more detail on the individuals concerned, see Pangonis, *Queens of Jerusalem*.

16   *Eracles*, p. 115. The event was so sudden that some other contemporaries seem to have been bemused about exactly how Henry and Isabelle's marriage came about: see *Ambroise*, pp. 152–4; *IP*, pp. 308–9.

17   The full text may be found on the Epistolae site, at epistolae.ctl. columbia.edu/letter/157.html, where it is described by the editors as 'a plea for help disguised as a complaint about all his friends and relatives who have not come to his aid'.

18   Scholarly opinion is divided on whether Eleanor and Marie met during December 1193. Evergates (*Marie of France*, p. 81) and McCash ('Marie de Champagne and Eleanor of Aquitaine', p. 710) tend towards the view that they did, Turner (*Eleanor of Aquitaine*, p. 198) and Labande ('Les filles d'Aliénor d'Aquitaine', p. 104) that they did not.

19   On this letter, see Evergates, *Marie of France*, p. 90.

20   For details of the many bequests, and some of Marie's contemporary obituaries, see Evergates, *Marie of France*, p. 91. Theobald III would later marry Blanca of Navarre, daughter of Sancho VI the Wise and sister of Berengaria, who features in Chapter 6 of the present volume; his descendants would become kings of Navarre in the thirteenth century.

21   The full text and translation is available on the Epistolae site, at epistolae.ctl.columbia.edu/letter/162.html.

Chapter 2

1   Matilda is not the subject of a dedicated book-length biography,
    though she has her own *ODNB* entry: see Kate Norgate, rev. Timothy
    Reuter, 'Matilda, duchess of Saxony (1156-1189)', *ODNB*. Matilda also
    features both in a biography of her husband (Jordan, *Henry the Lion*)
    and in a number of works that focus jointly on her and her sisters:
    see, for example, Bowie, *Daughters of Henry II*; Jasperse, *Medieval
    Women, Material Culture, and Power.*

2   A complete list of Matilda's travels with her mother (and, later, with
    her younger sisters as well) during these years may be found in
    Bowie, *Daughters of Henry II*, pp. 36-9.

3   Turner notes that 'while other great men in the twelfth century
    occasionally took some account of emotional compatibility in
    choosing their daughters' husbands, a powerful monarch could not
    afford such an indulgence, and political calculation prevailed' (*Eleanor
    of Aquitaine*, p. 144). For an interesting discussion on the topic of
    personal feelings in marriage, see Gillingham, 'Love, Marriage and
    Politics in the Twelfth Century'. Duke Henry and his first wife had
    produced a son, but he had died in infancy, apparently after falling off
    a table; see '(a) Heinrich' under Duke Henry's entry at the Foundation
    for Medieval Genealogy, at fmg.ac/Projects/MedLands/SAXONY.
    htm#Heinrichdied1195.

4   For more on the wedding and its advantages for Duke Henry, see
    Jordan, *Henry the Lion*, pp. 144-7.

5   See *UHL*, nos. 77 (where Matilda is styled *Machtildem filiam regis
    Anglie*), 83 (*gloriosissime domine Matildis, Bawarie et Saxonie ducisse*)
    and 94 (*uxoris mee ducisse Matildis, magnifici Anglorum regis filie*).

6   Matilda's imperial heritage is also emphasised in the gospel book of
    Henry the Lion, which we will discuss further below. For more on
    Empress Matilda, see Hanley, *Matilda*; Castor, *She-Wolves*, pp. 35-126.

7   Quote from RT, p. 106. Pipe Rolls PR 13 Henry II and PR 14 Henry II.
    More information about the Pipe Rolls, including which ones survive
    from the twelfth century and a list of those published, is available
    from the Pipe Roll Society; see piperollsociety.co.uk/.

8   One scholar estimates that 30 per cent of children died before the end
    of their first year, and that only half of those who survived the first
    year reached the age of 5 (Shahar, *Childhood in the Middle Ages*, p. 149).
    Bearing in mind that this does not even include the many pregnancies
    that ended in miscarriage, we can see that a successful conception
    was by no means a guarantee of a living child and thus not really - in
    the eyes of contemporaries - worth recording.

9   RT, p. 116.

10 RT, p. 145.

11   The gospel book is held by the Herzog August Bibliothek, Wolfenbüttel, Lower Saxony (Codex Guelf. 105 Noviss. 2°). The library bought it in 1983, following a fundraising campaign aimed at preserving national treasures; the £8.1 million price tag made it at the time the world's most expensive book.

12   The coronation image is on fol. 171v of the gospel book; Plate 9. The gospel book is analysed in detail in Jasperse, *Medieval Women, Material Culture, and Power*, pp. 63–89, and Jasperse, 'Matilda, Leonor and Joanna', in which she notes that in the coronation miniature, Matilda 'is portrayed as taller than her husband, thereby counterbalancing Henry's privileged position at Christ's right side, indicating that the royal princess was equally important from both a divine and dynastic perspective. Matilda's importance is stressed also by the crown that is conferred on her, which actually touches her head while Henry's crown hovers just above, suggesting that her royal status was considered crucial to Duke Henry because it enhanced his own prestige considerably' (p. 529).

13   For description and discussion of these vestments, together with an image from the cathedral chapter book listing the donation, see Jasperse, *Medieval Women, Material Culture, and Power*, pp. 93–7.

14   On Henry II's appropriation of the cult of Becket, see Bowie, *Daughters of Henry II*, pp. 145–9; Bowie, 'Matilda, Duchess of Saxony (1168–89) and the Cult of Thomas Becket'. For more on Becket himself, see Barlow, *Thomas Becket*; Guy, *Thomas Becket*.

15   *JF*, pp. 141 and 149 respectively.

16   For more on this point, see Bowie, *Daughters of Henry II*, p. 164.

17   For more detail on Duke Henry's disputes and his relationship with the emperor, see RH, vol. 1, pp. 523–4; Jordan, *Henry the Lion*, pp. 160–82; Bowie, *Daughters of Henry II*, pp. 103–4; Fuhrmann, *Germany in the High Middle Ages*, pp. 168–71.

18   RH, vol. 1, p. 524.

19   RH, vol. 2, p. 16.

20   The birth is mentioned in RH, vol. 2, p. 17.

21   RT, p. 145 and RW, vol. 2, p. 52 respectively.

22   RT, p. 145. Details on Henry II's negotiations on behalf of Duke Henry may also be found in RH, vol. 2, p. 35.

23   Details on Lothar are scarce, but what evidence there is for his life has been assembled at the Foundation for Medieval Genealogy, under his father's entry: see '(f) Lothar', at fmg.ac/Projects/MedLands/SAXONY.htm#Heinrichdied1195. On the subject of hostages and their treatment, see Kosto, *Hostages in the Middle Ages*; Bennett and Weikert (eds), *Medieval Hostageship*.

24   There is a wealth of literature on troubadours and courtly love; as a start, see Gaunt and Kay (eds), *The Troubadours: An Introduction*;

Akehurst and Davis (eds), *A Handbook of the Troubadours*; Boase, *The Origin and Meaning of Courtly Love*. Some 'rules' of courtly love are set out in AC, pp. 177–86.

25 *BB*, quotes from pp. 164 and 166 respectively.

26 *Rolandslied*, p. 340.

27 For more on the choices offered to the duke, see Jordan, *Henry the Lion*, p. 188.

28 AB, pp. 101–2.

29 More on the death of Thomas, count of Perche, at the Battle of Lincoln in 1217 may be found in McGlynn, *Blood Cries Afar*, pp. 208–14 and Hanley, *Louis*, pp. 159–63; see also Chapter 8.

30 Quote from *UHL*, no. 121.

31 Duke Henry's biographer notes that 'none of the German princely courts in the second half of the twelfth century were of such importance to the cultural life of the time as that of Henry the Lion', and that '[Henry's] family connection to the Angevins gave a decisive impulse to intellectual and artistic life in the ducal entourage' (Jordan, *Henry the Lion*, p. 200).

Chapter 3

1 Leonor, as we will call her (see the footnote where she is first mentioned in the introduction), is not the subject of a dedicated biography. She features in works that focus on all three sisters, such as Bowie, *Daughters of Henry II*; Jasperse, *Medieval Women, Material Culture, and Power*. She is also the subject of a chapter in a book about her eldest daughter: Shadis, *Berenguela of Castile*.

2 On the double betrothal, see RT, pp. 100–1; for more on this and on young Frederick's death after being passed over for the succession, see Fuhrmann, *Germany in the High Middle Ages*, pp. 159 and 163.

3 Shadis, *Berenguela of Castile*, p. 25.

4 Shadis, *Berenguela of Castile*, p. 26.

5 For more on the political background to the marriage, see Cerda, 'The Marriage of Alfonso VIII of Castile and Leonor Plantagenet'. Leonor's mother appears to have been an influential figure in the negotiations, which took place before her imprisonment by Henry II: see Turner, *Eleanor of Aquitaine*, pp. 194–5.

6 *GRH*, vol. 1, p. 139.

7 The most thorough account of Henry II's arbitration between the kings of Castile and Navarre is RH, vol. 1, pp. 439–51 (reference to Alfonso as 'our dearly beloved son' on p. 450); see also GW, pp. 553–5; Warren, *Henry II*, p. 603; Barber, *Henry Plantagenet*, pp. 194–5.

8 The names and dates of birth of Leonor's children who died in infancy, and indeed the number of children she bore in total, are

the subject of some confusion. The list given here is the one that
has been compiled from primary-source material by the Foundation
for Medieval Genealogy: see fmg.ac/Projects/MedLands/CASTILE.
htm#AlfonsoVIIIdied1214A. As noted there, two of the four children
who died in infancy between 1180 and 1186 may have been twins.

9   In an informal piece for *BBC History Magazine*'s website, medieval
queenship expert Dr Elena Woodacre makes the interesting point that
'beauty was obviously a huge part of a queen's role, and they were
expected to represent contemporary ideals. But queens were often
described in idealistic terms and referred to as being beautiful or fair
even if they weren't necessarily all that attractive. After all, no one
wants to be the one to say that their queen isn't a looker, so it's hard to
know how beautiful the woman was in absolute terms' (historyextra.
com/period/medieval/top-questions-medieval-queens-answered/).

10 On Leonor's relationship with Alfonso and the ruling partnership they
formed, see Shadis, *Berenguela of Castile*, pp. 34–9.

11 Shadis, *Berenguela of Castile*, p. 38.

12 Bowie, *Daughters of Henry II*, pp. 165–6.

13 These vestments are now in the Museo de Real Colegiata de San
Isidoro in León; they are discussed in Jasperse, 'Matilda, Leonor and
Joanna', pp. 532–6, with an image of them on p. 533.

14 Pipe Rolls, PR 27 Henry II. Sancho's birth is also recorded by the
Norman chronicler Robert de Torigni, who always had a special
interest in Leonor; as he noted twice in his work, he was her
godfather. RT, pp. 140 (Sancho), 94 and 145 (godfather).

15 The text of the Treaty of Le Goulet appears in Rigord, pp. 148–53; see
also Powicke, *Loss of Normandy*, pp. 200–5.

16 For more on Eleanor's part in the marriage arrangements, see RW,
vol. 2, pp. 186–7; Turner, *Eleanor of Aquitaine*, pp. 288–9.

17 RH, vol. 2, p. 480.

18 RH, vol. 2, pp. 480–1.

19 One scholar believes that Alfonso's claim was 'unlikely' and that he
was probably 'taking shrewd advantage of John's disinterest in and
difficulties with maintaining his continental lands' (Shadis, *Berenguela
of Castile*, p. 31).

20 RW, vol. 2, p. 219.

21 *CL*, p. 52; translation in Shadis, *Berenguela of Castile*, p. 31. For more on
Alfonso's Gascon interests, see Bowie, *Daughters of Henry II*, pp. 119–22.

22 Quotes from untranslated contemporary Castilian chronicles *De rebus
Hispaniae* and *Chronicon mundi*, as cited and translated in Bianchini,
Queen's Hand, pp. 288–9.

23 *CL*, pp. 55–5; translation in Shadis, *Berenguela of Castile*, p. 152. Shadis
sets this display of grief in the context of the overt mourning of
family members in medieval Castile: ibid., pp. 151–4.

24 For further discussion on this point, see Orme, *Medieval Children*, pp. 120–3.
25 The letter may be found in full (both in its original Latin and in English translation) on the Epistolae site, at epistolae.ctl.columbia.edu/letter/709.html. For more on the battle, see *PCG*, pp. 689–704 and James F. Powers, 'Las Navas de Tolosa, Battle of', in *OEMW*, vol. 2, pp. 489–91 (who describes the encounter as 'the great turning point in the conflict of Christian and Muslim states in the Hispanic reconquest').
26 On Henry's accidental death, see *PCG*, pp. 712–13.
27 For more on this rather unorthodox episode, see Hanley, *Louis*, pp. 179–80; Grant, *Blanche of Castile*, pp. 278–9.
28 RT, p. 145.
29 GW, p. 687.
30 *CL*, p. 43 and *PCG*, p. 683; both quotes translated in Bowie, *Daughters of Henry II*, p. 110.

Chapter 4

1 Joanna is the subject of a chapter in Alio, *Sicily's Queens* (pp. 194–216), and an *ODNB* article: D.S.H. Abulafia, 'Joanna [Joan, Joanna of England], countess of Toulouse (1165–1199)', *ODNB*. She also appears alongside Matilda and Leonor throughout Bowie, *Daughters of Henry II*; Jasperse, *Medieval Women, Material Culture, and Power*.
2 Detailed analysis of the whereabouts of Eleanor and her daughters during the girls' early lives may be found in Bowie, *Daughters of Henry II*, pp. 35–42.
3 This is necessarily a very brief overview; for more on Sicily and the Norman origins of its ruling dynasty, see Matthew, *The Norman Kingdom of Sicily*; Mendola, *The Kingdom of Sicily*.
4 *GRH*, vol. 1, p. 55.
5 *GRH*, vol. 1, p. 116. Joanna's first marriage, the reasons behind it and the negotiations for it are examined in most detail in Bowie, 'Shifting Patterns in Angevin Marriage Policies', and Bowie, *Daughters of Henry II*, pp. 81–94.
6 The charter in which William specifies Joanna's dower is reproduced in RT, pp. 129–30 and RH, vol. 1, pp. 414–16.
7 Pipe Rolls, PR 22 Henry II.
8 A map of Joanna's travels on the way to her wedding may be found in Alio, *Sicily's Queens*, p. 216.
9 RH, vol. 1, p. 413.
10 RT, p. 144 (my italics).
11 See Bowie, *Daughters of Henry II*, pp. 210–11, who notes that in the cases of both Joanna and her sister Leonor, 'whilst romantic love

may have been a minor consideration when engineering a politically significant dynastic match, it was not impossible to achieve' (p. 210).

12 RD, p. 17; see also RH, vol. 2, p. 163.

13 *IP*, p. 168.

14 *IP*, p. 168; RD, p. 25.

15 These negotiations are described in detail in RH, vol. 2, pp. 164-9 (quote from p. 165). We will meet Arthur, who was the son of Richard's brother Geoffrey and Geoffrey's wife Constance of Brittany, in Chapter 7.

16 Berengaria will be the subject of Chapter 6. For Eleanor's itinerary, see Turner, *Eleanor of Aquitaine*, p. 265. Turner believes that the queen insisted to Joanna that she should 'accompany her brother and his bride on the voyage to Palestine to see that Richard's wedding would actually take place' after she had taken such pains to bring Berengaria to him (ibid.).

17 *IP*, p. 178.

18 The encounter is described in *IP*, pp. 183-5; RD, pp. 35-7.

19 *IP*, pp. 193-4 (quote p. 193); RH, vol. 2, pp. 204-5. For more on Richard's time in Cyprus, see Gillingham, *Richard I*, pp. 144-54.

20 *IP*, p. 195.

21 For more on this monumental engagement, see *IP*, pp. 201-19; *Ambroise*, pp. 65-108; Hosler, *The Siege of Acre*.

22 Unsurprisingly, this action of Richard's has been the subject of much discussion over the years. It does not form part of our story here, but for a summary and references, see Gillingham, *Richard I*, pp. 167-71.

23 The negotiations are summarised (in a slightly garbled manner that indicates he was not privy to the minutiae of the discussions) in *Ambroise*, pp. 131-2. The fullest contemporary account is that of an Arab chronicler who was in Saladin's close household: Beha ed-Din, pp. 310-12. The whole episode is discussed, with additional references, in Gillingham, *Richard I*, pp. 184-9. Eleanor of Brittany was the sister of Arthur of Brittany, mentioned above; see note 15 above, and Chapter 7.

24 On the women's return journey, see RH, vol. 2, p. 307.

25 For more on Richard's time in captivity and Eleanor's efforts to raise the ransom, see Gillingham, *Richard I*, pp. 222-53; Turner, *Eleanor of Aquitaine*, pp. 270-5.

26 For more detail and a simplified family tree illustrating the claims, see Bowie, *Daughters of Henry II*, pp. 71-3.

27 There is a wealth of literature available on Catharism and the Albigensian Crusade. For an introduction, see Pegg, *A Most Holy War*; Oldenbourg, *Massacre at Montségur*; McGlynn, *Kill Them All*; Roquebert, *Histoire des Cathares*. On the specific question of Raymond VI's involvement in the conflict, see Déjean, *Comtes de Toulouse*, pp. 247-57.

28 William of Puylaurens gives the account of the siege that has Joanna acting on her husband's behalf, but he seems confused as to whether

it occurred in 1197 or 1199 (WP, pp. 18–19). Turner notes that an annalist of Winchester called Joanna 'a woman whose masculine spirit overcame the weakness of her sex' (*Annales monastici*, vol. 2, p. 64; translation in Turner, *Eleanor of Aquitaine*, p. 285), and he believes that Joanna's second marriage 'brought her no happiness' and that she was 'left to contend with a rebellion in her husband's domains alone, abandoned by him' and 'forced to flee from the county of Toulouse' (ibid.). The episode of the siege is examined in Déjean, *Comtes de Toulouse*, p. 259; Alio, *Sicily's Queens*, pp. 212–13.

29 An English translation of the document by which John confirmed this grant to Joanna may be found in *Calendar*, p. 391.

30 Joanna's original will has not survived, but a transcript of it is held at the Archives Départementales de Maine-et-Loire, 101.H.55, and a translation appears in *Calendar*, pp. 392–3. For discussion of the will, see Bowie, *Daughters of Henry II*, pp. 186–7, who notes that the 'touching tribute to her former husband says as much about Joanna's first marriage as it does her second' (p. 186).

31 Abulafia, 'Joanna', *ODNB*; see also Turner, *Eleanor of Aquitaine*, pp. 285–6 and Bowie, *Daughters of Henry II*, p. 188.

32 There were more female pilgrims and crusaders than has often been thought, although they were vastly outnumbered by men. For more on women and crusading, see Edgington and Lambert (eds), *Gendering the Crusades*; Hodgson, *Women, Crusading and the Holy Land*.

Chapter 5

1 Margaret is not the subject of a dedicated biography, but she features in a detailed work on her husband, Strickland, *Henry the Young King*, and in the chapter on Young Henry in Andrews, *Lost Heirs*, pp. 47–61.

2 *Becket*, pp. 46–7.

3 On the details of marriage arrangements, see RT, p. 84. For discussion, see Diggelmann, 'Marriage as Tactical Response'; Strickland, *Henry the Young King*, pp. 25–8; Turner, *Eleanor of Aquitaine*, pp. 135–6; Andrews, *Lost Heirs*, pp. 47–8.

4 WN, vol. 2, p. 99.

5 Sassier, *Louis VII*, p. 279.

6 RH, vol. 1, p. 258. For more on the unusual nature of this marriage, see Strickland, *Henry the Young King*, pp. 30–3.

7 RT, p. 92.

8 WN, vol. 2, p. 101.

9 For more on Matilda's claim, the oaths to support her and female succession in general, see Hanley, *Matilda*; Castor, *She-Wolves*; Beem, *The Lioness Roared*.

10 Quote from RT, p. 111. For more on the ceremony and a list of those present, see RT, pp. 111–12; Strickland, *Henry the Young King*, pp. 84–91.

11 Strickland believes this omission of Margaret from the ceremony was 'a calculated insult to Louis VII' (*Henry the Young King*, p. 81). Interestingly, clothing for Margaret to the extravagant amount of £26 17s 5d is listed in the Pipe Roll for this year (PR 16 Henry II); was this originally intended for her to wear to the coronation, or was it meant as some kind of compensation for her not being invited?

12 *GRH*, vol. 1, p. 6. For more on Louis's reaction, see RH, vol. 1, p. 326.

13 *GRH*, vol. 1, p. 31. Young Henry had already been anointed and consecrated, a rite that only needed to be performed once to confer kingship.

14 Quotes on the kings from RH, vol. 1, pp. 326 and 333. The Pipe Roll referring to Margaret is PR 20 Henry II; the charter may be found in *LCH*, vol. 3, pp. 389–90. On the wording of Margaret's charter, see also Strickland, *Henry the Young King*, p. 365 n. 171.

15 RT, p. 117; see also *GRH*, vol. 1, p. 34.

16 *JF*, p. 5.

17 One contemporary writes only of 'certain persons' who 'whispered in [Young Henry's] ear' (WN, vol. 2, p. 117), but another attributes the idea more completely to Louis: RH, vol. 1, pp. 362 and 367. On the additional suggestion that the couple should return to France, see *GRH*, vol. 1, p. 34.

18 On this separation, see Turner, *Eleanor of Aquitaine*, p. 231.

19 Of the available evidence, Strickland notes that 'the little that does [survive] nevertheless suggests that love developed within their marriage' (*Henry the Young King*, p. 31.)

20 RH, vol. 1, pp. 463–4. On Henry's demands and Louis's reaction, see also Gillingham, *Richard I*, p. 57; Hanley, *Two Houses, Two Kingdoms*, pp. 95–6.

21 *GRH*, vol. 1, p. 169. Young Henry's biographer thinks that 'it is hard to believe that Queen Margaret could have withdrawn to Paris without young Henry's knowledge or consent' (Strickland, *Henry the Young King*, p. 236).

22 For more on tournaments in the twelfth century, see Barber and Barker, *Tournaments*; Barker, *The Tournament in England*; Hanley, *War and Combat*, pp. 25–6; Asbridge, *Greatest Knight*, pp. 63–71.

23 Evergates, *Marie of France*, p. 29.

24 *HWM*, vol. 1, p. 267.

25 *HWM*, vol. 1, p. 277.

26 For discussion on this episode, and the likelihood of its having occurred at all, see Strickland, *Henry the Young King*, pp. 278–9.

27 RT, p. 146.

28 Rigord, pp. 67–8 (my translation).

29 RH, vol. 2, p. 55. For more on this conference, see Warren, *Henry II*, p. 598.

30 Cartulary of Rouen, fol. 73r-73v, as cited in Strickland, *Henry the Young King*, p. 316.

31 *GC*, pp. 149-50; Rigord, pp. 58-9; Nangis, p. 58.

32 For more on activity and culture in Hungary during the years after Margaret's arrival, see Engel, *The Realm of St Stephen*, pp. 53-4; on the preponderance of names from chivalric literature, see ibid., p. 86.

33 RT, pp. 132-3; RH, vol. 1, pp. 516-17. On Margaret's propagation of Becket's cult, see also Bowie, *Daughters of Henry II*, p. 167; Györffy, 'Thomas à Becket and Hungary'.

34 Engel, *The Realm of St Stephen*, p. 53.

35 See Engel, *The Realm of St Stephen*, pp. 88-9; Berend et al., *Central Europe in the High Middle Ages*, pp. 178 and 234.

36 We know the content of this letter because Marie's reply is extant; in it she accepts Margaret's decision and addresses her as *karissima soror mea* ('my dearest sister'). Archives Départementales de la Marne, 16 H 13, as cited in Evergates, *Marie of France*, p. 90.

37 *Eracles*, p. 143. On Henry's rather unexpected accession as king of Jerusalem (by marriage), see ibid., pp. 115-16; and above, Chapter 1.

Chapter 6

1 Perhaps surprisingly, given the dearth of available information, Berengaria is the subject of an academic biography: Trindade, *Berengaria: In Search of Richard the Lionheart's Queen*. Another full-length work is the markedly more fanciful and less scholarly Mitchell, *Berengaria: Enigmatic Queen of England*; shorter articles include Elizabeth Hallam, 'Berengaria [Berengaria of Navarre] (c. 1165-1230)', *ODNB*; Gillingham, 'Richard I and Berengaria of Navarre'. A forthcoming full-length academic work should add considerably to scholarship: Storey, *Berengaria of Navarre*.

2 Such information as can be gleaned about Berengaria's childhood, with reference to various contemporary Spanish records, is summarised in Trindade, *Berengaria*, pp. 32-7. On the specific question of either her or her sister Blanca considering a religious life, see ibid., p. 55.

3 *Ambroise*, p. 47 and *IP*, p. 173 respectively. A poem by the troubadour Bertran de Born (whom we encountered in Chapter 2) also alludes to a long-standing friendship between England and Navarre (*BB*, pp. 380-1).

4 On Sancho the Strong's height, see the detailed analysis in Del Campo, 'La estatura de Sancho el Fuerte' (the tables of measurements are intelligible even to those who do not read Spanish). Estimates of the year of Sancho's birth vary widely, from 1157 to 1170; a date towards the later end of the range is more likely.

5   For detailed discussion of Berengaria's dower, see Gillingham, 'Richard I and Berengaria', pp. 161-2; Trindade, *Berengaria*, pp. 142-3 and 151; Bowie, *Daughters of Henry II*, pp. 123-4.

6   War in Aquitaine was often brutal in nature, but Richard had taken it to new extremes. For example, in 1183, when in conflict with his brothers Henry and Geoffrey, Richard had a number of captives brought to the river outside Limoges, where they were staying, so they could be beheaded, drowned or blinded in full view as a warning (see *GRH*, vol. 1, p. 293; Hanley, *Two Houses, Two Kingdoms*, pp. 106-7; Strickland, *War and Chivalry*, pp. 52-3). Richard also had an unsavoury reputation for assaulting the wives and daughters of his Aquitanian nobles.

7   RH, vol. 2, p. 195.

8   RH, vol. 2, p. 196; see also Gillingham, *Richard I*, pp. 141-3.

9   RH, vol. 2, p. 196.

10 RD, p. 25 (who incidentally praises Eleanor of Aquitaine's beauty in the same sentence); *Ambroise*, p. 47; and RH, vol. 2, p. 196, respectively.

11 RD, p. 35.

12 *IP*, p. 182.

13 *IP*, p. 185.

14 RH, vol. 2, p. 204. The choice of celebrant is interesting: not only was a queen of England having her coronation in Cyprus, but the crown was placed on her head by a Norman bishop rather than an English one.

15 *IP*, p. 189 and Ambroise, pp. 55-6, respectively. On the wedding/ coronation ceremony, see also RD, p. 38; Trindade, *Berengaria*, pp. 86-7; Gillingham, *Richard I*, pp. 149-50.

16 *IP*, p. 221; *Ambroise*, p. 127; and *Eracles*, p. 121, respectively.

17 *IP*, p. 195.

18 See, for example, *Ambroise*, p. 127.

19 RD, p. 59; RH, vol. 2, pp. 277-8. For more on this, see Gillingham, *Richard I*, p. 230.

20 RH, vol. 2, p. 279.

21 Quote from RH, vol. 2, p. 307. The text and translation of the charter may be found on the Epistolae site, at epistolae.ctl.columbia.edu/ letter/763.html.

22 RH, vol. 2, p. 293.

23 On the subject of the hostages who were handed over as part of Richard's release arrangements, see Kosto, *Hostages in the Middle Ages*, pp. 171-6.

24 For a summary of the debate, with references, see Trindade, *Berengaria*, pp. 59-60 and 70-6 (who tends towards the view that Richard was homosexual or bisexual); Gillingham, *Richard I*, pp. 263-6, and Gillingham, 'Richard I and Berengaria', pp. 169-71 (who tends towards the view that he was not).

25 The passages are RH, vol. 2, p. 64 and pp. 356-7, respectively.

26 RH, vol. 2, pp. 356-7. For discussion of this episode, see also Gillingham, *Richard I*, pp. 263-4; Gillingham, 'Richard I and Berengaria', pp. 168-9; Trindade, *Berengaria*, pp. 120-4.

27 The text of the charter, with '*regina Berengaria*' as one of the witnesses, may be found on the Epistolae site, at epistolae.ctl.columbia.edu/letter/1326.html.

28 Epistolae, epistolae.ctl.columbia.edu/letter/767.html.

29 For more on this arrangement, see Trindade, *Berengaria*, pp. 146-7.

30 '*Berengaria, Dei gratia quondam humilis Angliae Regina*'; see Epistolae, epistolae.ctl.columbia.edu/letter/764.html.

31 Epistolae, epistolae.ctl.columbia.edu/letter/770.html.

32 AB, pp. 191-2. On this event, see also Carpenter, *Minority of Henry III*, p. 200.

33 Confirmation of the safe-conduct may be found on the Epistolae site, at epistolae.ctl.columbia.edu/letter/778.html; the text of the agreement about dower payments at epistolae.ctl.columbia.edu/letter/781.html.

34 The author of Berengaria's *ODNB* entry notes that Berengaria was 'strikingly generous to the religious orders even by the standards of her day' (Hallam, 'Berengaria [Berengaria of Navarre] (c. 1165-1230)', *ODNB*); her biographer believes that 'Berengaria's popularity was derived from her reputation as a protector of the poor and sick' (Trindade, *Berengaria*, p. 172). The manuscript archive of the abbey of L'Épau is BnF MS Latin 17124; it has been digitised and is freely available at gallica.bnf.fr/ark:/12148/btv1b52512553n/f1.item.

35 '*Dilecta dilectissima consanguinea et fidelis nostra Berengaria regina*'. Both Trindade (*Berengaria*, p. 183) and Mitchell (*Berengaria*, p. 121) quote this precise form of wording, though neither references the exact primary source.

36 The archaeological evidence and identification process is documented in Bouton, 'La reine perdue'; Bouton, 'La reine Bérengère perdue et retrouvée'; Térouane, 'A la quête d'une tombe sans nom'.

37 Quote from the chronicle of Archbishop Rodrigo Jiménez de Rada of Toledo, as translated in Trindade, *Berengaria*, p. 34.

Chapter 7

1 Constance is the subject of a biography written in French: Borgnis Desbordes, *Constance de Bretagne*. A shorter biographical piece in English is Michael Jones, 'Constance, duchess of Brittany (c. 1161-1201)', *ODNB*.

2 For more detail on the Breton succession crisis, see Dunbabin, *France in the Making*, pp. 331-2.

3   For an overview of Henry II's relationship with Brittany before 1166, see Everard, *Brittany and the Angevins*, pp. 34-44.

4   On the betrothal and the consequent rights this gave Henry II over Brittany, see RT, pp. 102-3; Borgnis Desbordes, *Constance de Bretagne*, pp. 86-90.

5   Turner writes of Constance's 'ferocious hostility [...] toward her Plantagenet in-laws' (*Eleanor of Aquitaine*, p. 263).

6   On the governance of Brittany during Constance's minority, see Everard, *Brittany and the Angevins*, pp. 76-92; it is noticeable that this chapter contains not a single mention of Constance. The dates of Geoffrey's visits to the duchy are given in ibid., pp. 95-6.

7   Borgnis Desbordes makes the interesting point that the literature popular at this time in England included many tales based on Breton heroes, so during her childhood Constance may have been able to hear stirring tales from her homeland (*Constance de Bretagne*, pp. 84-5).

8   *Constance*, p. 45 for Geoffrey's charter and pp. 45-6 for Constance's.

9   Constance's biographer believes that she and Geoffrey were 'in perfect accord' in their political goals (Borgnis Desbordes, *Constance de Bretagne*, p. 171, my translation).

10 RH, vol. 2, p. 25 and GW, p. 481, respectively.

11 GW, p. 479. The position of seneschal of France, as we noted in Chapter 1, was not hereditary and could be awarded or rescinded at the king's pleasure.

12 On the circumstances surrounding Geoffrey's death, see RH, vol. 2, p. 56 (who puts forward the tournament explanation); GW, p. 479 and Rigord, pp. 58-9 (both of whom put Geoffrey's death down to illness). For further discussion on Geoffrey's death and its causes, see Hanley, *Two Houses, Two Kingdoms*, pp. 110-11; Everard, *Brittany and the Angevins*, pp. 144-5; Borgnis Desbordes, *Constance de Bretagne*, pp. 205-9.

13 *Constantia, comitis Conani filia, ducissa Britannie, comitissa Richemondie* (*Constance*, p. 39).

14 On the significance of the name, see Favier, *Les Plantagenêts*, p. 536; Warren, *King John*, pp. 81-2; and Borgnis Desbordes, *Constance de Bretagne*, pp. 260-3, who later notes that the choice of Arthur's name indicates that Constance did not, at this point, harbour any ambitions towards the English crown for her son – because if she did, it would have been more sensible to call the baby Henry (ibid., p. 267).

15 On Constance and Ranulf's married life and the lack of evidence for any cohabitation, see Everard, *Brittany and the Angevins*, pp. 157-8.

16 See RH, vol. 2, pp. 164-9 (quote from p. 165).

17 RH, vol. 2, p. 61.

18 Gervase, vol. 1, pp. 336 and 346.

19 RH, vol. 2, pp. 295-6. On the subject of the hostages who were handed over as part of Richard's release arrangements, see Kosto, *Hostages in the Middle Ages*, pp. 171-6.

20 The Pipe Roll for the year that encompassed the end of Henry II's reign and the start of Richard's contains an entry for expenses relating to 'William, son of the duke of Saxony, and the daughter of Geoffrey, count [*sic*] of Brittany' (Pipe Roll PR 35 Henry II–1 Richard I); see also Borgnis Desbordes, *Constance de Bretagne*, p. 307.

21 RH, vol. 2, p. 389. Everard believes that Richard's original summons to Constance was 'a ruse' and that Ranulf captured her 'at Richard's behest' (*Brittany and the Angevins*, p. 160). For further discussion on this incident see Borgnis Desbordes, *Constance de Bretagne*, pp. 325-9 (who deems it 'unthinkable' that Ranulf could have acted without Richard's consent (p. 329)); Gillingham, *Richard I*, pp. 297-8; Bradbury, *Philip Augustus*, pp. 119-20.

22 Both Constance's and Arthur's biographers support this view: see Borgnis Desbordes, *Constance de Bretagne*, pp. 335-7; Michael Jones, 'Arthur, duke of Brittany (1187-1203)', *ODNB*. On Richard's invasion of Brittany, see RH, vol. 2, p. 389; Borgnis Desbordes, *Constance de Bretagne*, pp. 361-88.

23 The first two charters to be issued in Arthur's name, rather than Constance's, date from August 1196; in one of them he promises his Breton supporters that he will not make peace with King Richard without including them (*Constance*, p. 117).

24 See the itinerary based on charter evidence: *Constance*, p. 43.

25 On the charters, see, for example, the formulation *cum assensu et bona voluntate Arturi filii mei*, 'with the assent and goodwill of my son Arthur' (*Constance*, p. 67); and also similar wording in other charters in ibid., pp. 64, 66, 72 and 73.

26 RH, vol. 2, p. 427. See also Jones, 'Arthur, duke of Brittany', *ODNB*; Andrews, *Lost Heirs*, p. 65.

27 On Richard's death, see Rigord, pp. 145-6; RH, vol. 2, pp. 452-4.

28 One chronicler noted that 'when the king was now in despair of surviving, he devised to his brother John the kingdom of England and all his other territories' (RH, vol. 2, p. 453), though others do not mention it.

29 RH, vol. 2, p. 456.

30 RW, vol. 2, p. 180.

31 RH, vol. 2, pp. 462-3; RW, vol. 2, pp. 182-3.

32 For discussion on the importance of coronations at this time, see Andrews, *Lost Heirs*, p. 8; Hanley, *Louis*, pp. 243-6.

33 Turner notes that 'Eleanor found her grandson, Arthur of Brittany, poisoned by the anti-Plantagenet sentiments of his Breton mother Constance and his protector Philip II, unacceptable as Richard's heir', and adds that 'Constance's fury against the Angevin line had blinded

her to the advantage that an upbringing at Richard's court would have given her son' (*Eleanor of Aquitaine*, p. 274).

34 The complete text of the treaty may be found in Rigord, pp. 148–53.

35 RH, vol. 2, p. 481.

36 The circumstances of Constance's remarriage are discussed by Borgnis Desbordes, who tends towards some complex political explanations (*Constance de Bretagne*, pp. 418–22), and by Jones, who says that the union with Guy was 'a move probably designed to widen her political contacts, but which also brought her considerable personal happiness' ('Constance, duchess of Brittany', *ODNB*). A brief biographical sketch of Guy appears in *Constance*, pp. 134–6.

37 See the itinerary in *Constance*, p. 44.

38 See Chaillou, 'On Constance of Brittany's Family'. The confusion appears to have been caused by a line in a later chronicle in which it is not clear whether a person named Margaret, connected to Brittany, is the *sister* or the *sister-in-law* of Peter de Dreux, who married Alix, Constance's elder daughter by Guy. Even if this Margaret was Peter's sister-in-law, she might have been the daughter either of Constance and Guy, or of Guy by his second marriage. See the discussion at the Foundation for Medieval Genealogy, at fmg.ac/Projects/MedLands/BRITTANY.htm#MargueriteChesterMGeoffroyIRohan.

39 For a discussion on Constance's cause of death, see Borgnis Desbordes, *Constance de Bretagne*, pp. 436–8 and n. 200.

40 The circumstances of Arthur's disappearance and death are explored more fully in Andrews, *Lost Heirs*, pp. 71–3.

Chapter 8

1 Isabelle of Gloucester has historically not been the subject of much scholarly attention, but happily this is being remedied by a number of recent and forthcoming works. See Spong, 'Isabella of Gloucester and Isabella of Angoulême'; Spong, 'Isabella of Gloucester: Heiress, Lord, Forgotten Consort'; Vincent, 'A Queen in Rebel London'; Robert B. Patterson, 'Isabella, *suo jure* countess of Gloucester (c. 1160–1217)', *ODNB*; Louise J. Wilkinson, 'Isabella, first wife of King John (d. 1217)' on the Magna Carta Project website, at magnacarta800th.com/schools/biographies/women-of-magna-carta/isabella-of-gloucester/.

2 RW, vol. 2, p. 34 (who notes specifically that William named 'the king's son John' as his heir, not 'his daughter Isabelle and her husband' or any similar wording); *Gloucester*, p. 5.

3 RT, p. 148. The Pipe Rolls indicate that Henry received the income from Isabelle's lands: see for example PR 30 Henry II.

4 On Isabelle's place in Eleanor's household, see Pipe Roll PR 1 Richard I; Turner, *Eleanor of Aquitaine*, p. 260. On the wedding and Richard being the driving force behind it, see RW, vol. 2, pp. 78–9; RH, vol. 2, p. 115.

5   It is around this time that several of John's many illegitimate children were born. The summary of evidence about them by the Foundation for Medieval Genealogy is children nos 6-20 under his entry, at fmg.ac/Projects/MedLands/ENGLAND,%20Kings%201066-1603. htm#JohnKingdied1216A.

6   RW, vol. 2, p. 87; *GRH*, vol. 2, p. 78. See also Warren, *King John*, p. 66.

7   On John's abortive plan to ally himself with Philip at this stage, see RD, pp. 60-1 (who notes that it was Eleanor of Aquitaine who talked him out of it); *GRH*, vol. 2, pp. 236-7. See also Church, *King John*, p. 51; Turner, *Eleanor of Aquitaine*, p. 268; Hanley, *Two Houses, Two Kingdoms*, pp. 138-9.

8   RH, vol. 2, p. 483. The same error occurs in RW, vol. 2, p. 188, but as Roger of Wendover (who wrote slightly later) was relying on Roger of Howden for this part of his text, this is not surprising.

9   This treaty was discussed in Chapters 3 and 7. Its Clause 6 confirms that 'We [John] have given to the king of France everything that the count of Évreux possesses' (Rigord, p. 150). See also *Gloucester*, p. 6.

10 For evidence of the gifts, see Pipe Roll PR 4 John. On the possibility of Isabelle and Isabella living in the same household, see PR 7 John; PR 9 John; and Vincent, 'Isabella of Angoulême', pp. 196-7. Morris notes that 'the expenses of the two Isabellas were recorded as if they were staying together under the same roof' (*King John*, p. 137).

11 See Warren, *King John*, pp. 182-3; Hanley, *Louis*, p. 62. Morris writes of John 'forcing' Geoffrey to marry Isabelle and adds that 'never had John's exploitation of his powers of lordship been so brazen or so cynical' (*King John*, pp. 242-3).

12 There are, for example, charters that contain both names; see *Gloucester*, pp. 32 (granted by Isabelle, with the consent of Geoffrey), 36 (granted by Geoffrey, with the consent of Isabelle) and numerous other examples.

13 *Gloucester*, p. 8. A full list of these barons may be found on the Magna Carta Project website, at magnacarta800th.com/schools/biographies/the-25-barons-of-magna-carta/. Isabelle's own presence in London with the other rebel barons is attested by two charters that she issued from there in 1216 (see Vincent, 'A Queen in Rebel London', p. 39).

14 AB, p. 157; see also Hanley, *Louis*, p. 76.

15 The phrase *in libera viduitate mea* ('in my free widowhood') appears frequently in Isabelle's charters during this time; see all those listed on pp. 131-9 in *Gloucester*. For an example of *in libera viduitate mea et in ligia potestate mea* ('in my free widowhood and in my full power'), see ibid., p. 81.

16 The primary sources that mention Isabelle's death are summarised by the Foundation for Medieval Genealogy, and may be found in her sub-entry under her father's; see '(4) Isabel', at fmg.ac/Projects/

MedLands/ENGLISH%20NOBILITY%20MEDIEVAL.htm#WilliamFitz
Robertdied1183A.

17   Isabella of Angoulême has been the subject of more scholarly attention
     than Isabelle of Gloucester. Recent and forthcoming works include
     Spong, 'Isabella of Gloucester and Isabella of Angoulême'; Spong,
     'Isabella of Angoulême: The Vanishing Queen'; Nicholas Vincent,
     'Isabella [Isabella of Angoulême], *suo jure* countess of Angoulême (c.
     1188–1246)', *ODNB*; Vincent, 'Isabella of Angoulême: John's Jezebel';
     Richardson, 'The Marriage and Coronation of Isabella of Angoulême';
     Richardson, 'King John and Isabelle of Angoulême'; Louise J. Wilkinson,
     'Isabella of Angoulême, wife of King John' on the Magna Carta Project
     website, at magnacarta800th.com/schools/biographies/women-
     of-magna-carta/isabella-of-angouleme-wife-of-king-john/; Wilkinson,
     'Maternal Abandonment and Surrogate Caregivers'.
18   For more discussion on Isabella's date of birth, see Vincent, 'Isabella of
     Angoulême', pp. 174–5 (who notes that 'her officially declared age [...]
     was regarded with a certain degree of scepticism' by contemporaries);
     Morris, *King John*, pp. 119–21.
19   RH, vol. 2, p. 483.
20   For more discussion on John's motives for marrying Isabella, see
     Vincent, 'Isabella of Angoulême'; Church, *King John*, pp. 82–92; Morris,
     King John, pp. 119–21; Warren, *King John*, pp. 67–9. Turner notes that
     'Eleanor [of Aquitaine] had no love for the Lusignan clan, and her
     son's rash marriage that blocked a major expansion of their power
     must have pleased her' (*Eleanor of Aquitaine*, pp. 290–1).
21   On the marriage, see RH, vol. 2, p. 483; RW, vol. 2, pp. 187–8 (who
     claims that Isabella was formerly Hugh's actual wife rather than merely
     his betrothed); AB, p. 105 ('the king took her and stole her from the
     count'). On the coronation, see RH, vol. 2, p. 501; RW, vol. 2, p. 193.
22   For more on the Lusignans' appeal and the decision of Philip and his
     council of barons to deprive John of his lands, see Bradbury, *Philip
     Augustus*, pp. 135–6 and 140–3; Warren, *King John*, pp. 73–6.
23   'Was Isabella treated in a suitably royal fashion by her husband,
     King John?' asks Vincent ('Isabella of Angoulême', p. 184). 'The answer
     must be a resounding "no". What evidence we have suggests that the
     financial and other practical provisions made for her during John's
     lifetime were modest, even downright mean.'
24   RW, vol. 2, p. 206.
25   The York reference is RH, vol. 2, p. 518. See earlier in this chapter for
     discussion of the royal household accounts.
26   RW, vol. 2, pp. 207 and 214 respectively.
27   AB, pp. 115 and 116 respectively.
28   For more on the engagements at La-Roche-aux-Moines and Bouvines,
     see Hanley, *Louis*, pp. 54–9.

29 AB, p. 148.
30 RW, vol. 2, p. 363.
31 For more on Terric and the records that mention him, see Vincent, 'Isabella of Angoulême', pp. 199–200.
32 AB, p. 189.
33 The full letter may be found on the Epistolae site, at epistolae.ctl. columbia.edu/letter/457.html.
34 The full letter may be found on the Epistolae site, at epistolae.ctl. columbia.edu/letter/725.html.
35 More details on this campaign may be found in MP, vol. 1, pp. 394–6, 408–10 and 414–26; Vincent, 'Isabella of Angoulême', pp. 210–13; Hanley, *Two Houses, Two Kingdoms*, pp. 294–6.
36 MP, vol. 1, p. 454.
37 This subject is discussed in Wilkinson, 'Maternal Abandonment'; Woodacre, 'Between Regencies'.

BIBLIOGRAPHY

Primary sources and encyclopaedias

AB: Anonymous of Béthune, *History of the Dukes of Normandy and the Kings of England*, trans. Janet Shirley, with historical notes by Paul Webster (Oxford: Routledge, 2021)

AC: Andreas Capellanus, *The Art of Courtly Love*, trans. John J. Parry (New York: Columbia University Press, 1941)

Ambroise: *The History of the Holy War: Ambroise's Estoire de la Guerre Sainte*, trans. Marianne Ailes, introduction and notes by Marianne Ailes and Malcolm Barber (Woodbridge: Boydell, 2011; orig. 2003)

BB: *The Poems of the Troubadour Bertran de Born*, ed. and trans. William D. Paden, Tilde Sankovitch and Patricia H. Stäblein (Berkeley: University of California Press, 1986)

Becket: *The Life and Death of Thomas Becket, Chancellor of England and Archbishop of Canterbury, Based on the Account of William FitzStephen His Clerk, with Additions from Other Contemporary Sources*, trans. George Greenaway (London: Folio Society, 1961)

Beha ed-Din: Beha ed-Din, *What Befell Sultan Yusuf*, trans. C.W. Wilson (London: Palestine Pilgrims Text Society, 1897)

Calendar: *Calendar of Documents Preserved in France, Illustrative of the History of Great Britain and Ireland. Volume 1: AD 918-1206*, ed. Horace Round (London: HMSO, 1899)

CL: *Chronica latina regum Castellae*, in *Chronica Hispana Saeculi XIII*, ed. Luis Charlo Brea, Juan A. Estévez Sola, Rocío Carande Herrero (Turnhout: Brepols, 1997)

Constance: *The Charters of Duchess Constance of Brittany and Her Family, 1171-1221*, ed. Judith Everard and Michael Jones (Woodbridge: Boydell, 1999)

CT: Chrétien de Troyes, *Arthurian Romances*, trans. William W. Kibler and Carleton W. Carroll (London: Penguin Classics, 1991)

Epistolae: Epistolae: Medieval Women's Latin Letters, online, available at epistolae.ctl.columbia.edu/

Eracles: 'The Old French Continuation of William of Tyre [Lyon *Eracles*]', in *The Conquest of Jerusalem and the Third Crusade: Sources in Translation*, trans. Peter W. Edbury (Aldershot: Ashgate, 1998), pp. 11–145

GC: Les grandes chroniques de France, tome sixième, Louis VII le Jeune et Philippe II Auguste, ed. Jules Viard (Paris: Honoré Champion, 1930)

Gervase: Gervase of Canterbury, *The Historical Works of Gervase of Canterbury*, ed. W. Stubbs, 2 vols (London: Rolls Series, 1879–80)

Gloucester: Earldom of Gloucester Charters, ed. Robert B. Patterson (Oxford: Clarendon, 1974)

GRH: Gesta regis Henrici secundi Benedicti abbatis: The Chronicle of the Reigns of Henry II and Richard I, AD 1169-1192, ed. W. Stubbs, 2 vols (London: Rolls Series, 1867)

GS: Gesta Stephani, ed. and trans. K.R. Potter, with notes and introduction by R.H.C. Davis (Oxford: Clarendon, 1976)

GW: Gerald of Wales, *Instruction for a Ruler: De Principis Instructione*, ed. and trans. Robert Bartlett (Oxford: Clarendon, 2018)

HWM: History of William Marshal, ed. and trans. A.J. Holden, S. Gregory and D. Crouch, 3 vols (London: Anglo-Norman Text Society, 2002–06)

IP: *The Chronicle of the Third Crusade: The Itinerarium Peregrinorum et Gesta Regis Ricardi*, trans. Helen J. Nicholson (London and New York: Routledge, 2001; orig. 1997)

JF: Jordan Fantosme's Chronicle, ed. and trans. R.C. Johnston (Oxford: Clarendon Press, 1981; facsimile repr. Edinburgh: Birlinn, 2018)

JS: The Historia Pontificalis of John of Salisbury, ed. and trans. Marjorie Chibnall, Nelson Medieval Texts (London: Nelson & Sons, 1956)

LCH: Letters and Charters of Henry II, ed. Nicholas Vincent, 7 vols (Oxford: Oxford University Press, 2020)

MP: Matthew Paris, *Matthew Paris's English History*, trans. J.A. Giles, 3 vols (London: Henry G. Bohn, 1852–54)

Nangis: William of Nangis, *Chronique de Guillaume de Nangis*, ed. F. Guizot (Paris: Brière, 1825)

ODNB: Oxford Dictionary of National Biography, online, available at oxforddnb.com

OEMW: Oxford Encyclopaedia of Medieval Warfare and Military Technology, ed. Clifford J. Rogers, 3 vols (New York: Oxford University Press, 2010)

PCG: Primera Crónica General: Estoria de España, ed. Ramón Menéndez Pidal (Madrid: Bailly-Baillière, 1906)

PR: *The Pipe Rolls of Henry II*, 38 vols (London: Pipe Roll Society, 1884-1925). Pipe rolls each cover one regnal year, so they are referenced in the text as e.g. PR 22 Henry II (Pipe roll for the twenty-second year of the reign of Henry II)

RD: Richard of Devizes, *The Chronicle of Richard of Devizes*, ed. and trans. John T. Appleby (London: Nelson, 1963)

RH: Roger of Howden, *The Annals of Roger of Hoveden*, trans. Henry T. Riley, 2 vols (London: Henry Bohn, 1853; facsimile repr. Felinfach: Llanerch, 1997)

Rigord: Rigord, 'Vie de Philippe Auguste', ed. F. Guizot, in *Collection des Mémoires relatifs à l'histoire de France*, vol. 11 (Paris: Brière, 1825), pp. 9–180

Rolandslied: Conrad of Regensburg, *Das Rolandslied*, ed. Karl Bartsch (Leipzig: Brockhaus, 1874)

RT: Robert de Torigni, *The Chronicles of Robert de Monte*, trans. Joseph Stevenson (London: Seeleys, 1856; facsimile repr. Felinfach: Llanerch, 1991)

RW: Roger of Wendover, *Roger of Wendover's Flowers of History*, trans. J.A. Giles, 2 vols (London: Henry G. Bohn, 1849; facsimile repr. Felinfach: Llanerch, 1995-56)

UHL: *Die Urkunden Heinrichs des Löwen Herzog von Sachsen und Bayern*, ed. Karl Jordan (Stuttgart: Hiersemann, 1941-49)

WB: William the Breton, 'Vie de Philippe Auguste', ed. F. Guizot, in *Collection des Mémoires relatifs à l'histoire de France*, vol. 11 (Paris: Brière, 1825), pp. 181-354

WN: William of Newburgh, *The History of English Affairs*, ed. and trans. P.G. Walsh and M.J. Kennedy, 2 vols (Warminster: Aris & Phillips, 1988)

WP: William of Puylaurens, *The Chronicle of William of Puylaurens: The Albigensian Crusade and Its Aftermath*, trans. W.A. Sibley and M.D. Sibley (Woodbridge: Boydell, 2003)

Secondary sources

Akehurst, F.R.P., and Judith M. Davis (eds), *A Handbook of the Troubadours* (Berkeley: University of California Press, 1995)

Alio, Jacqueline, *Sicily's Queens 1061-1266: The Countesses and Queens of the Norman-Swabian Era* (New York: Trinacria Editions, 2020)

Andrews, J.F., *Lost Heirs of the Medieval Crown* (Barnsley: Pen & Sword, 2019)

Asbridge, Thomas, *The Greatest Knight: The Remarkable Life of William Marshal, the Power behind Five English Thrones* (London: Simon & Schuster, 2015)

Aurell, Martin, *L'Empire des Plantagenêt* (Paris: Tempus, 2017; orig. 2004)

Baldwin, John W., *Aristocratic Life in Medieval France* (Baltimore and London: Johns Hopkins University Press, 2000)

----- *The Government of Philip Augustus: Foundations of French Royal Power in the Middle Ages* (Berkeley: University of California Press, 1986)

----- *Paris, 1200* (Stanford: Stanford University Press, 2010; orig. Paris: Éditions Flammarion, 2006)

Barber, Richard, *Henry II: A Prince among Princes* (London: Allen Lane, 2015)

----- *Henry Plantagenet* (Woodbridge: Boydell, 2001; orig. 1964)

Barber, Richard, and Juliet Barker, *Tournaments* (Woodbridge: Boydell, 1989)

Barker, Juliet, *The Tournament in England 1100-1400* (Woodbridge: Boydell, 1982)

Barlow, Frank, *The Feudal Kingdom of England 1042-1216*, 5th rev. ed. (Harlow: Longman, 1999; orig. 1955)

----- *Thomas Becket* (Berkeley: University of California Press, 1986)

Bartlett, Robert, *Blood Royal: Dynastic Politics in Medieval Europe* (Cambridge: Cambridge University Press, 2020)

----- *England under the Norman and Angevin Kings, 1075-1225* (Oxford: Oxford University Press, 2000)

Bassett, Hayley, 'An Instrument of Diplomacy? The Curious Case of Princess Alice of France', in *Queens in Waiting: Potential and Prospective Queens*, ed. Sarah Betts and Chloe McKenzie (Basingstoke: Palgrave Macmillan, forthcoming)

Bates, David, and Anne Curry (eds), *England and Normandy in the Middle Ages* (London: Hambledon, 1994)

Beem, Charles, *The Lioness Roared: The Problem of Female Rule in English History* (New York: Palgrave Macmillan, 2006)

Benham, Jenny, *Peacemaking in the Middle Ages: Principles and Practice* (Manchester: Manchester University Press, 2007)

Bennett, Judith, *Medieval Women in Modern Perspective* (Washington, DC: American Historical Association, 2000)

Bennett, Matthew< and Katherine Weikert (eds), *Medieval Hostageship c. 700-c. 1500: Hostage, Captive, Prisoner of War, Guarantee, Peacemaker* (Oxford and New York: Routledge, 2016)

Berend, Nora, Przemysław Urbańczyk and Przemysław Wiszewski, *Central Europe in the High Middle Ages: Bohemia, Hungary and Poland, c. 900-c. 1300* (Cambridge: Cambridge University Press, 2013)

Bianchini, Janna, *The Queen's Hand: Power and Authority in the Reign of Berenguela of Castile* (Philadelphia: University of Pennsylvania Press, 2012)

Blythe, James M., 'Women in the Military: Scholastic Arguments and Medieval Images of Female Warriors', *History of Political Thought*, 22 (2001), pp. 242-69

Boase, Roger, *The Origin and Meaning of Courtly Love: A Critical Study of European Scholarship* (Manchester: Manchester University Press, 1977)

Borgnis Desbordes, Eric, *Constance de Bretagne (1161-1201), une duchesse face à Richard Coeur de Lion et Jean sans Terre* (Fouesnant, Brittany: Yoran Embanner, 2018)

Bouton, André, 'La reine Bérangère perdue et retrouvée', *Vie Mancelle*, 100 (1969), pp. 5-8

----- 'La reine perdue', *Vie Mancelle*, 41 (1962), pp. 8-10

Bowie, Colette, *The Daughters of Henry II and Eleanor of Aquitaine* (Turnhout: Brepols, 2014)

----- 'Matilda, Duchess of Saxony (1168-89) and the Cult of Thomas Becket: A Legacy of Appropriation', in *The Cult of St Thomas Becket in the Plantagenet World c. 1170-c. 1220*, ed. Paul Webster and Marie-Pierre Gelin (Woodbridge: Boydell, 2016), pp. 113-32

----- 'Shifting Patterns in Angevin Marriage Policies: The Political Motivations for Joanna Plantagenet's Marriages to William II of Sicily and Raymond VI of Toulouse', in *Les stratégies matrimoniales dans l'aristocratie (Xe-XIIIe siècles)*, ed. Martin Aurell (Turnhout: Brepols, 2013), pp. 155-67

----- 'To Have and Have Not: The Dower of Joanna Plantagenet, Queen of Sicily (1177-1189)', in *Queenship in the Mediterranean: Negotiating the Role of the Queen in the Medieval and Early Modern Eras*, ed. Elena Woodacre (London: Palgrave Macmillan, 2013), pp. 27-50

Bradbury, Jim, *The Capetians: Kings of France 987-1328* (London: Continuum, 2007)

----- *Philip Augustus* (London and New York: Longman, 1998)

Burnett, Charles, Alessandra Foscati and Constanza Gislon Dopfel (eds), *Pregnancy and Childbirth in the Premodern World: European and Middle Eastern Cultures, from Late Antiquity to the Renaissance* (Turnhout: Brepols, 2019)

Carpenter, David, *Magna Carta* (London: Penguin Classics, 2015)

----- *The Minority of Henry III* (London: Methuen, 1990)

Cassagnes-Brouquet, Sophie, *Chevaleresses: Une chevalerie au féminin* (Paris: Perrin, 2013)

Castor, Helen, *She-Wolves: The Women Who Ruled England before Elizabeth* (London: Faber & Faber, 2010)

Cerda, José Manuel, 'Leonor Plantagenet and the Cult of Thomas Becket in Castile', in *The Cult of St Thomas Becket in the Plantagenet World c. 1170-c. 1220*, ed. Paul Webster and Marie-Pierre Gelin (Woodbridge: Boydell, 2016), pp. 133-46

----- 'The Marriage of Alfonso VIII of Castile and Leonor Plantagenet: The First Bond between Spain and England in the Middle Ages', in *Les stratégies matrimoniales dans l'aristocratie (Xe-XIIIe siècles)*, ed. Martin Aurell (Turnhout: Brepols, 2013), pp. 143-54

Chaillou, Léa, 'On Constance of Brittany's Family', *Foundations*, 9 (2017), pp. 35-46

Chamberlin, E.R., *Life in Medieval France* (London: Batsford, 1967)

Cheney, Christopher, *Pope Innocent III and England* (Stuttgart: Hiersemann, 1976)

Church, S.D., 'The Date and Place of King John's Birth Together with a Codicil on His Name', *Notes and Queries*, 67 (2020), pp. 315-23

Church, Stephen, *King John: England, Magna Carta and the Making of a Tyrant* (Basingstoke: Macmillan, 2015)

Clanchy, M.T., *England and Its Rulers, 1066-1272* (London: Wiley-Blackwell, 1983)

Conklin, George, 'Ingeborg of Denmark, Queen of France, 1193-1223', in *Queens and Queenship in Medieval Europe*, ed. Anne J. Duggan (Woodbridge: Boydell, 1997), pp. 39-52

Coss, Peter, *The Lady in Medieval England 1000-1500* (Stroud: Sutton, 1998)

Danziger, Danny, and John Gillingham, *1215: The Year of Magna Carta* (London: Hodder, 2003)

Déjean, Jean-Luc, *Les comtes de Toulouse, 1050-1250* (Paris: Fayard, 1988; orig. 1979)

Del Campo, Luis, 'La estatura de Sancho el Fuerte', *Principe de Viana*, 48-9 (1952), pp. 481-94

Delorme, Philippe, *Blanche de Castille*, Histoire des Reines de France (Paris: Pygmalion, 2002)

Diggelmann, Lindsay, 'Marriage as a Tactical Response: Henry II and the Royal Wedding of 1160', *English Historical Review*, 119 (2004), pp. 954-64

Duby, Georges, *The Chivalrous Society*, trans. Cynthia Postan (London: Arnold, 1977)

----- *France in the Middle Ages 987-1460*, trans. Juliet Vale (Oxford: Blackwell, 1994)

----- 'Women and Power', in *Cultures of Power: Lordship, Status and Process in Twelfth-Century Europe*, ed. Thomas N. Bisson (Philadelphia: University of Pennsylvania Press, 1995), pp. 69-85

Duggan, Anne (ed.), *Queens and Queenship in Medieval Europe* (Woodbridge: Boydell, 1997)

Dunbabin, Jean, *France in the Making, 843-1180*, 2nd ed. (Oxford: Oxford University Press, 2000; orig. 1985)

Dyer, Christopher, *Making a Living in the Middle Ages: The People of Britain 850-1520* (New Haven and London: Yale University Press, 2009; orig. 2002)

Edgington, Susan, and Sarah Lambert (eds), *Gendering the Crusades* (Cardiff: University of Wales Press, 2001)

Engel, Pál, *The Realm of St Stephen: A History of Medieval Hungary, 895-1526* (London: I.B. Tauris, 2001)

Erler, Mary and Maryanne Kowaleski (eds), *Women and Power in the Middle Ages* (Athens, GA: University of Georgia Press, 1988)

Everard, Judith, *Brittany and the Angevins: Province and Empire, 1158-1203* (Cambridge: Cambridge University Press, 2000)

Evergates, Theodore, *The Aristocracy in the County of Champagne, 1100-1300* (Philadelphia: University of Pennsylvania Press, 2007)

----- *Marie of France: Countess of Champagne, 1145-1198* (Philadelphia: University of Pennsylvania Press, 2019)

Evergates, Theodore (ed.), *Aristocratic Women in Medieval France* (Philadelphia: University of Pennsylvania Press, 1999)

Favier, Jean, *Les Plantagenêts: Origines et destin d'un empire XIe-XIVe siècles* (Paris: Fayard, 2015; orig. 2004)

Fawtier, R., *The Capetian Kings of France: Monarchy and Nation 987-1328* (Basingstoke: Macmillan, 1960)

Fleiner, Carey, and Elena Woodacre (eds), *Virtuous or Villainess? The Image of the Royal Mother from the Early Medieval to the Early Modern Era* (New York: Palgrave Macmillan, 2016)

Flori, Jean, *Eleanor of Aquitaine: Queen and Rebel*, trans. Olive Classe (Edinburgh: Edinburgh University Press, 2007)

Foundation for Medieval Genealogy, online, at fmg.ac/

Fuhrmann, Horst, *Germany in the High Middle Ages c. 1050-1200*, trans. Timothy Reuter (Cambridge: Cambridge University Press, 1986)

Gaunt, Simon, and Sarah Kay (eds), *The Troubadours: An Introduction* (Cambridge: Cambridge University Press, 1999)

Gillingham, John, *The Angevin Empire*, 2nd ed. (London: Bloomsbury, 2001)

----- 'Love, Marriage and Politics in the Twelfth Century', *Forum for Modern Language Studies*, 25 (1989), pp. 292-303

----- *Richard I* (New Haven and London: Yale University Press, 1999)

----- 'Richard I and Berengaria of Navarre', *Bulletin of the Institute of Historical Research*, 53 (1980), pp. 157-73

Given-Wilson, Chris, and Alice Curteis, *The Royal Bastards of Medieval England* (London: Routledge & Kegan Paul, 1984)

Grant, Lindy, *Blanche of Castile: Queen of France* (New Haven and London: Yale University Press, 2016)

Guy, John, *Thomas Becket: Warrior, Priest, Rebel, Victim* (London: Viking, 2012)

Györffy, G., 'Thomas à Becket and Hungary', *Hungarian Studies in English*, 4 (1969), pp. 45-52

Hallam, Elizabeth M., and Judith Everard, *Capetian France 987-1328*, 2nd ed. (Harlow: Pearson, 2001; orig. London: Longman, 1980)

Hamilton, B., 'Women in the Crusader States: The Queens of Jerusalem, 1100-1190', in *Medieval Women*, ed. Derek Baker (Oxford: Studies in Church History, Subsidia I, 1978), pp. 143-74

Hanley, Catherine, *Louis: The French Prince Who Invaded England* (New Haven and London: Yale University Press, 2016)

----- *Matilda: Empress, Queen, Warrior* (New Haven and London: Yale University Press, 2019)

----- *Two Houses, Two Kingdoms: A History of France and England, 1100-1300* (New Haven and London: Yale University Press, forthcoming)

----- *War and Combat 1150-1270: The Evidence from Old French Literature* (Woodbridge: D.S. Brewer, 2003)

Hodgson, Natasha R., *Women, Crusading and the Holy Land in Historical Narrative* (Woodbridge: Boydell, 2007)

Holt, J.C., 'Aliénor d'Aquitaine, Jean sans Terre et la succession de 1199', *Cahiers de Civilisation Médiévale*, 29 (1986), pp. 95-9

----- *Magna Carta*, 2nd ed. (Cambridge: Cambridge University Press, 1992; orig. 1965)

Hornaday, Aline, 'A Capetian Queen as Street Demonstrator: Isabelle of Hainaut', in *Capetian Women*, ed. Kathleen Nolan (New York and Basingstoke: Palgrave Macmillan, 2003), pp. 77-97

Hosler, John D., *The Siege of Acre, 1189-1191: Saladin, Richard the Lionheart, and the Battle That Decided the Third Crusade* (New Haven and London: Yale University Press, 2018)

Jasperse, Jitske, 'Matilda, Leonor and Joanna: the Plantagenet sisters and the display of dynastic connections through material culture', *Journal of Medieval History*, 43 (2017), pp. 523-47

----- *Medieval Women, Material Culture, and Power: Matilda Plantagenet and Her Sisters* (Amsterdam: Arc Humanities Press, 2020)

----- 'With This Ring: Forming Plantagenet Family Ties', in *Relations of Power: Women's Networks in the Middle Ages*, ed. Emma O. Bérat, Rebecca Hardie and Irina Dumitrescu (Bonn: Bonn University Press, 2021), pp. 67-84

Johns, Susan M., *Noblewomen, Aristocracy and Power in the Twelfth-Century Anglo-Norman Realm* (Manchester: Manchester University Press, 2003)

Jordan, Karl, *Henry the Lion: A Biography*, trans. P.S. Falla (Oxford: Clarendon Press, 1986)

Kelly, Amy, *Eleanor of Aquitaine and the Four Kings* (Cambridge, MA: Harvard University Press, 1950)

Kersey, Shirley, 'Medieval Education of Girls and Women', *Educational Horizons*, 58 (1980), pp. 188-92

Kibler, William W. (ed.), *Eleanor of Aquitaine: Patron and Politician* (Austin: University of Texas Press, 1976)

Kosto, Adam J., *Hostages in the Middle Ages* (Oxford: Oxford University Press, 2012)

Labande, Edmond-René, 'Les filles d'Aliénor d'Aquitaine: Étude comparative', *Cahiers de Civilisation Médiévale*, 29 (1986), pp. 104-22

Lachaud, Frédérique, *Jean sans Terre* (Paris: Perrin, 2018)

Leyser, Henrietta, *Medieval Women: A Social History of Women in England 450-1500* (London: Weidenfeld & Nicolson, 1995)

Loud, G.A., 'The Kingdom of Sicily and the Kingdom of England, 1066–1266', *History*, 88 (2003), pp. 540–67

Lyon, Ann, 'The Place of Women in European Royal Succession in the Middle Ages', *Liverpool Law Review*, 27 (2006), pp. 361–93

Magna Carta Project, online, at magnacarta.cmp.uea.ac.uk/

Martindale, Jane, 'Eleanor of Aquitaine: The Last Years', in *King John: New Interpretations*, ed. S.D. Church (Woodbridge: Boydell, 1999), pp. 137–64

Matthew, Donald, *The Norman Kingdom of Sicily* (Cambridge: Cambridge University Press, 1992)

McCash, June Hall Martin, 'Marie de Champagne and Eleanor of Aquitaine: A Relationship Reexamined', *Speculum*, 54 (1979), pp. 698–711

McDougall, Sara, *Royal Bastards: The Birth of Illegitimacy, 800–1230* (Oxford: Oxford University Press, 2017)

McGlynn, Sean, *Blood Cries Afar: The Forgotten Invasion of England 1216* (Stroud: Spellmount, 2011)

----- *Kill Them All: Cathars and Carnage in the Albigensian Crusade* (Stroud: The History Press, 2015)

McLaughlin, Megan, 'The Woman Warrior: Gender, Warfare and Society in Medieval Europe', *Women's Studies*, 17 (1990), pp. 193–209

Meade, Marion, *Eleanor of Aquitaine: A Biography* (London: Phoenix, 2002; orig. 1977)

Menant, François, Hervé Martin, Bernard Merdrignac and Monique Chauvin, *Les Capétiens, 987–1326* (Paris: Tempus, 2018; orig. 2008)

Mendola, Louis, *The Kingdom of Sicily 1130–1860* (New York: Trinacria Editions, 2015)

Mitchell, Mairin, *Berengaria: Enigmatic Queen of England* (Burwash: A. Wright, 1986)

Morris, Marc, *King John: Treachery, Tyranny and the Road to Magna Carta* (London: Hutchinson, 2015)

Norton, Elizabeth, *England's Queens: The Biography* (Stroud: Amberley, 2012)

O'Callaghan, Joseph F., *Reconquest and Crusade in Medieval Spain* (Philadelphia: University of Pennsylvania Press, 2003)

Oldenbourg, Zoé, *Massacre at Montségur*, trans. Peter Green (London: Phoenix, 1998; orig. Weidenfeld & Nicolson, 1961)

Orme, Nicholas, *From Childhood to Chivalry: The Education of the English Kings and Aristocracy 1066–1530* (London: Methuen, 1984)

----- *Medieval Children* (New Haven and London: Yale University Press, 2001)

Owen, D.D.R., *Eleanor of Aquitaine: Queen and Legend* (London: Wiley, 1996)

Pangonis, Katherine, *Queens of Jerusalem: The Women Who Dared to Rule* (London: Weidenfeld & Nicolson, 2021)

Papin, Yves D., *Chronologie du moyen âge* (Paris: Editions Jean-Paul Gisserot, 2001)

Pegg, Mark Gregory, *A Most Holy War: The Albigensian Crusade and the Battle for Christendom* (Oxford: Oxford University Press, 2008)

Poulet, André, 'Capetian Women and the Regency: The Genesis of a Vocation', in *Medieval Queenship*, ed. John Carmi Parsons (Stroud: Sutton, 1998; orig. 1994), pp. 93–116

Powicke, F.M., *The Loss of Normandy (1189-1204): Studies in the History of the Angevin Empire* (Manchester: Manchester University Press, 1913)

----- *The Thirteenth Century*, 2nd ed. (Oxford: Oxford University Press, 1962)

Richardson, H.G., 'King John and Isabelle of Angoulême', *English Historical Review*, 65 (1950), pp. 360–71

----- 'The Marriage and Coronation of Isabella of Angoulême', *English Historical Review*, 61 (1946), pp. 289–314

Roquebert, Michel, *Histoire des Cathares* (Paris: Perrin, 2002)

Sassier, Yves, *Louis VII* (Paris: Fayard, 1991)

Saul, Nigel, *A Companion to Medieval England 1066-1485*, 3rd ed. (Stroud: Tempus, 2005; orig. 1983)

Seabourne, Gwen, *Imprisoning Medieval Women: The Non-Judicial Confinement and Abduction of Women in England, c. 1170-1509* (Farnham: Ashgate, 2011)

Searle, E., 'Women and the Legitimization of Succession of the Norman Conquest', *Anglo-Norman Studies*, 3 (1980), pp. 159–70

Shadis, Miriam, *Berenguela of Castile (1180-1246) and Political Women of the High Middle Ages* (New York: Palgrave Macmillan, 2009)

----- 'Piety, Politics and Power: The Patronage of Leonor of England and Her Daughters Berenguela of León and Blanche of Castile', in *The Cultural Patronage of Medieval Women*, ed. June Hall McCash (Athens, GA: University of Georgia Press, 1996), pp. 202–27

Shadis, Miriam, and Constance Hoffman Berman, 'A Taste of the Feast: Reconsidering Eleanor of Aquitaine's Female Descendants', in *Eleanor of Aquitaine: Lord and Lady*, ed. Bonnie Wheeler and John Carmi Parsons (London: Palgrave Macmillan, 2003), pp. 177–211

Shahar, Shulamith, *Childhood in the Middle Ages* (London: Routledge, 1990)

Sivéry, Gérard, *Blanche de Castille* (Paris: Fayard, 1990)

----- *Philippe Auguste* (Paris: Perrin, 2003; orig. Librairie Plon, 1993)

Spong, Sally, 'Isabella of Angloulême: The Vanishing Queen', in *English Consorts: Power, Influence, Dynasty. Volume 1: Early Medieval Consorts* (Basingstoke: Palgrave Macmillan, forthcoming)

----- 'Isabella of Gloucester and Isabella of Angoulême: Queenship and Female Lordship in England and France, 1189-1220', unpublished PhD thesis, University of East Anglia, 2022

----- 'Isabella of Gloucester: Heiress, Lord, Forgotten Consort', in *English Consorts: Power, Influence, Dynasty. Volume 1: Early Medieval Consorts* (Basingstoke: Palgrave Macmillan, forthcoming)

Storey, Gabrielle, *Berengaria of Navarre: Queen Consort of England and Lady of Le Mans* (Oxford and New York: Routledge, forthcoming)

Strickland, Matthew, *Henry the Young King, 1155-1183* (New Haven and London: Yale University Press, 2016)

----- *War and Chivalry* (Cambridge: Cambridge University Press, 1996)

Térouane, P., 'A la quête d'une tombe sans nom', *Bulletin de la Société d'Agriculture, Sciences et Arts de la Sarthe, Mémoires*, Vol. 4, 7 (1969), pp. 27-44

Tout, T.F., *France and England: Their Relations in the Middle Ages and Now* (London: Longmans, Green & Co., 1922)

Trindade, Ann, *Berengaria: In Search of Richard the Lionheart's Queen* (Dublin: Four Courts Press, 1999)

Truax, Jean A., 'Anglo-Norman Women at War: Valiant Soldiers, Prudent Strategists or Charismatic Leaders?', in *The Circle of War in the Middle Ages: Essays on Medieval Military and Naval History*, ed. Donald J. Kagay and L.J. Andrew Villalon (Woodbridge: Boydell, 1999), pp. 111-25

Turner, Ralph V., 'Eleanor of Aquitaine and Her Children: An Inquiry into Medieval Family Attachment', *Journal of Medieval History*, 14 (1988), pp. 321-35

----- *Eleanor of Aquitaine: Queen of France, Queen of England* (New Haven and London: Yale University Press, 2009)

Tyerman, Christopher, *Who's Who in Early Medieval England* (London: Shepheard-Walwyn, 1996)

Van Houts, Elisabeth, 'Les femmes dans le royaume Plantagenêt: Gendre, politique et nature', in *Plantagenêts et Capétiens: Confrontations et héritages*, ed. Martin Aurell and Noël-Yves Tonnerre (Turnhout: Brepols, 2006), pp. 95-112

Verbruggen, J.F., 'Women in Medieval Armies', *Journal of Medieval Military History*, 4 (2006), pp. 119-36

Vincent, Nicholas, 'Isabella of Angoulême: John's Jezebel', in *King John: New Interpretations*, ed. S.D. Church (Woodbridge: Boydell, 1999), pp. 165-219

----- 'A Queen in Rebel London, 1215-17', in *'A Verray Parfit Praktisour': Essays Presented to Carole Rawcliffe*, ed. Linda Clark and Elizabeth Danbury (Woodbridge: Boydell, 2017), pp. 23-50

Volkmann, Jean-Charles, *Généalogies complètes des rois de France* (Paris: Éditions Jean-Paul Gisserot, 1999)

Vollrath, Hannah, 'Aliénor d'Aquitaine et ses enfants: Une relation affective?', in *Plantagenêts et Capétiens: Confrontations et héritages*, ed. Martin Aurell and Noël-Yves Tonnerre (Turnhout: Brepols, 2006), pp. 113-23

Warren, W.L., *The Governance of Anglo-Norman and Angevin England, 1086-1272* (Stanford: Stanford University Press, 1987)

----- *Henry II*, 3rd ed. (New Haven and London: Yale University Press, 2000; orig. 1973)

----- *King John*, 2nd ed. (New Haven and London: Yale University Press, 1997; orig. 1961)

Wheeler, Bonnie, and John Carmi Parsons (eds), *Eleanor of Aquitaine: Lord and Lady* (London: Palgrave Macmillan, 2003)

Wilkinson, Louise J., 'Maternal Abandonment and Surrogate Caregivers: Isabella of Angoulême and Her Children by King John', in *Virtuous or Villainess? The Image of the Royal Mother from the Early Medieval to the Early Modern Era*, ed. Carey Fleiner and Elena Woodacre (New York: Palgrave Macmillan, 2016), pp. 101–24

Woodacre, Elena, 'Between Regencies and Lieutenancies: Catherine of Aragon (1513) and Kateryn Parr (1544)', in *Les alters ego des souverains: Vice-rois et lieutenants généraux en Europe et dans les Amériques (XVe-XVIIe siècles)*, ed. Philippe Chareyre, Álvaro Adot and Dénes Harai (Pau: Presses de l'Université de Pau et des Pays de l'Adour (PUPPA), 2021), pp. 185–206

INDEX

Note: All individuals are listed by first name. *Italicised* page references denote illustrations. The suffix 'n' indicates a note.

The History Press
The destination for history
www.thehistorypress.co.uk